LARGER THAN LIFE

❖

❖

Larger Than Life

New Mexico in the Twentieth Century

Ferenc M. Szasz

University of New Mexico Press ❖ Albuquerque

12 11 10 09 08 07 06   1 2 3 4 5 6 7

LIBRARY OF CONGRESS CATALOGING-IN-PUBLICATION DATA

Szasz, Ferenc Morton, 1940–
Larger than life : New Mexico in the twentieth century / Ferenc M. Szasz.
p. cm.
Includes bibliographical references and index.
ISBN-13: 978-0-8263-3883-9 (pbk. : alk. paper)
ISBN-10: 0-8263-3883-6 (pbk. : alk. paper)
1. New Mexico—History—20th century.
2. New Mexico—Biography. I. Title.
F801.S97 2006
978.9'053—dc22

2005027464

"The Cultures of Modern New Mexico, 1940 to the Early Twenty-first Century," is a totally revised version of an essay that first appeared in *Contemporary New Mexico, 1940–1990*, ed. Richard W. Etulain (Albuquerque: University of New Mexico Press, 1994), now out of print.

"New Mexico's Forgotten Nuclear Tests: Projects Gnome (1961) and Gasbuggy (1967)" first appeared in *New Mexico Historical Review* 73 (October 1998): 347–70. Reprinted by permission.

"The History of Atomic Photography" is a much-revised version of an essay review that first appeared under the title "The Photography of the Atomic Age: A Review Essay," in *New Mexico Historical Review* 70 (January 1995): 77–82.

"Francis Schlatter: The Spiritual Healer of the Southwest" is a much-revised version of an essay that originally appeared in *New Mexico Historical Review* 54 (April 1979): 89–104.

Front cover photo credits and captions—top: Gasbuggy, p. 169; second row, left to right: Francis Schlatter, p. 203; Tony Hillerman, p. 114; third row left to right: Bill Richardson, p. 51; Edith Warner, p. 31; Pershing II missile, p. 185; Norris Bradbury, p. 144; bottom row, left to right: Rudolfo Anaya, p. 105; Trinity p. 177; Concha Ortiz y Pino de Kleven, p. 96; J. Robert Oppenheimer, p. 36.

Book design and type composition by Kathleen Sparkes.
This book is typeset using Minion 10/14; 26P,
display type is Minion and Incognito families

For the family

Margaret

Eric, Chris, Scott, and Maria

Tyler, Sean, and Matthew

CONTENTS

ACKNOWLEDGMENTS

$\mathcal{A}$s the research for these essays has stretched over several decades, I find that I owe a great deal to a great many people. First, I would like to thank the excellent staff at Zimmerman Library, the Centennial Library, and the Fine Arts Library at the University of New Mexico. I would like to single out Kate Lugar and Dorothy Wonsmus for special accolades. Roger A. Meade, archivist at Los Alamos, has guided my research on atomic history for over two decades, and David Holtby, editor in chief of UNM Press, has been a source of publishing wisdom for even longer. The state will be much impoverished by their retirements. Graduate students Maria Szasz, Scott Meredith, and Nathan Wilson all helped with the typing, as did Chris G. Bradley and the late Penelope D. Katson, for which I remain profoundly grateful. Scott also graciously shared his expertise on the history of New Mexico music. Finally, I would like to thank my physicians Dr. Jonathan Lackner, Dr. Robert Galagan, Dr. David Clanon, and Dr. Steven Fuette for their combined aid in keeping me on this side of Jordan so that I could complete this project as planned.

Albuquerque
February 2005

INTRODUCTION

$\mathcal{T}$hese essays represent a thirty-year effort to come to grips with the history of modern New Mexico. Before I summarize their themes, however, I would like to sketch a bit of background. In July of 1964 I arrived in New Mexico via bus. But since I spent what seemed an eternity waiting in the Raton and Albuquerque bus depots, I cannot say for certain that I actually set foot on New Mexican soil. I was on my way to a two-week summer camp position at the Orme Ranch in northern Arizona, which served as my introduction to the Southwest. Even though it has been over forty years, I can still recall my first glimpse of the New Mexico sky and the Red Rock country east of Grants.

My next encounter with the state came in April of 1967, when I attended the Organization of American Historians annual convention in Chicago. My graduate school adviser, Milton Berman, had long been friends with Gerald D. Nash, the best-known American historian then teaching at the University of New Mexico. Berman graciously arranged an interview for me as Nash had been hastily selected to find someone to teach a relatively new subspecialty, American social and intellectual history. Nash and I chatted briefly, and when I handed him my vita, which consisted of my name, address, and phone number, plus a lone article that had been accepted by *New York History*, he said, "Good, you have an article accepted already." I can still recall his comment because no one at the University of Rochester in the mid-1960s encouraged graduate students to publish. Faculty were, of course, required to produce books and articles to gain tenure and promotion, but graduate students were expected to use their time solely to absorb the proffered wisdom. Within the graduate community, publishing was neither admired nor denigrated. It was simply not what one was there for. But those were the 1960s, and things were about to change.

About a week after my interview with Nash, I received a phone call from UNM department chair Edwin Liewen, a distinguished scholar of Latin American military history. In—what I would learn later—his typical gruff manner, he said, "If we offer you the job, will you take it?" I jumped at the chance and gladly signed on for a one-year, temporary position as a visiting instructor. My only other job offer came three days later from Northern Montana University in Havre, Montana. Luck was clearly on my side.

During the summer of 1967, I crammed all my worldly possessions into a 1964 green Plymouth Valiant and headed west for my first real job. I found the Albuquerque of the late 1960s to be a delightfully provincial city of about 150,000 with—excluding the numerous mom-and-pop New Mexican cafés—virtually no good restaurants, few department stores, and literally no bookstores. I could buy the Sunday *New York Times* only at the airport, and no newsstand carried either the *New York Review of Books* or *Commentary*, my essential reading at the time. Still, the charm of both city and campus captured me immediately. When I overheard UNM students conversing fluently in Spanish, it suddenly dawned on me that I had literally moved to another country. But, as my family and I would later learn from our years of teaching in Exeter, England, and Aberdeen, Scotland, when one lives in a foreign country, every act—from buying groceries to chatting with neighbors to touring the countryside—can prove an adventure. Red or green what? I became a fast learner.

I liked the University of New Mexico immediately. My UNM colleagues, the staff, and the students were open and friendly. Few UNM students of the late sixties/early seventies reflected the bitter cynicism of the Vietnam-Watergate era that made teaching American history increasingly difficult. Apparently UNM liked me as well, for the new History Department chair, Frank W. Iklé, a specialist in Asian history, soon shifted my appointment to a tenure track position. With this move, what began as a one-year, fill-in job stretched into an over-three-decade career. Luck was with me once again.

During my second year at UNM, I met Margaret Connell Garretson, a young widow with two children (Eric, ten, and Chris Ann, six), who had enrolled as a new PhD candidate. We married in 1969 and added Maria two years later. Margaret's historic links to New Mexico extended far deeper than mine. In the 1890s, her great-grandfather, George W. Carson, a pharmacist and Civil War veteran from New Sharon, Iowa, had developed tuberculosis and moved to Socorro to unsuccessfully "chase the cure." He died in Socorro in 1898. During his years there—so family legend has it—he edited the Socorro newspaper. George's brother, Charles, also lived for a while in Santa Fe, where he was similarly involved in publishing a Spanish-language newspaper. Margaret had completed her MA at the University of Washington and chose UNM for her PhD because her previous visits to the state had convinced her that she wanted to return. She joined the UNM History Department in 1987, and today we rank among the most senior of the nation's same-department husband-and-wife history teams.

Thus, Margaret and I embraced New Mexico with the zeal of two converts. Nobody phrased this sentiment better than famed war correspondent Ernie Pyle when he penned his 1942 essay "Why Albuquerque?"

> We like it because people are friendly and interested in you
> and yet they leave you alone. . . . And we like it because
> you can do almost anything you want to, within reason. . . .
> We like it because we can have Navajo rugs in our house and
> piñon and juniper bushes in our yard, and western pictures
> on our knotty-pine walls. We like it because you can take a
> Sunday afternoon spin in the mountains and see deer and
> wild turkey. . . . We have seen sunrises so violently beautiful
> they were almost frightening, and I'm only sorry I can't
> capture the sunsets and the thunderstorms and the first
> snows on the Sandias, and take them East and flaunt them
> in people's faces.
>
> We like it here because no more than half our friends
> who write us know how to spell Albuquerque. We like it here

because there aren't any street cars, and because you see lots
of men on Central Avenue in cowboy boots. We like it because
you can see Indians making silver jewelry, and you can see
sheepskins lying all over a vacant downtown lot drying in
the sun. . . .

We like it because Albuquerque is still small enough
that you always see someone you know when you go
downtown. . . . We like Albuquerque because, in spite of
the great comfortable sense of isolation you feel here, still
you do not suffer from over-isolation. For people here, too,
live lives that are complete and full. We want for little, even
in the nebulous realm of the mind. There is no famine of
thought in our surroundings. In the Southwest character
there is a sufficiency which though not complacent, has in
it something of the desert's charm.[1]

Margaret's historical specialties focused on the history of Native
American education, Indian-white relations, and Celtic–Native American
history. From the start she termed herself a "western historian," a designation that I came to adopt only much later. Her research interests drew us
to explore the Southwest, especially Pueblo and Navajo country, and we
spent many an hour traveling the state's little blue roads. We also hiked the
region's mountains whenever we got the chance. The challenging topography of the state—to borrow the Irish phrase—"gobsmacked" us on a
regular basis.

From her growing up in the Pacific Northwest, as well as her study of
Native American history, Margaret often emphasized the importance of
"place" for any writer of history. Place is very different from geography,
for it signifies an emotional attachment to the land. It speaks to roots. It
refers to a locale where a people have lived for generations. Place involves
belonging and often a "sense of being." To talk of place in a southwestern
context usually brushes up against the idea of the sacred, a concept that
most historians tend to shy away from.

It took us little time to discover that the Southwest is filled with
sacred places: Chaco Canyon, ancestral home of many of the Puebloan
peoples; Blue Lake of Taos Pueblo (returned to the pueblo in 1970); Puye

Ruins, sacred as the ancestral home of Santa Clara Pueblo; the stone lions near Los Alamos, sacred to Cochiti Pueblo; the four mountains of the Navajo, which mark the boundaries of Dinétah; the Roman Catholic healing shrine at Chimayó, a destination for pilgrims from around the world ("the Lourdes of North America"); Tomé Hill, which devout pilgrims climb every Easter; and many others.

A people have to live in a region for generations for it to evolve into sacred space. Much has to have happened there. As Professor W. Scott Olsen once suggested, tragedy forms an essential component of any sacred locale. Famed Kiowa writer N. Scott Momaday put it this way: "Where words touch the land, that is what makes a place sacred." If one is searching for sacred spaces, New Mexico offers a number of opportunities.[2]

Margaret also frequently pointed to the historically western—primarily, but not exclusively, Native American—concept of "reciprocity." I liked to think that my midwestern, Presbyterian upbringing—combined with the broader, continental worldviews of a Hungarian immigrant father—steeped me in the basic ideas of "fairness," but Margaret insisted that fairness and reciprocity are not really synonyms. Reciprocity usually implies a wider set of connections—between humans, animals, plants, rivers, and all other beings on earth. One sees this most vividly in Native American cultures. For example, when whale hunters from coastal tribes off Vancouver Island launch their boats, they understand that a specific whale has been selected for them to kill. Thus, if they chance upon a stray whale, they will pass it by until they meet the one that they feel has been designed for their purpose. Similarly, Native Americans from many Plains tribes are taught to ask forgiveness from the deer they kill; they do so, they remind it, so that they may feed their families.

Such ideas have met hard sledding in recent times. Whale hunting has been virtually forbidden, and deer hunting is enmeshed in a web of complex (and expensive) state regulations. But in a strange sense, for numerous southwesterners the idea of reciprocity has been "democratized." For many—Native and non-Native alike—reciprocity has begun to revolve around a quasi-emotional relationship to the land itself.

But this is a very sensitive concept. "New Age" enthusiasts have borrowed—some Natives say "stolen"—the idea of the sacredness of the earth to apply it to a variety of awkward personal and public situations.

Enthusiasts have erected large stone circles on public lands and have actually placed human remains in the kivas at Chaco Canyon. This perverse "democratization of the sacred" has driven U.S. Park Service and Bureau of Land Management officials to distraction.

Still, as newcomers to the Southwest, we have observed that many Native American and Hispanic farmers of the Rio Grande Valley do indeed view their relationship to the land through a different lens from that of mainstream Americans. Perhaps this can be traced to their inherited religious traditions, or perhaps it is somehow linked to the fact that arable land in the Southwest has always been hard to come by. The technology to work that land is so intricate, it took great skill to ensure community survival.[3] Still, reciprocity suggests that people are responsible to a world beyond their own self-interests.

In a sense, this collection of essays on modern New Mexican history falls somewhere between my inherited midwestern ideas of fairness and my incomplete understanding of reciprocity. I plan to donate all royalties from this book to the UNM Department of History to help fund a graduate student who will serve as an intern at UNM Press, which will oversee the next generation of books about the Land of Enchantment. I view this as but a small gesture of gratitude for having had the opportunity of teaching American history at UNM for over three decades.

■

I have grouped the essays into four sections. Part One deals with people. Here I will sketch the sagas of three often larger-than-life figures who have helped shape the state's recent history. The initial essay shows how America's first real "celebrities"—Charles A. and Anne Morrow Lindbergh— affected the out-of-the-way region of New Mexico and the Southwest during the 1920s and 1930s. In the second, I will argue that famed atomic physicist J. Robert Oppenheimer forged a reciprocal relationship with northern New Mexico. In essence, the Pecos Wilderness Area (then called the Pecos Forest Reserve) restored the health of the frail New York City youth, and, in return, he transformed Los Alamos into the first New Mexico city to be recognized around the globe. The last essay in this section argues that in 1984, newly elected congressman Bill Richardson (currently governor) met his first real political challenge when he successfully steered through Congress a bill to create the Bisti/ De-Na-Zin wilderness areas south of Farmington. He would later utilize these talents for much more delicate negotiations on an international level, but he first honed his compromising skills during a fiercely debated environmental issue in his newly adopted state.

Part Two, "Cultures," consists of a single lengthy essay on the cultures of modern New Mexico from 1940 to the early twenty-first century. Here I suggest that the standard interpretation of New Mexico's past— the "romantic balance" between Native American, Hispanic, and Anglo-pioneer cultures—needs a major updating. In the post–World War II years, several new "cultures"—such as big science, tourism, and literature—have all emerged to realign the famed "heroic triad" of the New Mexico past.

Part Three—"Atomic New Mexico"—reflects my long-term fascination with the origins of the nuclear age. A recent survey listed the creation of the atomic bomb as the most important single event of the twentieth century, and New Mexico, of course, played a vital role in this endeavor. When Los Alamos scientists detonated the Trinity Site blast on July 16, 1945, they literally drew a line across the pages of history. This section consists of three essays: how General Leslie R. Groves and Commander Norris Bradbury ensured that Los Alamos would remain permanent, the relatively unknown tale of two underground nuclear blasts near Carlsbad and near Farmington in the 1960s, and the emergence of atomic photography as an authentic subdiscipline.

I term the final section simply "Mysteries." The first of the three essays included here discusses the tale of German immigrant Francis Schlatter, an itinerant who in 1895 allegedly healed five thousand people simply by touching them. The second analyzes the story of the munitions train explosion that literally flattened the hamlet of Tolar, New Mexico, in 1944. The third deals with the over two-thousand-year-old story of "Threatening Rock" in Chaco Canyon. Virtually every New Mexican has heard of Chaco Canyon—now a World Heritage site—but few recognize the name of Threatening Rock. Yet every visitor to the site until January 1941 would have stood in awe of the thirty-thousand-ton wall of sandstone that seemed ready to collapse at any moment to destroy Pueblo Bonito and whatever else lay in its path.

PART ONE

People

INTRODUCTION

$\mathcal{A}$t 121,666 square miles, New Mexico ranks fifth among the states in size. But the 2000 census discovered only 1,819,046 people, which places it among the bottom tier in terms of population. Perhaps this gap between the vast, open spaces and the relatively few citizens accounts for the numerous high-profile personalities that have so often dotted New Mexico's colorful past.

Two examples will suffice: Socorro's Elfego Baca and Lincoln/Silver City's Billy the Kid.

Born in 1865, Elfego Baca lived as a youth in Topeka but returned to Socorro in his late teens. Over the course of his eighty years, he started a local detective agency, published a Spanish-language newspaper, *La Opinion Publica*, and joined the Huerta faction of the Mexican Revolution (Pancho Villa allegedly placed a price on his head). In addition, Baca successfully defended himself against three separate murder charges, dabbled in mine exploration and real estate, and served as sheriff, mayor, and district attorney for the Socorro region. When he died in Albuquerque in 1945, he had established a reputation as an excellent lawyer.[1]

All this is impressive enough, but Baca was catapulted into instant legend because of an incident that occurred in 1884, shortly after he turned nineteen. That year, the newly appointed deputy sheriff found himself trapped in a home in San Francisco Plaza (today's Reserve), where an estimated eighty Texas cowboys, who had been terrorizing the local Hispanic population, began firing at him. Secure behind adobe barricades, they peppered Baca's refuge with over four thousand shots, virtually shredding the building's walls. Not only did Baca survive the onslaught, he killed two of his attackers and wounded several others. When local authorities finally rode up to halt the thirty-six-hour melee, they discovered that the house contained a sunken floor that allowed Baca to emerge without a scratch. When he exited the cabin, he marched straight into the realm of western myth.

.Hispanic folksingers quickly penned ballads on his exploits, and he became an overnight hero for the local populace. In a 1936 WPA interview, Baca confessed that "I never wanted to kill anybody but if a man had it in his mind to kill me, I made it my business to get him first."[2] Many people consider Elfego Baca as perhaps the most "picturesque" character in all of New Mexico history.[3]

Baca's reputation extended well beyond his lifetime. In 1958, Walt Disney Corporation produced a short-lived TV series and several comic books on his career. Termed *The Nine Lives of Elfego Baca*, the TV show was accompanied by a theme song:

> *Elfego was wise and Elfego was strong*
> *Elfego, El Gato, who made a right from wrong*
> *And the legend is that*
> *Like El Gato the Cat*
> *Nine lives had Elfego Baca.*[4]

At the dawn of the twenty-first century, Socorro stages the annual Elfego Baca Golf Shoot, which tees off from the crest of Socorro Mountain. A large bronze sculpture of Baca is currently under construction, to be placed in a proposed museum in Reserve, New Mexico.

■

The legend of William H. Bonney, Billy the Kid, reached even farther afield. Born in New York in 1859, young William moved to the mining camp of Silver City in 1873 with his mother. Four years later he hired on as a ranch hand for John Tunstall in Lincoln and soon found himself drawn into the infamous Lincoln County War. After Tunstall was killed by local law officials, Billy helped shoot down both the sheriff and the deputy in Lincoln. It took two years to locate and capture him, but authorities then sentenced Bonney to hang and locked him in the Lincoln County jail. However, in 1881, he killed two guards and fled into the countryside, where he remained at large for three months until Sheriff Pat Garrett finally dispatched him on July 14, 1881. William Bonney was twenty-one years old.

As historian Robert Utley has noted, in real life, Billy the Kid should rank as a mere footnote to a violent era of New Mexico history. But in the realm of folklore, he instantly joined Kit Carson, Wyatt Earp, and Buffalo Bill as symbols of the vanishing frontier. Viewed equally as a cold-blooded murderer and kindhearted defender of Hispanic ranchers and sheepherders, Billy the Kid soon emerged as New Mexico's chief contribution to the legend of the Old West.[5]

By the middle of the twentieth century, New Mexico towns with links to Billy's life had all begun to capitalize on this connection. Ever since 1940, locals in the Lincoln area have performed a pageant, "The Last Escape of Billy the Kid." According to legend, the first man to play the role of Billy was famed San Patricio painter Peter Hurd. Similar to Tombstone, Arizona, the adobe houses and modest wooden stores of Lincoln have been frozen as they were during the Lincoln County War of 1878–81. The nearby roads of the Billy the Kid Trail achieved National Scenic Byway status in 1998.

Similarly, the Fort Sumner region houses Billy's grave and serves as the terminus of the annual "Last Ride of Billy the Kid" (from Lincoln to Fort Sumner) that is reenacted every year. Recently Silver City has inaugurated an annual "Billy and Milly Ball" (Mildred Clark Cusey was a noted regional madame). Historian Kathleen Chamberlain's 1997 bibliography extends to over 750 items.[6]

■

Other New Mexican figures have loomed almost as large: Cabeza de Baca, Francisco de Coronado, don Diego de Vargas, Fathers Dominguez and Escalante, Tula, Manuelito, Che Dodge, Narbona, Lew Wallace, Miguel Otero, Bishop Jean Baptiste Lamy, Manuel Abeyta, Clyde Tingley, Georgia O'Keeffe, Wendell Chino, Concha Ortiz y Pino de Kleven, and so on.

The following section will explore four prominent personalities who have helped shape the course of modern New Mexico history: aviators Charles A. and Anne Morrow Lindbergh, physicist J. Robert Oppenheimer, and Congressman (later Governor) William (Bill) Richardson. Their impact on the region has been extensive indeed.

CHAPTER ONE

Charles A. and Anne Morrow Lindbergh *and the* Shaping *of* New Mexican History

When twenty-five-year-old Charles A. Lindbergh touched *The Spirit of St. Louis* down at Le Bourget Aerodrome outside of Paris on May 21, 1927, he changed the course of American history. His daring feat not only marked the first solo flight across the Atlantic but also introduced the idea of "the celebrity" into national life. From that moment on, the rich, glamorous, and well connected sought out Lindbergh's company, and everything he did or said became instantly newsworthy.

In 1929, Charles Lindbergh married the beautiful Anne Morrow, daughter of Elizabeth C. and Dwight Morrow, the American ambassador to Mexico. For the next two years, the handsome young couple remained constantly on the move, flying here and there, opening various airports and helping lay out the nation's initial domestic air travel routes. The

American public delighted in their every move, and soon the Lindberghs emerged as celebrity icons, far more glamorous than contemporary film stars because their adventures were authentic.[1]

In March 1932, the Lindberghs suffered the ultimate family nightmare when their twenty-month-old son, Charles Jr., was kidnapped and murdered. The ensuing publicity proved so invasive that they fled in 1935 to the privacy of Great Britain and later to France. Invited by the American military attaché to investigate the growing German aircraft industry in the late 1930s, Charles became convinced of its technical superiority, and these views received considerable publicity as well. He also accepted a German medal of honor from Luftwaffe commander Herman Göring in 1938, which Anne presciently termed "the Albatross."

The following year the family returned to the States, where Lindbergh took on the role of chief spokesman for America First, a powerful noninterventionist organization. He was so well regarded that he could draw ten thousand listeners to an April 23, 1941, America First rally in Chicago. Turning a blind eye to Nazi atrocities, he argued vigorously that America should preserve its neutrality in the raging European conflict.

President Franklin D. Roosevelt was outraged. Unlike the twenty-first century, where presidents actively court celebrity support, Roosevelt considered Lindbergh a potential rival who, because of his unprecedented social power, could bring about great mischief. He once commented to a group of senators that he might have to "clip that young man's wings," and he gave the secretary of the interior, Harold L. Ickes, a green light to do so. Ickes responded with alacrity. He branded Lindbergh the "number one Nazi fellow traveler." The president himself termed the pilot a "copperhead." The negative comments from Washington goaded Lindbergh into resigning his commission as a colonel in the U.S. Air Corps Reserve (which was precisely what Roosevelt wanted).[2] When the Japanese attacked Pearl Harbor, Lindbergh immediately offered to serve, but Roosevelt refused to restore his commission. Thus, Lindbergh participated in the war as a civilian, flying fifty combat missions in that capacity. Not until 1954 did President Dwight D. Eisenhower return him to rank. Unable to shake the "Nazi fellow traveler" accusations, Lindbergh retired to Hawaii, where he gradually regained some of his earlier reputation by support for various ecological causes. He died in Maui in 1974.

But the Lindbergh legend did not die with him. It continued to flourish through the five-volume *Diaries and Letters of Anne Morrow Lindbergh* (1922–80) as well as the poignant memoirs by their youngest daughter, Reeve: *Under a Wing* (about Charles, 1998) and *No More Words* (about Anne, 2001). On the seventy-fifth anniversary of his grandfather's historic 1927 flight, Erik Lindbergh replicated the journey from New York to Le Bourget. In the fall of 2003, three German siblings claimed that Lindbergh had fallen in love with their hatmaker mother in 1957 and had fathered them all. A later DNA test confirmed this to be true. The respected Charles and Anne Morrow Lindbergh Foundation, which supports aerospace research, was stunned. Thus, for over three-quarters of a century, the Lindbergh legend has permeated all aspects of American life.[3]

■

The power of the Lindbergh legend also reached out to shape the course of New Mexican history, and it did so in three important areas. First, Charles's 1928 "goodwill" aircraft touchdowns in Lordsburg and Santa Fe helped establish the region's initial airports and considerably heightened state concern over aviation issues. Second, a visit to Pecos Pueblo and Chaco Canyon the next year by the newly married couple produced the first aerial photographs of key southwestern archaeological sites, thus inaugurating a whole new subspecialty of the discipline. Finally, Charles's public and (especially) private support for the dreams of Massachusetts scientist Robert H. Goddard enabled him to move to Roswell in 1930 and turn southeastern New Mexico into the rocket-testing center of the nation for most of the decade. Thus, the state of New Mexico owes a good deal to the all-pervasive celebrity status of Charles and Anne Morrow Lindbergh.

■

The hundred thousand cheering French who greeted the *Spirit of St. Louis* upon landing proved only the beginning. President Calvin Coolidge immediately dispatched the warship *Memphis* to return Lindbergh and his plane to the States, whereupon, as a further crowd-pleaser, he flew into New York Harbor in a seaplane. Afterward, Lindbergh received a larger Fifth Avenue ticker tape parade than had greeted the returning veterans of the Great War.

The elite of New York clamored for his attention. Mrs. Vanderbilt reportedly fainted when she learned that he would not attend her party, but he did visit extensively with Mayor Jimmy Walker and with publisher William Randolph Hearst and his actress consort Marion Davies.[4] Philanthropist Daniel F. Guggenheim invited him to stay at his mansion on New York's fabulous Gold Coast, where, in a feverish burst of activity—sometimes as much as eighteen hours a day—Lindbergh, who had never before written a line, penned the dramatic story of his pioneering flight. Titled "*We*" (the pilot and the plane), the book zoomed to the top of the bestseller list, much to the delight of publisher G. P. Putnam.[5]

At this time Guggenheim served as head of the private Daniel F. Guggenheim Fund for the Promotion of Aeronautics and, after brief consultation with the U.S. State Department of Commerce Aeronautics Division, decided to capitalize on Lindbergh's unprecedented national popularity. They had little trouble convincing him that it would give a tremendous boost to American aviation if he could fly his beloved aircraft all around the nation.

The schedule soon fell into place. An advance plane containing a pilot, mechanic, and overall manager, Donald E. Keyhoe, would precede Lindbergh in *The Spirit of St. Louis* for a three-month tour of the country. The planes would make eighty-two landings, at least one in every state. A few would be brief "touchdowns," but the majority would involve overnight layovers plus, of course, countless speeches on aviation by Lindbergh. Both Lordsburg and Santa Fe were delighted to discover they were included on the list of scheduled stops. Albuquerque, much to its dismay, found itself bypassed because it did not possess a proper landing field.[6]

At 11 A.M. on September 24, 1928, Lindbergh touched down in Lordsburg, then a town of about sixteen hundred people. His arrival provided one of the most exciting moments in southern New Mexico history. Planners for the event invited representatives from the entire low desert region, and the welcoming dais contained not just the mayor and other dignitaries of Lordsburg but also various officials from Douglas, Tombstone, and Willcox, Arizona, as well as representatives of local women's clubs and regional cattle interests. All Lordsburg businesses closed from ten thirty to twelve, and smartly dressed, mounted teams of local cowboys and cowgirls, along with the Boy Scouts, formed the official line of welcome. The crowd was estimated at ten thousand. Everything went like clockwork. *The Spirit of St. Louis* flew over the veterans' hospital at Fort Bayard, buzzed Silver City, and then, after circling the landing field six or seven times, touched down on the six-hundred-acre site that the mayor later proclaimed "Lindbergh Airport." Surviving photographs show a tall, awkward young man dressed in a business suit standing by his plane or being escorted around by local dignitaries.[7]

Lindbergh played his part well. He waved to the mile-long crowd, amid gasps of, "Oh, isn't he adorable." He took time to write a brief note to a young lad too sick to attend and chatted with several other young New Mexicans—"the pilots of the future"—before making a brief speech. In part, he said: "Mr. Chairman, citizens of New Mexico, Lordsburg is one of the smallest cities included in this tour of the United States. We do not believe in measuring a city by its size as much as by what it does, and by establishing this airport you have set an example for the cities of the United States."[8]

Tour organizer Donald Keyhoe heaped praise on Lordsburg as well. He commended the local arrangements people for holding the crowds behind the rope barricades. This proved especially crucial because the design of *The Spirit of St. Louis* did not allow the pilot to see directly in front of the aircraft, and at a previous stop a reporter had wandered within inches of the whirling propeller. Keyhoe also lived in constant fear that crowds might somehow storm the gates and damage the plane, as they had initially done at Le Bourget.[9]

At precisely eleven thirty-six the two planes taxied across the low desert and lifted off for the next stop, El Paso. For those who wished to see more of their hero, the city of El Paso chartered excursion buses to transport visitors to the El Paso High School stadium, where Lindbergh was scheduled to speak that evening.

Lordsburg basked in the reflected glory of Lindbergh's visit for several weeks. Alva N. Hollinger, of the nearby State College of New Mexico in Las Cruces, praised the pilot as providing a fine example for the youth of the day through his clean life and indomitable spirit. Another writer from Steins, New Mexico, observed that people turned out to see Lindbergh who would not have bothered to attend a glee club performance by "Babe Ruth,

Gene Tunney, President Coolidge, King Edward, and Charlie Chaplin." The reason: not only was Lindbergh modest and unassuming, he was also the ultimate master of his craft.[10] Although Lindbergh's visit to Lordsburg lasted less than two hours, for a brief moment the tiny New Mexican community cherished hopes of evolving into a major center of American aviation.

Lindbergh's arrival in Santa Fe two days later proved even more exciting. Although he circled Albuquerque several times, he only dropped a note to express his regrets over being unable to land. Then he headed up the Rio Grande Valley, where, spotting a lengthy line of cars stuck on La Bajada hill, he lightheartedly "leapfrogged" a number of vehicles. Santa Fe had hastily constructed a new airfield only three days previously, and after circling, Lindbergh landed at 2 P.M. without incident. When *The Spirit of St. Louis* finally came to a stop, someone noticed a tumbleweed stuck to the tail.

As befitting the capital city, Santa Feans gave Lindbergh an overwhelming welcome. The crowd was estimated at ten thousand, with perhaps two thousand vehicles, and the welcoming dais included not only the governor, R. C. Dillon, and the mayor, but also Katherine Stinson Otero, probably the nation's most well-known female pilot. Afterward, Lindbergh sat on the backseat of an open car that took him to La Fonda Hotel— through a seemingly endless crowd of waving parochial and public school children. After a brief rest, he was escorted to the state capitol for the official program.[11]

From the west steps of the Capitol Building, Lindbergh praised New Mexico's future in aviation. He noted that Santa Fe's seven-thousand-foot altitude no longer presented any hardship since new supercharged engines had overcome that barrier. Because the state was so large, he predicted that area ranchers would soon be utilizing aircraft for personal travel. In 1928, he said, the airplane was in the same situation that the automobile had been in a decade or so earlier—before the advent of paved roads. Europeans were slightly ahead of Americans, he noted, because their governments had all subsidized their aircraft industries. He closed by urging each New Mexico city to create an airport and to encourage people to travel by air.[12]

After the speech, Lindbergh retired to La Fonda early, for the next day—destination Abilene, Texas—proved one of the most challenging.

Charles A. Lindbergh at the state capitol in Santa Fe,
September 25, 1928. Photographer unknown. Courtesy
Palace of the Governors (MNM/DCA). Neg. no. 147105.

The two pilots arrived at the Santa Fe airport for a 2 A.M. takeoff—a moderate miscalculation as they had not intended to do any night flying. The problem lay with *The Spirit of St. Louis*, which had no navigation lights, but a number of Santa Feans brought out their automobiles, and their headlights allowed the planes to safely take off. Once airborne, Lindbergh waved a flashlight back and forth so that the support plane knew precisely where he was. It was with relief that the pilots greeted the sunrise, but the scheduled landing at Abilene came off as smoothly as all the previous ones.[13]

As with southern New Mexico, the northern part of the state also gloried in Lindbergh's visit. The *Santa Fe New Mexican* carried a full-page welcome from various organizations and carefully listed all the technical aspects of his plane, including a discussion of the oil circulation system,

*Charles A. Lindbergh with Mayor Clyde Tingley of Albuquerque,
1929. Photographer unknown. Courtesy Palace of the Governors
(MNM/DCA). Neg. no. 128713.*

the carburetor, and the air-cooling apparatus. A local poet compared
his accomplishment with that of Columbus. Editorial writers praised
Lindbergh's spiritual values and marveled at his mysterious hold on the
American people. Said one: "He is the living spirit of all that the world
needs today."[14]

The impact of this visit reverberated throughout the state long after
the celebration faded. At the request of U.S. Secretary of Commerce

The Spirit of St. Louis *in Santa Fe, September 1928. Photographer unknown. Courtesy Palace of the Governors (MNM/DCA). Neg. no. 147104.*

Herbert Hoover, Governor Dillon wrote local chambers of commerce to ask them to make certain that all New Mexican cities prominently displayed their names on appropriate rooftops. Local businesses proved eager to cooperate. The Santa Fe Builders Supply Company put an eight-foot-high *Santa Fe* on its roof, and the First National Bank in Albuquerque responded in kind. Large automobile garages in Carlsbad and Fort Sumner followed suit, while Tucumcari, Alamogordo, and Raton all promised to have their names displayed in the near future.

Citizens of Albuquerque went even further. Stung that Santa Fe had eclipsed their glory, editorial writers in the *Albuquerque Journal* urged the city to construct a proper airfield to encourage cross-country pilots to land there.[15] Airfields were not that difficult to create in the 1920s, and by the next year Albuquerque had established a respectable landing strip, which was quickly rewarded by an official visit from Anne and Charles Lindbergh.[16]

In this regard, Lordsburg proved a step ahead of the Duke City. In September 1929, their Lindbergh Airport served as a highly publicized stopover point for the New York to Los Angeles International Air Race. Amelia Earhart later visited Lordsburg as well. There is no question that Charles A. Lindbergh's 1928 landings in Lordsburg and Santa Fe provided a crucial impetus for aviation throughout the entire Southwest.

In the late 1920s, such a bold publicity crusade for aviation filled a real need, for flying in that era involved an incredible number of risks. The same papers that celebrated Lindbergh's glowing predictions of regular air-mail and increased domestic airline travel also carried articles on a bizarre set of aerial activities: a ninety-three-year-old "flying grandmother" from North Dakota who had just entered a cross-country air race, nine men who had safely parachuted simultaneously from a navy transport plane in Washington State—setting a new record, a German aviator whose chute had unfortunately failed to open, and an ongoing investigation regarding a plane crash that had killed Germany's ambassador to the United States: "Witnesses say wings suddenly folded up and aircraft shot downward to earth."[17] Indeed, the first major disaster of the Lindbergh-backed transcontinental Air Transport line occurred in the Southwest in September 1929, when a trimotor filled with travelers on the Albuquerque to Los Angeles route crashed into Mount Taylor with no survivors.[18] It would take several years before American airlines could follow, in Keyhoe's words, "the invisible air trails along which Colonel Lindbergh passed in his nationwide tour."[19] In his profession, as Lindbergh once remarked to daughter Reeve, a person only fails once.[20]

In addition to fostering new and improved regional airports, Lindbergh's visit must have inspired untold numbers of young New Mexicans to follow in his footsteps. Santa Fean Laughlin Barker proved one of these. Fascinated by the Santa Fe stopover, young Barker decided to make aviation his career and, after graduating from the U.S. Naval Academy in 1943, went on to become a noted carrier pilot and later chief of Naval Operations at the Pentagon, from which he retired in 1964 with the rank of commander. How many other New Mexicans shared this dream cannot now be determined, but it is doubtful if Barker was unique. The Lindbergh visit also affected the life of Laguna Pueblo native Mariano Pedro. From that time forward until his death, his family always called him "Lindy."[21]

◾

The second area where the Lindbergh legend helped shape New Mexican history occurred the following year. In the summer of 1929, the newly married Charles and Anne conducted some of the first aerial archaeological surveys of the American Southwest. In so doing, they pioneered a technique that is now deemed essential to the profession. Later that fall, archaeologist Earl H. Morris displayed a number of these Lindbergh images during a lecture at the Carnegie Institution in Washington, praising the airplane as having "great usefulness" in unraveling the secrets of the Southwest.[22] In 1932 archaeologist A. V. Kidder similarly entranced a Santa Fe audience at the Laboratory of Anthropology by showing aerial slides that the Lindberghs had taken over Central America. Said Kidder: "Now a new and unique instrument has appeared to revolutionize the gathering of archaeological data—the airplane."[23]

The Lindberghs, of course, were hardly the first to stumble upon the idea of aerial photography. English archaeologist Sir Henry Wellcome had photographed Near Eastern sites from a box kite as early as 1913, and five years later British scientist O. G. S. Crawford had teamed with the Royal Air Force to survey scores of ancient sites in Hampshire. Indeed, Crawford published a book, *Air Photography for Archaeologists*, in 1929, although there is no evidence that the Lindberghs had read it.[24] During the previous summer, archaeologists Olaf Emblem and Carlos Viera had taken a few aerial shots of Chaco Canyon for the School of American Research, but they received no publicity whatsoever. It took the charisma of the Lindbergh name to bring this innovative technique to the attention of the nation.

Since Anne grew up as the daughter of the U.S. ambassador to Mexico, it was surely she and her family who introduced the decidedly provincial Charles to the field of archaeology. But it was A. V. Kidder who first invited the Lindberghs to try their hand at photographing southwestern ruins from the air. Heralded as the man who single-handedly shifted archaeology from "pot hunting" to a science, in 1929 Kidder was completing his final summer of excavation at the Pecos Pueblo ruins northeast of Santa Fe. A critic of excessive "digging," he instantly realized how valuable aerial photos might be.[25]

Flying an open cockpit two-seater bi-wing Curtis Falcon, Charles and Anne landed at Kidder's Forked Lightning Ranch site near Pecos in the early summer of 1929. Anne later described the atmosphere there as resembling a Boston boy's school and the camp itself as "a heavenly high cool green valley between mountains and the cliffs of a mesa."[26] Surviving photos show that the Lindberghs wrapped the cowling of their Falcon with canvas to keep out dust and wind. The Pecos National Historic Park Archive contains thirteen aerial photographs that either Charles or Anne took of the Pecos region, including Dick's Ruin, Pajarito Plateau Canyon, and various images of Pecos proper. Although these pioneering photos may well have served as valuable tools for archaeologists by revealing average distances between dwellings and gardens, etc., none of the images is visually impressive.[27]

From Pecos, the Lindberghs flew to Canyon del Muerto, a side canyon of the far better-known Canyon de Chelly in northeastern Arizona. Along the way they snapped the first aerial view of the top of Black Mesa north of Santa Fe, revealing the locations where San Ildefonso Natives had fled after the 1592 Reconquest by don Diego de Vargas, as well as considerable evidence of illegal pot hunting.[28] They also photographed several images of Chaco Canyon (to be discussed later), as well as a number of photos of abandoned cliff dwellings in Canyon del Muerto and in Canyon de Chelly. Archaeologists Ann Axtel Morris and Earl H. Morris were then working on a site at Canyon del Muerto, and when the plane flew overhead, they shouted and flapped their arms in a vain attempt to attract its attention. Here, however, we have two conflicting accounts of what happened next. According to Ann Morris, the Lindberghs decided against landing their Falcon in the canyon proper and brought it down on a nearby mesa top. Later, at dusk, she saw two young people approach to politely inquire if this were the Morris camp, the man saying that he came from Dr. Kidder and "my name is Lindbergh."[29]

According to Edward Moffat Weyer, Jr., however, Ann and Earl Morris had both left Canyon del Muerto on July 25 with two of the expedition's three cars, and subsequent rains and flash floods had made the roads impassible for the third. So team members Weyer, Oscar Tatman, and one Omar (Olaf Emblem?), plus their Navajo guides, had been stuck in the region for several days. Weyer notes that it was they who first heard the aircraft and saw it disappear over the horizon. When the sound suddenly ceased, they feared a possible crash. Later they watched a tall man carrying a bulky load (which turned out to be Anne) wade across a low-level stream and approach the camp. The initial greeting from Charles: "How are you fixed for grub? . . . Er . . . you'll have to excuse me, this is Mrs. Lindbergh—it's for her."[30]

Charles then told Weyer that he had spotted a hitherto unknown hand-and-foothold trail to their base camp, so he decided to land the Falcon on the mesa nearby. He also spotted a previously unknown ruin in Canyon de Chelly that Oscar Tatman suggested should now be termed "Lindbergh's Cave," which the team explored the following day. "From my ship I can find one undiscovered ruin for every one that has been located on the ground," Charles boasted.[31] Since Charles and Anne also delivered some letters from Kidder to the Morrises, this flight provided the first (and last) airmail service from Pecos Pueblo, New Mexico, to Canyon del Muerto, Arizona.[32]

These southwestern aerial photographs so impressed Kidder that he urged the Lindberghs to consider other venues. Consequently, in October 1929, Kidder (on his first flight) and the Lindberghs made a five-day aerial survey of Yucatán and Guatemala. The Pan American Corporation supplied the Sikorsky Amphibian and the Carnegie Institution provided the film. Both Anne and Charles took turns piloting the aircraft, and the resulting photographs proved startling. In addition to locating several hitherto unexplored sites, the Lindberghs radioed their discoveries directly to Pan American International Airport at Miami, which passed them on to the Science News Service and hence to the popular press.[33] The nation's papers were fascinated by this venture. As a *New York Times* editor observed, Lindbergh was a "pioneer of aerial archaeology."[34]

In 1930 and 1931 Kidder and the Lindberghs again flew over parts of Central America and again Anne took many of the photographs. Lindbergh also agreed to aid anthropologist A. L. Kroeber by flying him over Peru, but all this came to a sudden end with the tragic 1932 kidnapping of their son.[35]

Of the perhaps one hundred photographs of southwestern archaeological sites taken by the Lindberghs, only one has achieved the status of minor classic. This is the powerful aerial image of Chaco Canyon's largest ruin, Pueblo Bonito, with a clear view of the towering "Threatening

Rock," a huge sandstone cliff, directly behind it. On January 22, 1941, the thirty thousand tons of Threatening Rock collapsed into the back wall of the pueblo, damaging about sixty-five rooms. The 1929 aerial photo clearly reveals an archaeological disaster ready to happen.

The question of who actually snapped the shutter on this classic image of Threatening Rock and Pueblo Bonito has always been a bit of a puzzle. Most accounts credit the photograph to Charles, but this is open to doubt. If the Lindberghs took the image on their flight to Canyon del Muerto, which seems likely, it was Charles who sat at the controls. Thus, it is highly probable that Anne Morrow Lindbergh should be given credit for clicking the shutter on Threatening Rock and Pueblo Bonito twelve years before the fall—still the most famous of all their 1929 pioneering photographs of southwestern archaeological ruins.

█

The final area where the Lindberghs helped shape the course of modern New Mexican history drew less on their popular celebrity status than on their quiet influence with the nation's rich and powerful. Both Charles and Anne grew up in distinguished families—she slightly more than he—but the pressures of the celebrity life meant that they were pushed more and more into the circles of the wealthy. The young couple actually had to don disguises when they visited New York, and later in life Charles had to periodically turn away disturbed young men who claimed to be their kidnapped son. Only by consorting with the elite could Charles and Anne find any sort of real privacy. But moving amid the circles of power has its advantages, and Charles (less so Anne) drew upon them to obtain consistent support for Massachusetts scientist Robert H. Goddard's dream of eventually sending a rocket into space.

In the late 1920s, the mild-mannered Robert H. Goddard was unknown to the general public, but he was widely recognized by a small group of rocket scientists. His modest fame rested largely on the publication of a single scientific paper, "A Method of Reaching Extreme Altitudes" (1919), which appeared from the Smithsonian Institution. This article proved mathematically that a liquid fuel rocket could indeed reach the upper atmosphere. The same newspaper publicity that so glorified the Lindberghs drove the shy Goddard to distraction. He often found himself described as the "Moon Rocket Man," ridiculed as an eccentric scientist who planned to transport passengers to outer space or Mars.[36] Goddard persisted in conducting his various local experiments, but his rocket test of July 17, 1929, in Auburn, Massachusetts, crashed with such furor that the neighbors reported the downing of a plane.[37]

An article on this mishap caught Lindbergh's eye, and he phoned Goddard to request an interview. The two met shortly afterward and Lindbergh became an instant convert. As the airplane represented an advance over the automobile, Lindbergh reasoned, so too would the rocket advance the airplane. Consequently, Lindbergh prevailed on Daniel F. Guggenheim to assist Goddard, which the foundation proceeded to do with an $18,000-a-year grant. In addition, Lindbergh used his influence on the Carnegie Institution in Washington to add an additional $5,000.[38]

Goddard realized that crowded Massachusetts was not ideal for future experiments with rocketry. Since Lindbergh knew well the nation's geography from his 1928 tour, he also helped Goddard choose his new test locale, urging him to consider relocating to the southern Great Plains. After consulting U.S. Weather Bureau reports as to dust and wind conditions, Goddard decided that the southwestern edge of the plains would be his best bet. So in 1930 Esther and Robert Goddard moved to Roswell, New Mexico. As Esther later recalled, they always termed the landscape of southern New Mexico "prairies"—"We didn't dare call them deserts." An eastern reporter of 1934, however, proved far less circumspect. He described the Roswell region as "a haunting world of alkaline gray, holy, profane, grim, although exquisite with a haunting stillness."[39]

From that moment forward, Robert H. Goddard and Roswell, New Mexico, became forever linked in the public eye. Although Goddard remained officially on the faculty at Clark University in Worcester, Massachusetts, thanks largely to Guggenheim funding, he spent most of the 1930s in New Mexico, periodically firing off his rockets in the Eden Valley north of Roswell. Esther dutifully shot film of virtually every flight. Over the years, the shy, reserved scientist and his wife became respected members of the community. He especially enjoyed the time he spent with various service clubs.

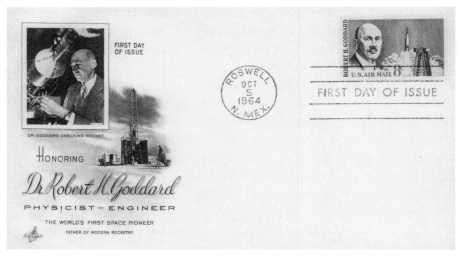

First-day cover (1964), honoring Roswell's Robert H. Goddard as the "father of modern rocketry." Collection of the author.

After his death in 1945, Goddard would be ranked with Alexander Graham Bell, Samuel F. B. Morse, Thomas Edison, and the Wright brothers as an authentic American genius. He is justly celebrated as the father of the space age, for his 214 patents provided the basis of American military and space age technology. His public patents—especially those regarding multiple-stage rockets and gyroscope guiding systems—easily found their way to German laboratories. When he and his staff examined a captured German V-2 rocket in early 1945, they recognized every feature. "This is your rocket, Dr. Goddard," a colleague remarked. "It seems to be," he replied.[40] In 1960, the John F. Kennedy administration settled all claims with his widow and with the Guggenheim Foundation for a million dollars. In September 1964, the U.S. Post Office issued an eight-cent air mail stamp in his honor. Today the Goddard Space Flight Center and Roswell Goddard High School perpetuate his name on both a national and a local level.

Given this success, it is difficult to realize how hard Goddard struggled all through the 1930s as experiment after experiment failed to perform as expected. His modest Roswell workshop measured only thirty-five-by-fifty feet, and Esther actually hand-sewed parachutes for the rockets' return. Part of this situation may well be his own doing, for he consistently refused to share his ideas and technical breakthroughs with his fellow scientists.[41] Indeed, Cal Tech émigré physicist Theodore von Karmen later faulted Goddard for not participating more fully in the larger rocket scientific community.[42] Given this isolation, the subsequent Guggenheim six-year grant of $25,000—again at Lindbergh's urging—proved crucial to his dogged experimentation.

Anne and Charles Lindbergh visited Roswell on several occasions, and Charles and Daniel Guggenheim both journeyed there to witness a special rocket test in September of 1935, which, like so many of the others, did not come up to expectations. By 1938, the Guggenheim Foundation had invested $148,000 in Goddard with very little to show for it. Had the foundation decided to pull the plug, Goddard would have had little recourse.

Goddard knew well how important Lindbergh's support was to his continued funding. Thus, he periodically mailed him reports and/or rocket films and tried hard to keep him abreast of every development. The collected Goddard papers reflect his fear that Lindbergh might somehow lose interest in the rocket project.[43]

Painfully aware of the value of publicity, Lindbergh periodically urged Goddard to make his experiments better known to the public. But when the scientist refused to do so, Lindbergh never wavered in his support. On his trips to Germany, Lindbergh also made inquiries about German rocket research and, from the vague replies he received, concluded (correctly, as it turns out) that they had a secret program under way. These findings he reported to Roswell.[44] In 1937, Charles wrote from Europe to praise Robert H. Goddard, and a university official read the statement at a Clark University commencement exercise. The letter was also published in the *New York Times*.[45] Goddard kept his end of the bargain as well. In 1937 he wrote Lindbergh, "Your continued interest in the rocket work is very encouraging. I wish it were possible for you to drop in occasionally and see what is being done."[46]

Lindbergh's public support of Goddard, it should be noted, occurred at the precise time when his own popular reputation began to plummet. His infamous remark at a Des Moines, Iowa, America First rally that the only groups who wanted U.S. involvement in the war were "the British, Jewish, and the Roosevelt Administration" does not seem to have broken his relationship with the Guggenheims, but it certainly soured feelings with vast segments of the American public. As his sister-in-law later noted, he went "from Jesus to Judas" in fifteen years.[47]

In 1963, with his reputation at least partially rehabilitated, Lindbergh wrote the preface to the first biography of the scientist, Milton Lehman's *This High Man: The Life of Robert H. Goddard*. Here Lindbergh noted that whenever he watched a rocket leave Cape Canaveral, he wondered if Goddard were dreaming in the 1930s or if he were dreaming now.[48] Surely Lindbergh knew full well how crucial he had been to Goddard's eventual success. Esther Goddard always praised his continual support of her husband's efforts.

■

For over a decade after his historic 1927 flight, Charles A. Lindbergh flourished as America's greatest celebrity. When he wed Anne Morrow in 1929, the aura precisely doubled. Everything the Lindberghs said or did became worthy of discussion, and this gave them an unprecedented cultural power. This cultural power of celebrity affected faraway New Mexico in that it provided the first sustained impetus for early state airports, encouraged young people to take up aviation, and gave incredible publicity to both the idea of aerial photography and the ancient southwestern sites so photographed. And without Lindbergh's continued private support, Robert H. Goddard's rocket experiments (literally) might not have gotten off the ground. Although over six thousand miles separate Le Bourget Aerodrome from the mountains and deserts of New Mexico, the Lindbergh legend had no difficulty bridging the distance.

CHAPTER TWO

J. Robert Oppenheimer *and the* State of New Mexico

A Reciprocal Relationship

$\mathcal{T}$he sagas of famed atomic physicist J. Robert Oppenheimer and the state of New Mexico have long been intertwined. Although the scientist lived most of his life in New York, California, and New Jersey, the Oppenheimer family leased and subsequently purchased a second home in the northern Pecos Valley during the late 1920s. A generation after his death, Oppenheimer's name still echoes throughout the region. Los Alamos boasts an Oppenheimer Avenue, and the J. Robert Oppenheimer Memorial Committee sponsors a prestigious lecture series that brings speakers to the Hill from around the world. In 1983, on the fortieth anniversary of the founding of the community, the Los Alamos National Laboratory (LANL) renamed their scientific library the J. Robert Oppenheimer Study Center (currently the third-largest library in the state). Today the scientist's son, Peter, lives quietly in the Santa Fe region.[1]

Even in the early twenty-first century, the name Oppenheimer still calls forth a flood of contradictory images. Throughout his sixty-two years, J. Robert Oppenheimer wore a number of hats. He was a child prodigy, a Harvard polymath, a pioneer in the emerging field of theoretical physics, the man who put West Coast physics on the world map, and the famed director of the secret Los Alamos Scientific Laboratory (LASL) from 1943 to 1945. After the war, reporters termed him "the father of the atomic bomb," and for almost a decade, he carried the mantle of public voice of nuclear wisdom. In 1947 he became director of the Institute for Advanced Study at Princeton and, several years later, suffered the indignity of a witch-hunt "trial" before the Personnel Security Board of the U.S. Atomic Energy Commission (AEC). Because of his well-known left-wing connections in the 1930s, plus his recent opposition to the creation of a U.S. hydrogen bomb, the AEC deprived him of his security clearance. Nine years later, however, the AEC partially apologized by awarding him its prestigious Fermi Medal. In 1994, twenty-seven years after Oppenheimer's death, a former Soviet spymaster, Pavel Sudaplatov, publicly claimed that Oppenheimer—as well as several others—had delivered atomic secrets to the Soviet Union during the war. But Sudaplatov produced no documentary evidence to support the claim, and the charges were hotly denied by both historians and Oppenheimer's colleagues.[2] A British commentator once compared Oppenheimer's post-AEC-hearings treatment to that of the infamous Alfred Dreyfus affair, but the template reaches well beyond the anti-Semitic France of the 1890s. Indeed, the saga of his life seems ripped from the pages of Sophocles or Aeschylus: J. Robert Oppenheimer as tragic hero of the early nuclear age.[3]

International figure though he may have been, J. Robert Oppenheimer also directly shaped the course of New Mexico history. In fact, the Oppenheimer/New Mexico stories overlapped in a myriad of ways. Over the years, Oppenheimer forged a number of links to his adopted state. From his first visit to the Pecos Forest Reserve in 1922 to the purchase of a summer retreat in the upper Pecos Valley in 1929 to his directorship of the lab during the war years to his honorary degree from the University of New Mexico in 1947 to his poignant last speech in Los Alamos in 1964, the sagas of man and state have long been intertwined. In a strange sense, the relationship proved reciprocal. The natural wonders of northern New

Mexico helped restore J. Robert Oppenheimer to both mental and physical health, and his scientific management catapulted Los Alamos into a city that is now recognized around the globe.

Born into a wealthy New York German-Jewish family on April 22, 1904, young Robert's first contact with New Mexico—like so many of his generation—came because of illness. For all his brilliance, Oppenheimer suffered from a variety of health problems. His parents cautioned his young friends to simply let him alone during his periodic bouts of depression. His high school classmate and long-term friend Francis Fergusson even claimed that Oppenheimer had once tried to strangle him with a belt.

Shortly after he graduated from New York City's famed Ethical Culture School, Oppenheimer contracted a severe case of trench dysentery while on a mineralogical trip to the Herz Mountains of Germany. Too ill to attend Harvard that fall as planned, he spent most of the year in the family apartment on Riverside Drive, where he was largely confined to his room, the prescribed treatment of the day. This would have been hard on any teenager, but for a budding genius it approached the impossible. He increasingly began to behave in a sullen and boorish manner. In desperation, his father begged Herbert W. Smith, his former English teacher, to take him west during the summer of 1922 to try to restore his equilibrium. For almost two months the pair rode through what is now the Pecos Wilderness of northern New Mexico—then called the Pecos Forest Reserve. A guest ranch in Cowles, New Mexico, run by Winthrop and Katherine Chaves Page, served as their base.[4]

That Smith and Oppenheimer ended up in the mountains of New Mexico rather than those of Montana, Wyoming, or Idaho may largely be credited to fellow Ethical Culture student and Albuquerque resident Francis Fergusson. Fergusson belonged to one of the state's most eminent families. His mother was Clara Huning, daughter of pioneer Fritz Huning, whose Albuquerque mansion—the Huning Castle—once ranked among the state's most elegant homes. His father was lawyer Harvey B. Fergusson, who served in Washington, D.C., as both territorial delegate (from 1896 forward) and, after statehood in 1912, as its first elected congressman.

Francis's older brother, Harvey, later became a respected southwestern novelist, while his older sister, Erna, gained even greater fame as the chief interpreter of the region to outsiders. Her Santa Fe–based Koshare Tour Services (1920–27) and her books—especially *Our Southwest* (1940)—introduced thousands to the famed "three cultures" of the area. Francis had attended Albuquerque schools, but he transferred to the Ethical Culture School for his high school senior year to better prepare for admission to an Ivy League university.

Francis and Robert shared a schoolboy interest in poetry and drama, and surely it was he who urged the Oppenheimer family to consider the healing charms of his home state. Francis obviously knew a good deal about the Koshare tours—where elegantly dressed young women, decked to the nines with Indian jewelry, escorted La Fonda Hotel visitors to nearby Indian pueblos and ancient Native and Hispanic sites. Through family connections, the Fergussons also had links with the Chaves/Page clans.[5] Moreover, ever since the late nineteenth century, New Mexico had earned a deserved reputation as a place to regain one's health. During the preantibiotic days of the 1930s, the fledgling *New Mexico Magazine* frequently ran articles touting the state as a "land of almost perpetual sunshine."[6]

Oppenheimer's first lengthy visit to New Mexico in the summer of 1922 had a number of consequences. First, Katherine Chaves Page—a twenty-eight-year-old upper-class Hispanic woman blessed with great charm of manner—welcomed the frail, insecure boy into her family circle. Women often responded to Oppenheimer—on a variety of levels—and some historians argue that he had his first schoolboy crush on her.[7] Although perhaps overstated, Herbert W. Smith later told historian Alice Kimball Smith that when the warm, aristocratic Chaves family embraced the frail Oppenheimer, he found himself loved and admired "for the first time in his life."[8]

Second, Oppenheimer's long rides through the Pecos Forest Reserve—still one of the most spectacular regions of the state—helped restore his mental and physical balance. The young men camped amid mountain forests of spruce, pine, piñon, and aspen. They rode by thirteen-thousand-foot peaks, such as Santa Fe Baldy and Pecos Baldy, that stretched well above timberline. They crisscrossed the high meadows of Hamilton Mesa, Round Mountain, and Grady's Mountain, which dazzle the eye every summer with wild hollyhocks, red skyrockets, bluebells, jack-in-the-pulpits, purple asters, shooting stars, mountain pinks, and bluewood violets. The area also abounds with lupine, bluebonnets, buttercups, dwarf lobelias, coreopsis, columbines, thistles, and evening primrose. The forks of the Rio La Casa contain forty- to sixty-foot waterfalls, while bear, mountain lion, deer, and elk all drink at sundown from the region's scattered lakes.[9] As nature writer Lou Hernandez once observed, "In spring a visitor can enjoy the feeling that he is the first to set foot in a virgin wilderness."[10]

Smith later reported that Oppenheimer relished the challenges of this mountain experience and accepted his responsibilities like a mature adult. The trip must have helped restore both body and soul, for Oppenheimer entered Harvard in the fall of 1923 and completed the rigorous four-year curriculum in only three years. After graduation, he studied in Cambridge, England, before earning his PhD in theoretical physics at Göttingen University in 1927, when he was only twenty-three. His performance at the oral examination proved so dazzling that one of his professors, James Franck, jested, "I got out of there just in time. He was beginning to ask *me* questions."

By switching to theoretical physics, young Oppenheimer finally discovered his calling. After two years of further study, he accepted simultaneous appointments at the University of California, Berkeley, and the California Institute of Technology in Pasadena. Alternating semesters at each university, during the next decade Oppenheimer helped put West Coast physics on the international scientific map. Initially apolitical, from the mid-1930s on Oppenheimer increasingly moved amid radical left-wing circles. Whether he officially joined the Communist Party remains an issue of some dispute.[11]

Once his sons were back in the States for good, Oppenheimer's father purchased a summer home for them in the upper Pecos Valley in 1929. Thus, Oppenheimer and his younger brother, Frank—also a physicist—shared a New Mexico summer retreat to which they would escape as often as possible. The Oppenheimer brothers grew to love the region, and this also allowed Oppenheimer to maintain contact with Katherine Chaves Page until her tragic murder in 1961. It is no exaggeration to say that the foremost impact that New Mexico had on Oppenheimer was to restore him to health.

Oppenheimer's 1922 trip to New Mexico also expanded his circle of friends to include his first westerners. He and Smith renewed contact with Francis Fergusson in Albuquerque, and there he met Harvey and Erna, as well as their friend Paul Horgan. Horgan, who would later gain international fame as both novelist and historian, formed a close relationship with Oppenheimer. He visited the Oppenheimers' Long Island summer home for extensive stays at least twice, and he and Oppenheimer—who at that time voiced serious literary aspirations—enjoyed themselves immensely. On one visit, the two were out sailing on Oppenheimer's sloop the *Trimethy* and got caught in a riptide that carried them far out to sea. When they failed to return on time, Oppenheimer's father dispatched the family yacht for a search mission. In a later interview, Horgan termed the youthful Fergusson-Oppenheimer-Horgan relationship a "pigmy triumvirate." He also confessed that Oppenheimer was the most brilliant person he had ever met. In retrospect, Horgan regretted that their careers had so diverged. Although Horgan taught on the faculty at Wesleyan and Fergusson became a professor of literature at Princeton (with Oppenheimer nearby), the three seldom saw much of one another.[12]

Perhaps the most remarkable New Mexico friendship that Oppenheimer forged, however, came during the summer of 1937. Exhausted from his West Coast teaching, he had returned to the Pecos region for an extended vacation. While horseback riding through the Valle Grande area, he stopped at Edith Warner's modest tearoom on the west side of the Rio Grande, near the lone wooden Otowi Bridge crossing. Daughter of a Pennsylvania Baptist minister, the quasi-mystical Warner had escaped to New Mexico to write essays and eke out a living in the shadow of San Ildefonso Pueblo. From a rented adobe home on pueblo land, she served as the Otowi "station agent" for the narrow-gauge Denver and Rio Grande Western Railroad (the Chili Line). Translated, this meant that the headmaster of the Los Alamos Ranch School, A. J. Connell, had hired her to watch over the extensive Ranch School supplies and luggage until a truck could collect the goods on its thrice-weekly, three-and-a-half-hour journey up the only dirt road to the Hill. The Chili Line railway storage facility consisted of a boxcar.

In addition, Warner operated a small tea shop from her home, where she sold gasoline, ice, candy, and sandwiches to the steady stream of

Edith Warner by her home at Otowi, New Mexico, about the
time that Oppenheimer first met her. Photographer unknown.
Courtesy Palace of the Governors (MNM/DCA). Neg. no. 47537.

tourists who ventured from Santa Fe to the Frijoles Canyon Indian ruins
(now Bandelier National Monument). Warner's pleasant manner, plus
her famed recipe for chocolate cake, charmed Oppenheimer, and he
never forgot her.

This chance meeting bore fruit six years later. By early 1943, the Chili Line had gone bankrupt, the Los Alamos Ranch School had been taken over by the federal government, and wartime travel restrictions had cut the Santa Fe tourist trade to a trickle. Thus, Warner faced genuine destitution. In a gesture of great magnanimity, Oppenheimer, now director of the secret laboratory Site Y, encouraged her to establish a "reservations-only" restaurant to serve special meals—up to ten people at a time—to a select clientele. Because of security concerns, the clientele consisted exclusively of the Los Alamos scientists and their wives.

Both sides benefited from this experience. Hill residents relished the fifteen-mile drive at sunset down to her home by the Rio Grande, "where the river makes a noise." They especially enjoyed the simple meals that she prepared on her wood-burning stove for—as she phrased it—her "hungry scientists." Since she and her San Ildefonso partner, Tilano, drew most of the produce from their extensive garden, the dinners abounded with five kinds of squash, beans, raspberries, and fresh corn. For all this, she charged only two dollars per person and refused all tips. As this modest sum barely enabled her to cover expenses, several Hill wives helped sell her excess produce to their neighbors.[13]

Dining on Native American foods before an open fire in a home without telephone or electricity charmed the LASL scientists. The tranquil setting seemed to provide needed respite from their frenzied pace of life on the Hill. Their regular custom not only allowed Warner to survive the lean war years; it also enabled her to forge friendships with some of the finest minds of the day. She became especially close to Alice Kimball and Cyril Smith, Carson and Kay Mark, Edward and Mici Teller, Niels Bohr, Stan and François Ulam, and Robert and Kitty Oppenheimer (Tilano always referred to the laboratory director as "Mr. Op."). Fittingly, it was Kitty Oppenheimer who drove down to inform her of the bombing of Hiroshima. Along the way, Warner alerted the scientists and their wives to San Ildefonso traditions and cautioned them to avoid certain sacred areas when they hiked throughout the region.[14]

Numerous Los Alamos memoirs recall the charm of dining at Edith Warner's home. Reservations became highly sought after as Hill residents relished the good food and quiet conversations. Eventually the steady demand overburdened the frail Warner and she had to reduce her meal

Edith Warner and Tilano, 1949. Photographer unknown.
Courtesy Palace of the Governors (MNM/DCA). Neg. no. 47542.

offerings from five days a week to three. But she always found time to feed Robert and Kitty Oppenheimer whenever they asked.

After the war, when a new metal bridge across the Rio Grande threatened to disrupt Edith and Tilano's tranquil lifestyle, Los Alamos scientists joined with San Ildefonso builders to erect a new adobe house at a more distant location. The building stands today.

Edith Warner did not long survive the war. In spite of treatment at Los Alamos, she died of cancer in 1951. But her story has evolved into a New Mexico legend, one that drew on Hispanic, Native, and Anglo-American traditions. In 1951, sensing that the end was near, she ordered Tilano a two years' supply of blue jeans from Montgomery Ward. He died precisely two years later. Whether their relationship was platonic or physical has never been clear, but everyone agrees that it was deep and enduring. A modern observer has called the saga of Edith and Tilano "one of the great love stories of all time."[15]

Taos novelist Frank Waters fictionalized this story in his clumsy *The Woman at Otowi Crossing* (1966).[16] But Warner found her Boswell in Peggy Pond Church's *The House at Otowi Bridge* (1959), a southwestern classic that has never gone out of print.[17]

Oppenheimer's role in this myth has never been given proper credit. Yet it was his chance encounter with Warner during the summer of 1937 that laid the groundwork for the emergence of a New Mexico legend. On a deeper level, Warner's nourishing meals of traditional Native foods provided yet another way by which the charm of New Mexico allowed the pressured scientists to restore their own delicate balance—not just Oppenheimer this time, but scores of others as well. As Cyril Smith once remarked to his wife, Alice, "You can't possibly talk about Los Alamos without her."[18]

The official headquarters of the Manhattan Engineering District, or "Manhattan Project," the cover name for the American effort to build an atomic bomb, lay initially on the sixty-seventh floor of the Empire State Building and, later, in the new War Building in Washington, D.C. But the major scientific and technological work took place at dozens of locations scattered across the nation. Military laboratories and major universities such as the University of California, Columbia, the University of Chicago, the Massachusetts Institute of Technology, the University of Minnesota, and the University of Rochester all played crucial roles. When Major General Leslie R. Groves assumed overall command of this program on September 12, 1942, he tried to bring order to this diffuse enterprise. Groves insisted that all project activities be compressed to a single goal: to create a combat-ready atomic weapon in the shortest-possible time.[19]

From the onset, Groves insisted on absolute secrecy. He did so for two reasons. First, obviously, was to stem any scientific or technical leaks to the Axis powers (or to the Soviets, who were similarly excluded); second was to increase the absolute shock value whenever the weapon first saw combat use. Thus, Groves insisted on a policy of strict compart-mentalization: that is, a person should know only enough to perform his or her specific assignment. Only a handful of people knew the overall purpose of the Manhattan Project. Most workers had no idea what the person on the hall above them was working on. Until Hiroshima, many Los Alamos wives did not know what their husbands were engaged in. Even Groves's wife and two children remained completely in the dark.

But numerous scientists protested. Several said they would not move to Los Alamos if they could not tell their wives everything (Groves relented). Others argued that since the many problems they faced were so interrelated, the policy of compartmentalization would actually delay the final outcome. They insisted that the Manhattan Project create a spot where all issues could be discussed in a no-holds-barred scientific atmosphere.

Groves bent with the prevailing winds and agreed to set up such a venue. But the requirements were strict: the new location had to be isolated from major urban centers, easily protected by army security forces, convenient to major transportation networks, and (preferably) already on federally owned land so as to minimize the difficulties of the appropriation of property.[20]

Over the objection of many of his advisers, Groves selected Oppenheimer to head this new installation. Opponents pointed to Oppenheimer's well-known radical past, but Groves argued that Oppenheimer knew so much about the project anyway that it would be far better to have him at Los Alamos under constant surveillance. Moreover, he sensed that Oppenheimer's relentless ambition for fame would cause him to drop all previous radical contacts.[21]

Although Groves would later claim that he knew well the region of northern New Mexico from his time spent in Arizona, it was clearly Oppenheimer who alerted him to the possibility of New Mexico as a spot for the proposed Site Y. (A California venue had already been rejected as not sufficiently isolated.) In the fall of 1942, Oppenheimer and Groves seriously explored two New Mexico locations. The first was Jemez Springs, but Groves felt that the cliffs bordering the town might hamper future expansion, while Oppenheimer argued that they would stifle creativity by making the scientists claustrophobic.

The second choice lay with the nearby Los Alamos Ranch School, which by 1942 had fallen on hard times. Many of the staff had departed for the military, and student enrollment suffered accordingly.[22] One often reads that Oppenheimer chose the location because he had graduated from the Ranch School—even Paul Horgan held this view—but this

*J. Robert Oppenheimer
in his early forties
when he served as
head of Los Alamos.
Courtesy Los Alamos
National Laboratory.*

is not so. Oppenheimer knew the region only through horseback visits from his Pecos Valley home.

Groves responded favorably. He liked the fact that Los Alamos could be approached only by a single, easily guarded dirt road, and he deemed the Hill sufficiently isolated from mainstream American life. Initially the modest Ranch School buildings seemed appropriate to house the estimated one hundred scientists and their families needed to complete the task. Although the Ranch School, the nearby Anchor Ranch, and the properties of scores of Hispanic ranchers would have to be appropriated, much of the land lay in Forest Service hands. Oppenheimer also argued that the breathtaking views from the mesas would spur scientific creativity. Both were proven correct. With numerous MPs, many on horseback, a team of guard dogs (the K-9 Squad), and scattered G-2 (army intelligence) agents in Albuquerque and Santa Fe, Los Alamos proved relatively easy to secure from outsiders. And numerous scientists recalled the spectacular environment as the linchpin of their experience. As metallurgist Cyril Smith observed, "To my mind the landscape is as much a part of the project as Groves' management. The environment has an immense effect, I think, on one's general state of mind. Weekend hikes made it possible for us to maintain this intense level of work during the war."[23]

Thus, on December 7, 1942, Ranch School headmaster A. J. Connell, who had long seen the handwriting on the wall, received official notice that the federal government planned to confiscate the Ranch School properties for the war effort. After considerable dickering as to the date of transfer, the army agreed that the four seniors could take accelerated classes and graduate on January 21, 1943. Accordingly, the four received their diplomas in a formal graduation ceremony and departed, respectively, for Cornell, Harvard, Stanford, and the Newark College of Engineering.[24] The dust had not settled before the army arrived en masse to create the top-secret Site Y. Without Oppenheimer's deep affection for northern New Mexico, the nation's premier weapons laboratory would not be situated where it is today.

Oppenheimer's major impact on the state of New Mexico, of course, lay with his role as director of the Los Alamos Scientific Laboratory from 1943 to 1945. One of the first decisions he made in early 1943 involved trees. Contractors' bulldozers had begun to level the terrain for various buildings, but he stopped this immediately, insisting that every possible tree remain in place. This proved among the first of thousands of decisions in what became nothing less than an administrative miracle. Oppenheimer's fair and balanced decision making proved even more remarkable when one realizes that he had no previous administrative experience. (He had never even served as head of a university physics department.)

The issues he dealt with ranged from the mundane to the cosmic. Because of the isolation and relatively primitive living conditions, he spent countless hours assuring scientists—especially their wives— that the ultimate goal was a worthy one and that the harsh circumstances were only temporary.[25] When Edward Teller refused to cooperate,

*Oppenheimer's badge photo
at Los Alamos. Courtesy
Los Alamos National
Laboratory.*

J. R. Oppenheimer

Oppenheimer wisely gave him his own group to head. Along the way he composed a little prayer: "May the Lord preserve us from the enemy without and the Hungarians within."[26]

The ever-present army security measures proved a constant annoyance. All incoming and outgoing mail passed under censors' eyes, state driver's licenses carried numbers rather than names, and the numerous babies were registered as born at Box 1663, Santa Fe, N.M. Cameras were discouraged and diaries forbidden. Everyone visiting Santa Fe shops and museums had instructions not to speak to people more than necessary. When Hill wives dined at La Fonda Hotel for lunch, they were well aware that they remained under constant G-2 surveillance.[27] One final example: the Girl Scouts formed a chapter, but the troop had to pretend to be in Santa Fe (as Los Alamos did not officially exist). Moreover, all girls who had scientist fathers were instructed to register under fake names, lest spies discover where their fathers were.[28]

The technical and scientific dilemmas that Oppenheimer faced, of course, dwarfed all the other problems combined. From 1943 to 1945, Manhattan Project scientists stood at the very edge of human knowledge. This proved true for every step of the process. On a technical level, skilled machinists had to devise delicate beryllium-copper tools to drill high explosives, lest a steel tool accidentally spark and send the building up in flames. Metallurgists dealing with plutonium had no precedent to guide them as they painstakingly shaped the man-made radioactive element into hemispheres for the Trinity/Nagasaki weapons. Many of Oppenheimer's most creative administrative decisions came with his plan to restructure the entire laboratory to focus on the implosion weapon when it became clear that plutonium could not be used in the planned uranium-235 gun-type bomb.[29]

Along with administrative and technical questions, Oppenheimer faced a number of cosmic questions as well. Should the U-235 weapon be dropped in combat without any prior field test? Could a "super" or hydrogen weapon—hundreds of times more powerful—be created along with a fission bomb? How could the laboratory best defend its workers against potential radiation dangers? And the ultimate question: Could a nuclear bomb somehow ignite the atmosphere and destroy all life on earth? When Los Alamos historian David Hawkins first raised this last question with Edward Teller, Teller responded, with his usual dry wit: "Oh, David, there are worse things that could happen."[30] Oppenheimer had a role in virtually every LASL decision, large or small.

But Los Alamos allowed time for play as well as work. The lab closed down on Sundays, and the scientists took advantage of the time off to hike the extensive mountains of the region. They visited the ruins of Frijoles Canyon so often that it became virtually their private playground. In winter they skated Ashley Pond and skied the nearby mountains slopes. Oppenheimer and his wife, Kitty, took several two-day horseback rides across the Rio Grande to their Pecos home, much to the dismay of the FBI agents who had to accompany them. He usually rode a horse named Crisis, so feisty that he alone could handle it.

All the Los Alamos memoirs laud Oppenheimer's administrative skills. Rather than govern from an office desk, Oppenheimer spent his time constantly attending meetings and visiting laboratories. He seemed to know a bit about every problem on hand. People especially remembered his consideration and evenhandedness. For example, in one instance he went out of his way to thank the MPs for keeping the project safe. In another case, when he had to choose between two equally qualified scientists for a key position, he simply asked them to draw straws. As project veteran Jo Ann Foley once observed, Oppenheimer should have gotten an award for "cross cultural communication. He kept everybody on an even keel, even the teenagers."[31]

His administrative reputation has not faded with time. As Atomic Energy Commission head Glenn T. Seaborg observed in 1965, to a large extent "the greatness [of Los Alamos] lay in Robert Oppenheimer."[32] One of the approximately twenty British scientists stationed there, James Tuck, remained convinced that "a lesser man could not have done it." As another Los Alamos alumnus observed, "The work certainly would have been completed without Oppenheimer, but it wouldn't have been done so soon. He was very close to being indispensable. You think someone else might have come along—but you never know."[33]

Oppenheimer made thousands of decisions that affected New Mexico, but few proved more important than his acceptance of the plan to test the world's first atomic weapon at Trinity Site, about thirty-five miles east of Socorro. He even chose the name Trinity for the spot, and today *Trinity Site* appears on most state maps. What Oppenheimer meant by this term has never been clear. Even he professed uncertainty, although he told General Groves that he drew the name from a John Donne poem he had just read that contained the lines

Batter my heart
Three person'd God;

Los Alamos historian Marjorie Bell Chambers, however, has offered another explanation. She argues that the reference to Trinity has Hindu rather than Christian roots. In this sense, the term refers to something that is destroyed, and is later revived again.[34] The issue will probably never be resolved. When I posed this question to Frank Oppenheimer in the early 1980s, he confessed that he simply did not know.

■

In the tense hours before the Trinity test on Monday, July 16, 1945, Oppen-heimer seemed on the verge of collapse. Gaunt and exhausted, he held on to a pole to steady himself as the Trinity countdown approached zero. During the final seconds, he hardly breathed.[35] When the huge ball of fire rose forty thousand feet in the air—proving that the scientists' theories had been correct—he confessed to a colleague that "my confidence in the human mind is somewhat restored." To his brother, Frank, he simply said, "It worked."[36] Three weeks later, on August 6 and August 9, the specially modified B-29s *Enola Gay* and *Bock's Car* dropped their respective weapons on Hiroshima and Nagasaki. On August 14, Japan surrendered. Although the atomic bombs may not have won the war, they certainly ended it. Under Oppenheimer's direction, the Los Alamos scientists had been given an impossible assignment. And they delivered.

Exhausted by his ordeal, Oppenheimer told Groves that he hoped to resign as soon as possible. On October 16, 1945, his last day as director, Oppenheimer spoke to virtually the entire Los Alamos community in a gigantic outdoor ceremony. General Groves presented a certificate of appreciation from the secretary of war, which Oppenheimer accepted on behalf of the laboratory with a brief speech. In it he noted:

> If atomic bombs are to be added as new weapons to the
> arsenals of a warring world, or to the arsenals of nations
> preparing for war, then the time will come when mankind
> will curse the names of Los Alamos and of Hiroshima.
> The peoples of the world must unite, or they will perish.[37]

Three weeks later, on November 5, 1945, he gave his final Los Alamos speech to the approximately five hundred members of the newly formed Association of Los Alamos Scientists (ALAS). Since he had officially turned the laboratory over to his successor, naval commander Norris Bradbury, he felt a little more free to express his thoughts. Emphasizing both the "peril" and "hope" of atomic energy, he pleaded for scientific openness as the key to world unity. It remains one his best-remembered addresses.[38]

Over the years, many of Oppenheimer's scientific colleagues have recorded their impressions of his wartime leadership of the laboratory. Charles Crutchfield noted that at the start, Oppenheimer seemed to view

J. Robert Oppenheimer speaking in front of Fuller Lodge, 1945.
Photographer unknown. Courtesy Palace of the Governors
(MNM/DCA). Neg. no. 40769.

the Manhattan Project with virtual indifference. He considered it as a
purely scientific inquiry to see if the Allies could crack the nuclear secrets
of nature. (If they could not, of course, then neither could the Germans.)
But as time wore on, Oppenheimer became more emotionally involved,
until by 1945 he had staked everything he had on the successful outcome
of the Trinity test.[39] Scientist Louis Rosen recalled his former director as
a man with the brain of an Einstein and the soul of a poet.[40]

Long-term assistant John Manley provided yet another perspective on
Oppenheimer's leadership during those years when he highlighted
Oppenheimer's great flair for the dramatic. When Oppenheimer began
recruiting scientists to come to Los Alamos, it almost seemed as if he were
casting them as actors in a play. On virtually every major occasion, he

came up with a poignant, quotable phrase. For example, when President Franklin Delano Roosevelt died on April 12, 1945, Oppenheimer quoted from the Hindu sacred writings, the Bhagavad-Gita, "Man is a creature whose substance is faith. What his faith is, he is."[41] After the Trinity test, he delivered an even more-famous quotation from the same source: "I am become death, the shatterer of worlds." (He admired this skill in others as well. He later told the daughter of Trinity Site director Kenneth T. Bainbridge that her father's comment—"Now we're all sons of bitches"— was the best thing ever said at Trinity.)[42]

This propensity for delivering the on-target, dramatic phrase became a central part of his postwar persona. On August 17, 1945, he said, "A scientist cannot hold back progress because of fears of what the world will do with his discoveries."[43] When he met President Harry S Truman, he said he had "blood on his hands." Later he achieved notoriety for the remark: "In some sort of crude sense, which no vulgarity, no humor, no overstatement can quite extinguish, the physicists have known sin, and this is a knowledge which they cannot lose." (Truman was not pleased at such public displays of guilt and supposedly refused to ever see him again.) In March 1946, Oppenheimer advised University of Pennsylvania students that because nuclear war had become "unendurable," the atomic bombs would produce a "better world."[44] In another speech he noted that the "book of the past is closed and one has a fresh page to write on."[45] When asked to characterize his position as director of the Institute for Advanced Studies, he described himself as simply an "academic innkeeper." On another occasion, he described the issue of lingering radioactivity in the soil as "a nontrivial problem." After the war he honed this ability into a fine art. In 1949 he noted, "As long as men are free to ask what they must, free to say what they think, free to think what they will, freedom can never be lost, and science will never regress." In 1953 he described the world situation as: "We may be likened to two scorpions in a battle, each capable of killing the other but only at the risk of his own life." Three years later he observed, "In a free world, if it is to remain free, we must maintain, with our lives if need be yet surely by our lives, the opportunity for a man to learn anything." On Einstein's death in 1955 he said, "Any man whose errors take ten years to correct is quite a man." When he accepted the AEC award from Lyndon Johnson in 1963, he wryly noted, "I think it is just possible, Mr. President, that it may have taken some charity and some courage for you to make this award today." A number of his sayings have virtually entered the language.[46]

Although Oppenheimer may have lacked a sense of humor, he compensated for it by his flair for the piercing bon mot. As reporter Eric Sevareid observed in 1963, he was a "scientist who wrote like a poet and speaks like a prophet."[47] And this largely began with his years as LASL director.

In his autobiography, General Groves suggested that at war's end he was eager to see Oppenheimer leave LASL for two reasons. First, everything afterward would be anticlimactic for him and second, Groves expressed concern over the ever-present problem of Oppenheimer's radical past.[48] But the exhausted Oppenheimer was more than ready to return to academic life at Cal Tech, which eagerly welcomed him back. To his dismay, he found this impossible. During 1947, for example, he flew from California to Washington fifteen times. He spent endless hours writing the Acheson-Lillenthal report—the basis for the (failed) Baruch Plan presented to the United Nations in 1946. This proposal embodied America's attempt to avoid an arms race by creating the International Atomic Energy Committee under UN auspices. Unfortunately, the Soviet Union refused to cooperate. Congress also called on Oppenheimer on numerous occasions. From director of an obscure secret laboratory in northern New Mexico, Oppenheimer had suddenly assumed the mantle of public spokesman on issues of nuclear science and government.

With the possible exception of Albert Einstein, Oppenheimer emerged in the postwar period as the world's most highly profiled scientist. His distinctive porkpie hat—adopted at Los Alamos because Groves felt he stood out too prominently wearing his traditional cowboy hat—appeared without caption on the cover of the inaugural issue of *Physics Today*. *Life* also put him on the cover of its October 1949 issue with the sidebar "No. 1 Thinker on Atomic Energy."

Given the increased public demands, Oppenheimer made relatively few official trips back to New Mexico after 1945. He did visit the Hill in August of 1946 for a six-day conference on nuclear physics and again the next year to report (favorably) on the status of the now-permanent, Bradbury-run laboratory. We know that he stayed several days with his former secretary Dorothy McKibben during the time, but his later visits to the state all remain undocumented. In 1947 he assumed the position of director of the Institute for Advanced Study at Princeton, and in the mid-1950s he and Kitty purchased another summer house in the Virgin Islands. This island home, which allowed him to indulge his passion for sailing, seems to have replaced the Pecos Valley cabin as his primary retreat. Although he must have visited his brother Frank's Pagosa Springs, Colorado, ranch on occasion, Oppenheimer did not make another official public visit to New Mexico until May of 1964.

The fledgling University of New Mexico in Albuquerque had attempted to entice him back in 1947 but without success. From the onset, the academic "manager" of LASL had been the University of California, Berkeley, which oversaw all equipment purchases for the Manhattan Project years. At the dawn of the twenty-first century, with the university LANL contract now open to bids, some have wondered why Groves did not consider the much-closer University of New Mexico in Albuquerque for this assignment. One reason for the Berkeley choice surely lay with Oppenheimer's long-term links to the school, but another lay with the respective sizes of the two institutions in the 1940s. The University of New Mexico then housed fewer than one hundred faculty and under fifteen hundred students. The 350 graduates who donned caps and gowns in 1947 represented the largest graduating class in the school's fifty-eight-year history. (That same year, UNM awarded its first two PhDs.)[49] From a security point of view, any attempt to funnel gigantic amounts of scientific equipment through UNM in the 1940s would have instantly raised eyebrows. Only an institution the size of Berkeley could have served as an appropriate cover. Indeed, the first Berkeley contract, signed April 20, 1943, and backdated to January 1, spoke of 250 workers and $7.5 million in expenses.[50] The University of California has successfully managed Los Alamos for over sixty years.

But postwar UNM had its eyes fixed firmly on the future, and in the spring of 1947, President J. P. Wernette wrote Oppenheimer to ask him if he could come to Albuquerque to speak at commencement and also receive an honorary degree. Unfortunately, the invitation was delayed in the mail and by the time it arrived, Oppenheimer had made other plans. Still, as he wrote Wernette, New Mexico "is almost a home state to me for many reasons."[51]

Although disappointed, the UNM faculty voted to award him the degree in absentia. Accordingly, Wernette read the following at commencement exercises in Zimmerman Stadium on Saturday, June 7, 1947:

> J. Robert Oppenheimer, inspiring teacher, brilliant theorist in contemporary physics, former director of Los Alamos Scientific Laboratory, leader in the development of atomic energy, scientific statesman, determined to make this fabulous power serve the peacetime needs of humanity. Upon the recommendation of the Faculty of the University and by vote of the Regents, I confer upon him, in absentia, the honorary degree of Doctor of Science.[52]

The last thirteen years of Oppenheimer's life, 1954–67, were not especially pleasant. The publicity surrounding the 1954 AEC hearings, which sullied his reputation, aged him terribly and seemingly broke his heart. It also made him persona non grata in many official circles. A 1955 proffered invitation to speak at the University of Washington was hastily withdrawn, although he did speak to the nearby University of Oregon in Eugene shortly afterward. Nuclear politics were so sensitive that lab director Norris Bradbury could not extend him an official invitation to return to the Hill until after Oppenheimer had received the AEC Fermi Award in 1963. With this, Oppenheimer became somewhat "rehabilitated," and Bradbury officially invited him back for a public talk. Oppenheimer chose the subject "Niels Bohr and Atomic Weapons."[53]

On their two-day visit to Los Alamos in mid-May of 1964, Kitty and Robert Oppenheimer received the red-carpet treatment. They were treated to a special screening of the documentary film *Ten Seconds That Shook the World* and took a private tour of the newly erected LASL Museum. When Oppenheimer sat again in his old director's chair—now a museum exhibit—he quipped to Bradbury that it was "still very hard."[54]

The turnout for his talk proved overwhelming. Although Oppenheimer had been absent from the Hill for almost fifteen years, a thousand people filled the Civic Auditorium that Monday night. The standing ovations that he received at both start and finish brought tears to his eyes. Norris Bradbury introduced him as "Mr. Los Alamos."

During his speech, he emphasized the need for an "open world" of free interchange of scientific information. In passing, he observed that the leaders of the Manhattan Project were "not free of misgivings. . . . We were troubled about what we were up to." Several reporters rushed up afterward, but he refused to respond to any questions. All he would say was: "I love my country, if that's what you want to know."[55]

When Oppenheimer died on February 18, 1967, after months of battling throat cancer, accolades poured in from around the world. Among the most insightful was that of Norris Bradbury. Said his successor: "His stamp upon the character of Los Alamos was profound and permanent; his impression upon those who knew him was no less so. . . . Such men are incredibly rare."[56]

■

The links between J. Robert Oppenheimer and the state of New Mexico stretched over four and a half decades, and in many ways they proved reciprocal. The magnificent silences of the Pecos Forest Reserve helped restore Oppenheimer's physical and psychic balance, and he developed a lifelong affection for the state. In a sense, he must have linked New Mexico with the idea of renewed health. His consideration for the woman at the Otowi Bridge, whom he met on a 1937 horseback ride, not only allowed Edith Warner to survive the war economically but also enabled his fellow LASL scientists to retain their delicate mental balance. It is no exaggeration to say that Oppenheimer provided the canvas on which Peggy Pond Church would later create an authentic New Mexico legend. Oppenheimer's acquaintance with the Los Alamos Ranch School helped convince General Groves to situate Site Y on the Pajarito Plateau. And his directorship of Los Alamos during the war years still serves as the template for effective scientific management.

In 1948, the AEC officially decided to keep Los Alamos National Laboratory where it was and inaugurated a $100 million rebuilding program. In 1949, Los Alamos became a separate county. Five years later, the town ranked as the eighth-largest city in the state, with over twelve thousand in population. By the mid-1950s, it represented a $250 million federal investment. In 2004, its annual budget was $2 billion.

The influx of federal monies to a poor region of a generally impoverished state has been without precedent. A 1996 economic survey of the
impact of Los Alamos National Laboratory on northern New Mexico concluded that one of every twenty-three state jobs was either created or supported by the laboratory. The $1.1 billion funding for the fiscal year 1996
multiplied into about $4 billion, or about 5 percent of the total economic
activity for the entire state.[57] In an unforeseen way, the spread of this
income throughout northern New Mexico has allowed traditional Native
American and Hispanic crafts to revive and flourish. The lab provided
steady employment for the craftspeople as well as potential purchasers for
their various artworks.

Yet there is a dark side to the Oppenheimer link with New Mexico.
Since the Manhattan Project was viewed as a crash program, few gave
much concern to the long-term environmental consequences. Its successor agency, the Atomic Energy Commission, could not institute its
first committee along these lines until 1947.[58] At the dawn of the twenty-
first century, however, environmental issues have come to virtually dominate national and state concerns. The terrible Cerro Grande fire of 2000
allegedly uncovered three hundred toxic sites on the Hill. In 2005, the
New Mexico State Environment Department, aided by various private
organizations, remained locked in conflict with the laboratory over environmental pollution, especially over potential contamination of the Rio
Grande by creeping plutonium.[59]

Although Oppenheimer once ruefully remarked that he was responsible for ruining a beautiful place, not all of these environmental problems can be laid at his doorstep. But he does bear responsibility for a few.
In 1975, the successor to the AEC, the U.S. Energy Research and Development Administration (ERDA), discovered a plutonium "pocket" south
of the Los Alamos Inn. Further research concluded that the now-open
location originally housed the Technical Area laundry. As plutonium
washed off workers' clothes, it ended up lodged in the drain. Eventually,
the contamination was removed to a burial site.[60]

The main area of radioactive contamination from the Oppenheimer
years remains that of the Trinity Site, for the July 16, 1945, detonation
surely fell under his watch. Since the Trinity "gadget" exploded only one
hundred feet above the ground, the ball of fire touched the earth, fusing

the sand into radioactive greenish gray glass and driving the plutonium deep into the soil. Since the half-life of plutonium is about twenty-four thousand years, the fenced-in area of Trinity Site in central New Mexico will reflect the legacy of J. Robert Oppenheimer essentially forever.

A theologian once observed that the concept of forgiveness should lie at the heart of any just society, for one can never anticipate the consequences of one's actions. Although that observation holds true for the conventional areas of life, because of the extended time periods involved, it seems to resonate with special intensity whenever one speaks of things nuclear. It certainly should apply to Oppenheimer as well.

Although the first generation of atomic scientists overflowed with brilliance, with the passing of years Oppenheimer has assumed the highest profile of them all. Similarly, although the Manhattan Project could never have succeeded without the contributions of Oak Ridge, Tennessee, and Hanford, Washington, the community most remembered today is Los Alamos. Perhaps the reciprocal relationship between the state and the man may be summarized as this: the awesome splendor of northern New Mexico restored J. Robert Oppenheimer to health, and in return the state now houses both Trinity Site and a magnificent scientific laboratory that is recognized, for better or worse, around the globe.[61] Whether this ranks as a fair exchange depends largely on the perspective of the observer.

Congressman Bill Richardson *and the* 1984 Creation *of the* Bisti and De-Na-Zin Wilderness Areas in Northwest New Mexico

On November 5, 2002, Democrat William Blaine (Bill) Richardson defeated Republican John Sanchez to become the governor of New Mexico. He brought to this office a lengthy career of public service. Born in Pasadena, California, in 1947 to a Mexican mother and an Anglo-American father, he grew up in Mexico City (his father worked for Citibank there) before moving to Concord, Massachusetts, at the age of thirteen. He attended Choate preparatory school in Connecticut and graduated from Tufts University (BA, 1970) and the Fletcher School of Law and Diplomacy (MA, 1971).

After serving as a low-level staff member in Washington, D.C., Richardson moved to Santa Fe in 1978 to head the local Democratic Party. Two years later he challenged Republican incumbent Manuel

*In November of 2002 Bill Richardson celebrated his election as
governor of New Mexico with his wife, Barbara* (left), *and
Lieutenant Governor–elect Diane Denish. Photo by Greg Serber.
Copyright: the* Albuquerque Journal. *Reprinted with permission.*

Lujan, Jr. for the state's northern congressional seat but went down in the
Ronald Reagan landslide of 1980. Shortly thereafter, however, federal
redistricting awarded New Mexico a third congressional district, which
Richardson won easily in 1982. His northern New Mexico constituency
reelected him seven more times. For years he functioned as the highest-
profile Democrat of Hispanic origins.

In 1997, President Bill Clinton tapped him to become American
ambassador to the United Nations. He performed well in that role, and
the following year Clinton asked him to join the cabinet as head of the
Department of Energy. In his nomination speech, the president jested,
"If there's one word that comes to mind when I think of Bill Richardson,
it really is energy."[1] After the George W. Bush Republican victory of 2000,
Richardson taught briefly at Harvard and at the United World College in
Las Vegas, New Mexico, before deciding to run for governor in 2002.

Impressive though these credentials are, Richardson earned an even
greater reputation through his skills at negotiation. In 1994, Clinton

tapped him as special envoy to negotiate with the North Korean government over the release of a captured air force pilot. Later he twice more returned to North Korea to discuss delicate nuclear-related matters. In addition, Clinton sent him to secure the release of hostages from Bangladesh, Burma, the Sudan, Cuba, and Iraq. During the latter two discussions, he negotiated face-to-face with both Fidel Castro and Saddam Hussein. In yet another high-profile maneuver, Clinton sent him to central Africa, where he brought together, for the first time, two hated rivals for power in Zaire: President Mobutu and rebel Alliance leader Laurent Kabila. This bold move allowed at least a semipeaceful transfer of power in Zaire (today known as the Democratic Republic of Congo).

Although officially only a congressman from a small-population western state, Richardson's ability to achieve compromise in tense political situations catapulted him to international fame. His staff jokingly termed him "Clark Kent" and "007."[2] Four times—1995, 1997, 2000, and 2001—he received the nomination for the Nobel Peace Prize. Indeed, only two weeks after he became governor of New Mexico, a delegation of North Koreans—frustrated by the policies of the George W. Bush administration—visited Santa Fe to seek his aid, which he provided with full support from the State Department. At the onset of the twenty-first century, Bill Richardson has donned the mantle of his nineteenth-century counterpart, Henry Clay. He has become the "Great Compromiser" of the contemporary political scene.

■

Richardson faced the first serious challenge to these yet-untested negotiation skills shortly after he was sworn in as a freshman congressman in 1983. As his first crisis, he inherited a long-simmering standoff over the future of energy development in the San Juan Basin of northwest New Mexico. The sides of this fifteen-year controversy proved complex and varied. Fueled by the energy crisis of the 1970s, the Bureau of Land Management (BLM) began plans to allow various energy companies to mine the estimated two hundred billion tons of basin coal within the next several decades. In 1980 Reagan's newly appointed secretary of the interior, James Watt (1980–83), accelerated the process by instituting plans to mine three areas of the basin badlands that had all previously been designated "Wilderness Study Areas" (WSAs).[3]

The areas in question were (1) the Bisti Badlands WSA (*Bisti*—pronounced "bis-tah"—is Navajo for "strange rocks"), which consists of an approximately six-thousand-acre region about thirty-nine miles south of Farmington on State Highway 371; (2) the De-Na-Zin WSA, a much larger section of the same badlands topography that lies to the east on County Road 7500; (3) the Ah-Shi-Sle-Pah WSA, located north of Chaco Canyon and west of state Highway 57; and (4) a smaller region south of De-Na-Zin termed the "Fossil Forest" because it abounded with numerous fossilized tree trunks, many still in situ. The area with the highest profile remained the Bisti Badlands, easiest to reach by automobile and long famous in the Four Corners region for its striking colors and unusual rock formations, virtually a "natural Disneyland." During the 1960s, the San Juan Museum Society had launched a campaign to turn the Bisti Badlands into a National Park, initially as a means to stop locals from hauling away the petrified logs for fences.[4] With the onset of the energy crisis, concern over protecting the Bisti shifted from looting to the dangers of potential strip-mining.

The United States had long earned the reputation as "the Saudi Arabia of coal," and in the 1960s the estimated two hundred billion tons of coal in the San Juan Basin attracted national attention.[5] The De-Na-Zin mine on the eastern edge of the Navajo Reservation and the proposed Gateway mine were to supply coal for the Four Corners power plant. The state's largest supplier of energy, the Public Service Company of New Mexico (PNM), also laid plans to erect a new power station in the area. There was even talk of building a railroad. These ventures promised to bring hundreds of jobs to one of the poorer sections of the state, the majority of which would go to Navajo or Hispanic workers.

Environmentalists, archaeologists, anthropologists, geologists, and numerous others, however, became outraged. They argued that the proposed strip-mine would destroy irreplaceable archaeological, paleontological, and natural treasures. The Navajo Nation also had a major stake in this issue. First, about 125 Navajo families used the area to run their sheep, and most of them would have to be relocated. (Another "Long Walk," critics claimed.) Moreover, as part of the proposed resolution of the long-term Navajo-Hopi land dispute on Black Mesa in Arizona, the Navajo laid claims to several large sections of all three WSAs, plus the Fossil Forest. The environmentalists and the energy advocates were barely speaking to one another. In spring 1983, the *Albuquerque Journal* ran a lengthy series titled "Battle Over the Basin."

Since this formed part of his former congressional district, Republican congressman Manuel Lujan had attempted to find a solution. Working with Republican senator Pete Domenici, Lujan introduced legislation in Congress to set aside about four thousand acres of the Bisti WSA as a federally protected wilderness area. Environmental groups denounced this move as far too conservative. They demanded that two hundred thousand acres be set aside in all three WSAs, plus the Fossil Forest. Lujan's bill went nowhere. With the redistricting of New Mexico, the most intense energy-preservationist standoff since World War II suddenly fell into Richardson's lap. It would form his first real challenge.

■

The San Juan Basin consists of a roughly circular region of depressed sedimentary rock approximately one hundred miles in diameter. Bounded by mountains or uplifts, the basin includes parts of San Juan, Rio Arriba, McKinley, and Sandoval counties in New Mexico and Montezuma, La Plata, Archuleta, and Conejos counties in Colorado. Although not widely recognized by the average American citizen, specialists from a variety of disciplines have long been aware of its riches. Archaeologists and anthropologists treasure the region as the home of ancestral Puebloan peoples and their architectural masterpieces, Chaco Canyon and Mesa Verde. In addition to these wonders, the area is dotted with scores of outlying settlements, a number of which remain unexcavated. Paleontologists have long prized the area as one of the richest fossil regions on the globe. The sandstone strata abound with dinosaur remains. The Ghost Ranch quarry of Rio Arriba County has provided dinosaur specimens for dozens of museums. The basin ranks among the top three areas in the world where rocks from the end of the Cretaceous period and the beginning of the Tertiary era both lie exposed. (The only rivals are in China and Montana.) This time period—roughly sixty-six million years ago—witnessed the extinction of the dinosaurs and the emergence of mammals and thus provides an ideal place to study this transition. The Navajo Nation, which lies in the western part of the basin, has drawn on the San Juan River to create the state's largest irrigation program, the Navajo Indian Irrigation Project (first planting, 1979). And finally, national energy companies have long recognized the larger basin region as one of the richest oil, natural gas, and coal areas of the West.

Energy in the form of methane gas literally seeped from the basin. During the early twentieth century, ranchers could create "fireworks" by holding an open flame under their water faucets or tossing a match into a hole chopped in the ice over one of the streams. During the early 1940s, a group of local teenagers threw a burning log into Los Pinos River of southern Colorado and watched in amazement as the surface of the water exploded.[6] The region's economy still largely revolves around energy extraction.

The San Juan Basin underwent a major population boom during the 1950s, but it did not come to widespread national attention for another two decades. Beginning in the 1960s, the local environmental movement began to publicize the seemingly desolate and barren badlands and geological wonders. The move to turn the Bisti Badlands into a park or wilderness area gained widespread regional support.

New Mexico, of course, helped pioneer the idea of national wilderness. In 1924, Aldo Leopold convinced the nation to set aside thousands of acres of the Gila Mountains as the country's first federal wilderness area. The Pecos Wilderness northeast of Santa Fe and others followed in due course. But the Gila and Pecos regions looked like a "wilderness" was supposed to look: they abounded in wildflowers, streams, majestic mountains, and reams of conifers, pine, cedars, aspen, and fir. The proposed San Juan Basin Badlands, however, looked nothing like that. Cold in winter and beastly hot in summer, the area lacked permanent streams or mountains. Thus, the advocates for the Bisti Badlands Wilderness Area had their work cut out for them.

When New Mexico scientists declared 1978 as the "Year of the Fossil," the region gained additional publicity. Not only did numerous amateurs and professionals comb the area for specimens, the state government funded the first scientific study of the Bisti region.[7] In 1980 the legislature provided the first funds for the projected New Mexico Natural History Museum in Albuquerque. Interest began to grow.

The catalyst, however, came with James Watt's controversial plans to reopen the region to coal exploration. A Wyoming native long familiar with the intermountain West, one of Watt's first actions as secretary of the interior was to lease—at "bargain basement prices," his enemies claimed—several BLM lands in Wyoming for coal mining. Now he planned to do the same for the San Juan Basin. Although the San Juan coal was not as high grade as the Wyoming coal, it lay largely in the Fruitland formation, a sedimentary layer that carried minimal over-burden and thus could be strip-mined with relative ease.[8] Coal compa-nies eagerly explored their options, and PNM announced plans to build an elaborate new coal-fired facility nearby.

These actions drew together a variety of opponents. Although local environmentalists readily acknowledged that oil and gas drilling lay at the heart of the region's economy, they maintained a far more critical view of coal mining. Oil and gas wells produced minimal surface damage, but strip-mining of the Fruitland formation proved quite another story. In spite of repeated promises by the energy companies that they could restore the surface, critics denied that this could ever be done in such a fragile terrain as the badlands. Even the coal companies admitted that such restoration remained an untested, inexact science.

This polarized standoff was enmeshed in yet another complicated issue, that of land ownership. Due to its unique history, the San Juan Basin boasts some of the most convoluted land ownership patterns in the nation. The Navajo Nation and the state of New Mexico both own lands in the area, all "checkerboarded" with private, individual Navajo 160-acre allotments, interspersed with an occasional Anglo-American ranch. In certain regions, completely different people own the subsurface mineral rights as well. Still, most of the Bisti region remains in federal hands, and this meant that the BLM found itself at the center of the controversy, with no solution in sight.

By the 1970s, the government had enacted a number of laws that man-dated extensive surveys and environmental impact statements before any drastic action could occur on federal lands. The laws ranged from the famed Antiquities Act of 1906 to the Historic Preservation Act of 1966 to the National Environmental Policy Act of 1969 and also included a crucial executive order from President Richard M. Nixon in May of 1971. The rise of contract anthropological firms facilitated this time-consuming process.[9]

Consequently, during the 1970s the BLM was obligated by law to contract for a variety of regional surveys. Since PNM had plans to construct a power plant, it too had to contract for similar appraisals.[10]

Various energy interests also conducted surveys of their own. The State Bureau of Mines and Mineral Resources published the *Guidebook to the Core Geology of Northwest New Mexico* in 1976, and the Western Coal Company of Albuquerque produced its own *Mine Plan: Bisti Project* two years later. Geologist Peter John Hutchinson finished his thorough master's thesis on the stratigraphy and paleontology of the Bisti Badlands area in 1981.[11] All told, the various survey teams had produced numerous scientific surveys of specific areas of the San Juan Basin by 1982.[12]

Still, the sides remained polarized. PNM's hopes for a New Mexico generation station and the Albuquerque Coal Company's plans to strip-mine four prominent coal seams to produce approximately eighty million tons over the next decades contrasted sharply with a 1978 survey that concluded, "The destruction of this region without further research will mean the irreplaceable loss of a unique tradition in the prehistory of the Southwest."[13] Sierra Club lawyers prepared plans to test any action in the court system.

■

By the time Richardson assumed office, the investigators had compiled a mountain of survey data on the San Juan Basin. The government did not lack scientific information, but most of the data remained locked up in lengthy official reports. The final environmental impact statement on PNM's proposed power plant weighed more than a Chicago phone book. Moreover, the reports were filled with complex jargon and lengthy charts. Laced with passive voice, they presented a genuine challenge to read.

In an astute move, Richardson decided to bring all sides of the issue together in a common forum. To do so, he argued, would mean that "New Mexicans will be able to decide the fate of their lands, the fate of their wilderness area, and the fate of coal leasing in the state."[14] Thus, he scheduled public hearings on May 21, 1983, in Santa Fe and on June 7, 1983, in Washington. The Santa Fe gathering proved enormously popular, so much so that the over seventy speakers were limited to five minutes each, although they could include any additional material they wished for the final publication. A number of contributors to the various official surveys testified, along with Governor Toney Anaya and other state officials. Representatives from the Navajo Nation spoke out as well. Thus, coal company officials, PNM officers, Navajo sheepherders (whose comments had to be translated), and interested local citizens all had their say. The published version of the hearings (1984) ran to over nine hundred pages.

The Farmington Chamber of Commerce joined with various energy spokesmen to put forth a balanced case. The San Juan Basin held the key to the state's economic future, they said. Since the coal-leasing moratorium of 1971, over four hundred New Mexico miners had been thrown out of work, and state revenues had suddenly stagnated. Since the nuclear power alternatives, such as the WPPSS plant in the Pacific Northwest and Palos Verdes Two in Arizona, had proven financial catastrophes, the mining of coal would remain central to both state and nation for the foreseeable future (estimated reserves: thirty to forty years). Modern equipment allowed for both coal mining and environmental protection, said the spokesman for the Arch Mineral Corporation of St. Louis. The Ah-Shi-Sle-Pah area abounded with easily mined coal sources. If needed, they could draw on slant drilling techniques to minimize damage. Coal company spokesmen also denied that the Ah-Shi-Sle-Pah area merited a wilderness designation. "That is not a wilderness area," said one officer. "[It is] barren, desolate land, perfect for strip-mining."[15] Another pointed out that a few years previously, a National Science Foundation survey had actually recommended making the San Juan Basin into a "national sacrifice area" for the development of energy.[16] Both state and nation needed additional coal resources, they said, and the San Juan Basin offered the best area of supply.

Articulate though these advocates might have been, the brunt of the testifiers in Santa Fe felt otherwise. There is a Russian saying that quantity provides a quality in itself, and this certainly proved true for the majority of the assembled witnesses. Governor Toney Anaya spoke derisively of "Watt's Folly." Louis Denet Sosie, an attorney for the Navajo tribe's Justice Department, decried the venture as again forcing Native American families to be relocated from sacred places; he also denounced the "whole-sale giveaway" of resources.[17] "Coal is abundant," said Jim Baca, state land commissioner. "Wilderness in New Mexico is not."[18] Even the out-of-work miners from Raton joined the chorus. They feared that the proposed boomtown atmosphere would bring in out-of-state miners. Instead, they argued that the government should utilize the existing coal in the Raton region.[19] The San Juan Basin, said archaeologist Mark Michel, contains the ruins of a great precontact culture, with its two main focal points at Mesa Verde and the Chaco Culture National Historic Park. The region is dotted with outlying sites, he noted, containing the "largest concentration of prehistoric ruins in the United States."[20] Strip-mining would do irreplaceable damage. A panel of archaeologists testified that reverberations from coal mining in the Ah-Shi-Sle-Pah region might also cause crumbling of the nearby Chaco Canyon ruins. Geologist Barry Kues noted that the proposed mining would destroy perhaps two thousand fossil localities. Fellow geologist Spencer Lucas called the undisturbed fossil record in the San Juan Basin "fundamental to the science of paleontology and, thus, to the earth sciences as a whole."[21] An articulate spokesman for the Sierra Club insisted that the Bisti, De-Na-Zin, and Ah-Shi-Sle-Pah WSAs all be designated wilderness and that the Fossil Forest be protected as well.[22] The opposition proved overwhelming, and Richardson interpreted it as providing him with a public mandate.

After talking with the various sides, listening to hours of testimony, and reading reams of official studies and opinion pieces, Richardson made his move. First, he had to confront the political realities of the day. To diffuse vigorous opposition from a Farmington "Miners and Prospectors" group, he helped them resolve a local hunting issue. Since he was then at arm's length with Republican senator Pete Domenici—who feared that Richardson might try to unseat him in the next election—he worked primarily with Congressman Lujan and Democratic senator Bingaman until Domenici reluctantly came on board. Fortunately for Richardson, the Democrats controlled the House of Congress and his friend John Sieberling of Ohio chaired the Wilderness subcommittee.[23] In August of 1983 he introduced HR 3766 into Congress. This bill—far more extensive than the previous Lujan-Domenici legislation—provided wilderness protection for the Bisti, De-Na-Zin, and Ah-Shi-Sle-Pah regions, as well as special protection for the Fossil Forest.[24] With strong support from fellow congressman Lujan (who remained prominent on Interior Department committees), Richardson's bill passed the House. But it stalled in the Senate, and by the fall of 1984 it looked as if Congress would adjourn without any further action. This meant that any San Juan Wilderness Act would have to wait until the next Congress, with its fate hinging on the results of the forthcoming election.

Realizing full well that delay might unseat the Democratic majority and favor the Watt contingent (which he opposed), Richardson again made a decisive move. He hurriedly contacted his fellow New Mexico legislators—Lujan, Domenici, and Jeff Bingaman—as well as various environmental groups and the Navajo tribe, and he received a general agreement to introduce an entirely new piece of legislation, HR 6296. This he did on October 3, 1984.

This new bill was similar but not identical to his previous one. It advanced the Bisti (3,968 acres) and De-Na-Zin (23,872 acres) from WSA to full wilderness status. It also protected the Fossil Forest region (2,720 acres) from further mineral leasing or mining. Overall, 30,350 acres fell under these new categories.

But the new bill carried limitations. Richardson delegated the ultimate fate of the Fossil Forest to Congress, as the new bill instructed the secretary of the interior to complete a long-range study of the region's aesthetic, natural, educational, and paleontological value by 2002. The main change, however, concerned the Ah-Shi-Sle-Pah WSA (7,193 acres). The coal companies had long eyed this region, and the situation became complicated further when the Navajo Nation refused to relinquish their proposed land claims therein from the Navajo-Hopi settlement. As a result, the Ah-Shi-Sle-Pah remained only as a Wilderness Study Area.[25] "I am disappointed in the result," Richardson confessed to the House, "but I am convinced that the substitute before us today reflects the best possible compromise that can be reached under the circumstances."[26]

In the Senate, Jeff Bingaman agreed. On October 5, 1984, he urged passage of Richardson's new measure "to ensure that the wilderness option would not be precluded by other conflicting land use decisions in the region."[27] With unanimous support from the New Mexican delegation, the bill sailed through. On October 30, 1984, President Reagan signed the San Juan Wilderness Protection Act into law.

Bill Richardson deserves a great deal of credit for the passage of this act. As he later recalled, it involved a great deal of "hard negotiations."[28] The final act was filled with compromises. The future of the coal-rich Ah-Shi-Sle-Pah region remained in limbo, although hopes were high that the state, the Navajos, and environmentalists could find some way to protect it. The state of New Mexico contributed 2,520 acres to the De-Na-Zin Wilderness so as to provide better geographical and topographical unity, with the understanding that the BLM would compensate with other land of equal value. New Mexico also agreed to close two small coal mines on state-owned sections of the wilderness. The coal companies acquiesced because the projected set-aside acreage proved much smaller than the initial proposal of approximately two hundred thousand acres. The Navajo Nation compromised as well. They relinquished their proposed land claims in the Bisti, De-Na-Zin, and Fossil Forest areas in return for subsurface mineral rights on the approximately thirty-five thousand acres to the south and west, all part of the Navajo-Hopi land exchange. They also acknowledged that smaller Navajo inholdings should be negotiated on an individual basis. With the legislation, everyone agreed that the "gems" of the San Juan Basin Badlands were now safe from potential destruction.

The signing of the San Juan Wilderness Protection Act brought to a close one of the state's most heated environmental clashes since World War II. Moreover, it did so in the best of the democratic tradition: negotiated compromise. Through his persistent discussions, Richardson helped forge a "consensus bill of the New Mexico delegation," as Manuel Lujan phrased it. The legislation was, as Jeff Bingaman noted, "a compromise of the many diverse interests in New Mexico."[29] Indeed, the coal companies, PNM, the San Juan County Commission, the Sierra Club, the Wilderness Society, the BLM, the Navajo Nation, and the state of New Mexico could all claim at least partial victory. There is an old adage in diplomatic circles that "it is a good and fair settlement when neither party likes the outcome, but each agrees to it."[30] Certainly this proved true here. Through continued effort, Congressman Bill Richardson helped find a common ground.

The rocks at Bisti framed the official wilderness dedication ceremonies in May 1985. This was Richardson's first major triumph. Photo by Richard Pipes. Copyright: the Albuquerque Journal. *Reprinted with permission.*

Perhaps the most symbolic representation of this sentiment could be seen in the formal designation of the Bisti Wilderness Area. The ceremony was held on May 4, 1985, at the edge of the new wilderness about thirty-seven miles south of Farmington. Jeff Bingaman's office sent an official representative, and although he arrived over two hours late, Bill Richardson presented the main address. In the talk he graciously praised the cooperative effort that had brought about the occasion. As a final symbol of the spirit of compromise, the approximately one hundred people gathered there (largely environmentalists) enjoyed a free lunch—all hosted by the Public Service Company of New Mexico and the Sun Belt Mining Company.[31]

■

The passage of the 1984 San Juan Wilderness Protection Act had a number of long-term consequences. First, as one of the first wilderness areas to fall under BLM jurisdiction, it provided Congress with a clear precedent for future cases. Since Congress tends to repeat itself, having a proper model in place often influences subsequent legislation. Sierra Club spokesman Debbie Sease noted that wilderness groups were very pleased with the precedent set by the Bisti decision.[32]

Second, the legislation instructed the local BLM office in Farmington to devise a plan of land management for this new area. After two years of study, the BLM issued *Bisti: Wilderness Management Plan*. The study called for creating a primitive parking area, the fencing of the boundary, and the erection of appropriate signs.[33] Public hearings on the proposal also went smoothly. Shortly afterward, the BLM negotiated with the Navajos to exchange ten thousand acres that had previously divided the two wilderness areas. In 1996 they were combined into one, now termed the Bisti/De-Na-Zin Wilderness, which more than doubled the initial set-aside region. The current assignment of the BLM is to ensure that the fragile wilderness will be respected by the increasing number of tourists, although no one can quite determine how many there are. Unofficial estimates place the number of visitors at about ten thousand a year, but these are only educated guesses.[34] No permits are required to visit or camp there, although those who seek to do scientific research, guide others, or make commercial films must obtain permission. Visitors to the region are advised to carry plenty of water and good maps, as there are no established trails. Some advice books recommend carrying a GPS system.

Third, the federal protection of the area ensured that it would remain one of the nation's most fruitful dinosaur-hunting grounds. Over the next two decades, scientists have made scores of discoveries there. For example, in 1998 they uncovered a gigantic specimen—nicknamed "The

Bisti Beast"—that necessitated a National Guard helicopter to haul it from its wilderness locale. That same year, famed dinosaur scout Paul Sealey and paleontologist Tom Williamson uncovered a boneheaded dinosaur (called a pachycephalosaur) that five years later was officially confirmed as an entirely new genus.[35] What the future will reveal is anyone's guess.

Fourth, passage of the Wilderness Act lowered the controversy level in the San Juan Basin by several degrees. No single law can bring complete harmony to this volatile region, of course, but the subsequent disputes provoked much less emotional outrage than did the Bisti controversy. Periodic reports criticize the BLM for not keeping off-road vehicles out of the wilderness areas, but they usually acknowledge the difficulties therein.

Much to its embarrassment, the BLM discovered that it had mistakenly sold (in 1981) the rights for thirteen oil and gas wells and 5.5 miles of road in what is now the Bisti Wilderness. "It was a slip-up," confessed the BLM manager. The case has been tied up in the courts for over seven years and produced public hearings in both Farmington and Santa Fe. Still, the oil company, Sperex, admitted that it would be absurd to drill in a wilderness area, and even though the Forest Guardians have threatened legal action, the case has caused no major local repercussions.[36] Although extensive oil and gas drilling continues north of the wilderness area, as well as sporadic coal mining, PNM has never constructed its proposed power plant. It is unlikely to do so in the foreseeable future. The Ah-Shi-Sle-Pah region retains its WSA status, and there has been no further talk of mining there.[37] For the moment, the region is relatively peaceful.

The 1984 act also dramatically increased publicity for the Bisti and in so doing attracted a bevy of fine nature photographers. Although the *Denver Post* and *New Mexico Magazine* had carried occasional photo-essays on the area before 1984, the official designation alerted national photographers to its haunting beauty as well.[38]

New Mexico has long been home to a range of world-class nature photographers, and it was not long before they brought their skills to the Bisti region. In 1987, David Scheinbaum, former assistant to famed photographer Elliot Porter, contributed several black-and-white images to a book titled simply *Bisti*.[39] In 2003, Eduardo Fuss teamed with *New*

Mexico Magazine to create the first collection of color images in his *Wonderland: A Photographer's Journey into the Bisti.*[40] With the advent of electronic imagery, the San Juan Basin has begun to attract even more photographic attention. Today one can take a "visual tour" of the Bisti Badlands via the Internet.[41]

These haunting images of the Bisti often speak with a clearer voice than the halting prose that accompanies them. Indeed, many photographers seem almost at a loss for words when they try to convey the impact of the badlands landscape. Jay W. Sharp called it "eerie," more of a "dreamscape than a landscape."[42] Another termed it "surreal."[43] Still another confessed that he had never seen anything as "strange."[44]

The more articulate photographers confess that when they try to capture the essence of the Bisti with their cameras, their emotions range between awe and mysticism. "The landscape is haunting in its beauty and timelessness," confessed David Scheinbaum. It is "among the most beautiful and surprising landscapes in the world," said Mark Nohl of *New Mexico Magazine.* It is a venue where one can expect the unexpected, admitted Eduardo Fuss. Although it seems to be a land of "nothing there," the color, light, and odd rock formations loom as almost magical. Both Scheinbaum and Fuss agree that the Bisti/De-Na-Zin Wilderness Area demands an interpretive way of seeing. Its haunting beauty has to be discovered on an individual basis.[45]

Finally, the complex negotiations behind the passage of the 1984 legislation provided the first real test of Bill Richardson's skills at compromise. Although this bill was not the first passed by the freshman congressman—that involved a return of some land to Cochiti Pueblo—this one proved far more important. Over two decades later, Sierra Club representative Deborah Sease marveled at Richardson's skill along these lines. As she remembered, he never appeared inflexible in any of his stands. Alternatively he pushed or stood firm, always seeking a way to bring each group aboard a path to eventual compromise.[46]

Through endless meetings and discussions, Richardson stumbled upon what he would later describe as the fundamental rules of any successful negotiation: bringing groups with opposing points of view together to search for a common goal; acknowledging that finding a solution takes time; and holding on to a firm position, but always with a willingness to compromise at the end.[47] Although he would later bring these negotiating skills to the international arena, Congressman Bill Richardson initially applied them to the long-term environmental standoff of the San Juan Basin. His affection for the landscape of his newly adopted state of New Mexico had taken a giant leap forward.

PART TWO

Cultures

INTRODUCTION

❖

*I*n the 1980s, a number of universities, both here and abroad, established "cultural studies" programs and/or departments. Even with this hasty institutionalization, it remains a challenge to adequately define the term *culture*. The dictionary definition "the sum total of ways of living built up by a group of human beings and transmitted from one generation to another" seems too broad to be useful, while the more traditional understanding—that of a person familiar with the worlds of "literature, the fine arts, and proper manners" seems far too narrow. Historically, however, New Mexico has prided itself on having three "grand cultures": Native American, Hispanic, and Anglo-pioneer. (The state's African American community has argued that black culture should be included here as well.)

My graduate school training concentrated essentially on the history of "cultures" under what was then described as "American social and intellectual history." Although this term has long since been tossed into the historical wastebasket, I still believe that the history of ideas as placed in their social context remains a viable approach to any valid understanding of the past. As I suggest here in this extended essay, since 1940 New Mexico has witnessed the arrival of a whole new set of "cultures," and these have forever altered the intersections of the three grand traditions of the region's past.

Author's note: This section was written without endnotes, but one can turn to pages 254–60 for an annotated bibliography of classic works that deal with the various cultures of New Mexico.

CHAPTER FOUR

The Cultures *of* Modern
New Mexico, 1940 *to the*
Early Twenty-first Century

New Mexico is a unique land. Both long-time residents and first-time visitors agree on that. But exactly where does the uniqueness lie? Here there is no agreement. The most common interpretation has been that of the "three cultures." It is the presence of Native American, Hispanic, and Anglo-pioneer cultures, this argument goes, that accounts for New Mexico's distinctive qualities. Albuquerque writer Erna Fergusson voiced this eloquently in her *New Mexico: A Pageant of Three Peoples* (1951), as did Roswell native Paul Horgan in *The Heroic Triad* (1965). The annual Taos fiesta once reflected this theme by selecting *three* queens, one from each ethnic group.

Historians have spilled a good deal of ink discussing exactly how these cultures have interacted with each other over time. Many an early twentieth-century study suggested that all three blended in easy harmony. Fergusson and Horgan both emphasized their relatively peaceful coexistence. But a 1993 analysis was a bit more cautious, suggesting that "although the three cultures intermingle, they never completely blend."

The "three-cultures" approach to New Mexico has become virtual orthodoxy. Historians have come up with no other frame of analysis. For someone to argue that the over sixty years since World War II have altered the "three-culture" equation is tantamount to heresy. It might compare with questioning the centrality of scripture in the *Southern Baptist Newsletter*. But historians often rush in where angels fear to tread, and I plan to do precisely that. The thesis of this essay is both simple and complex: during the past six decades, New Mexicans have had to confront several new "cultures." In turn, these cultures have fostered, overlapped, blended with, and, at times, transformed the "heroic triad" of New Mexico's ancient past.

■

The first new "culture" might be termed the culture of landscape. From the frying pan flatness of the Llano Estacado to the alpine beauty of the northern mountains, New Mexico's landforms have ever inflamed the imagination. Modern scientists have counted six of the seven climate zones in the state, from the Lower Sonoran along the southern border to the Arctic-Alpine atop Wheeler Peak. The Bisti/De-Na-Zin Badlands, south of Farmington, have achieved international fame as the best fossil bed on the globe to study the end of the Cretaceous period. The land of New Mexico has always been a source of wonder.

While the landforms themselves have changed little since the 1930s, the landscape itself has altered considerably. After the war, the federal government withdrew millions of acres to create military bases and missile ranges at Clovis, Albuquerque, Alamogordo, and Roswell. Ironically, only in these federally protected areas can one find examples of the pristine New Mexico landscape of over a half-century ago. The White Sands Missile Range has inadvertently evolved into a "nuclear nature preserve," although access, of course, remains severely limited. In addition, increased regulations by the National Forest Service, National Park Service, Bureau of Land Management, and various state agencies have become a fact of life. Simultaneously, as easy access to public lands diminished, the state population has increased steadily.

The statistics tell a relentless tale. From a small town of about forty-five thousand in 1942, Albuquerque mushroomed into a sprawling metropolis approaching half a million by 2000. During the 1980s, the Las Cruces area was hailed as one of the fastest-growing regions of the nation. The overall state population increased accordingly:

1940:	531,818
1950:	681,187
1960:	951,023
1970:	1,017,055
1980:	1,303,393
1990:	1,515,069
2000:	1,819,046

Faced with such pressures, all levels of government found themselves "managing" the natural resources via increasingly complex rules and regulations. Consider the role of the state Department of Game and Fish as an example. Although concern over the fate of local trout, bear, beaver, elk, and deer reached back to the early years of the century, wildlife management programs increased steadily after World War II. In the late 1940s, for example, the department released a herd of bighorn sheep into the Sandia Mountains to replenish the original stock; a few years later they repeated the process with Barbary sheep in the Guadalupe Mountains. In the 1960s, they set loose yet more bighorn into the Pecos Wilderness. From the 1950s to the 1970s, the Department of Game and Fish also released such exotic animals as kudu, Siberian ibex, and Siberian gemsboks (oryx) into the New Mexican terrain. In the 1980s, officials laid plans to reintroduce the Mexican wolf (lobo) and the mountain lion—both of which drew heated protests from state ranchers and sheepmen.

With few exceptions, these programs of wildlife reintroductions have met with only modest success. The state abandoned its pheasant and prairie chicken release program in the 1950s and actually had to recapture and treat some disease-plagued Barbary sheep in the Guadalupes. In the late 1970s, public opinion so turned against the introduction of exotic species that the entire project was shelved. Only the successful fish hatchery program has escaped criticism.

Although most New Mexicans admit that some variety of land and wildlife management is necessary, there is little agreement on details. Virtually every issue—from banding mountain lions with radio collars to "thinning" the feral burro herd at Bandelier National Monument— brings forth heated controversy. Some programs, such as the 1991 fitting of Jornada Angora goats with radioactive collars to determine which coyote ate which goat (the "Atomic Goat" project), have been complete fiascoes. Perhaps the situation was best illustrated in a 1986 near-fatal bear attack on a Philmont Ranch Boy Scout camper. A Santa Fe spokesman saw this incident as a metaphor for the state's dilemma: "Everybody is running out of room."

◼

Few artists have captured the beauty of the New Mexican landscape better than the region's photographers. In fact, New Mexico has attracted more famous photographers than any other state except, perhaps, California. Much of this attraction can be traced to, in the words of author Charles F. Lummis, "that ineffable clarity, that luminousness, which makes a photographic light to be matched in no other civilized country."

During the 1940s, the state's most well-known photographers, John Candelario, Ernest Knee, and Laura Gilpin, all lived in the vicinity of Santa Fe. Gilpin's classic portrayal of Native peoples in *The Pueblos: A Camera Chronicle* (1941) and *The Enduring Navajo* (1968) were each the product of over a decade of effort. Her *Rio Grande: River of Destiny* (1949) portrayed in black-and-white photographs what Paul Horgan's *The Great River* (1954) conveyed in words.

The Fine Arts section of the University of New Mexico gave local photography a boost when it introduced new majors in the discipline during the early 1960s. Professor Van Deren Coke brought in talented professional photographers, such as Anne Noggle and Betty Hahn, and, especially, art historian Beaumont Newhall. Widely acknowledged as the "founder" of the history of photography, Newhall attracted a large number of graduate students to the field. Albuquerque galleries, such as White Oak, Quivira, and the University Art Museum, plus Camera West and the Andrew Smith Gallery in Santa Fe, provided the public with numerous opportunities to view photographic images. The first New Mexico Photographers Exhibition was not staged until 1956, but within twelve years a New York City art judge declared the state's photography of "very high caliber—as good as anything in the country." The photographs of Todd Webb, Meridel Rubenstein, Paul Caponigro, and Patrick Nagatani, plus the publishing emphasis of the University of New Mexico Press, have kept the town of Santa Fe, and much of the state, "synonymous with photography over the years."

Two of America's most famous nature photographers, Ansel Adams and Eliot Porter, have strong New Mexico links. Born in California and trained as a classical musician, Adams fell in love with the state on his first visit to Taos and returned to photograph thousands of New Mexican scenes. In fact, Adams's most widely known photograph is his black-and-white rendition *Moonrise, Hernandez, New Mexico*, which he shot one late afternoon in 1941. For nearly fifty years, this brooding, majestic village scene has stood as testimony both to the mystery of New Mexico as well as to the vision of the photographer. Yet as Adams confessed in 1974, *Moonrise* owed as much to his darkroom skills as to the placement of his camera. The actual sky was not so dark, he admitted, nor did the crosses in the cemetery shine quite so brightly. *Moonrise* thus became "a distortion, but not a distortion." "Reality was not that way at all," Adams admitted. "But it felt that way."

Even more famous than Ansel Adams was longtime Tesuque resident Eliot Porter. Born in Illinois, Porter, like Adams, came to photography via another discipline, having first trained as a physician and taught biochemistry at Harvard until 1939. That year, art impresario Alfred Stieglitz gave Porter his first show—twenty-nine black-and-white images—at Stieglitz's famous gallery, An American Place, in New York City. Afterward, Porter resigned his teaching job to devote the rest of his life to photography. Although he began with large-scale landscapes, he soon turned to depicting the more intimate details of nature, almost a "miniaturization" of the world around him. "Only in fragments of the whole is nature's order apparent," Porter wrote in 1990.

Moving to New Mexico permanently in 1946, Porter proceeded to master the difficult art of the dye transfer color-printing process. In fact, his ability to manipulate color in the darkroom soon elevated the dye transfer procedure to a genuine art form. Porter's first book, *In Wildness Is the Preservation of the World* (1962), helped to establish the Sierra Club's

Porter's black-and-white rendition "Barbershop, Mesilla, New Mexico, 1940." Courtesy Jonathan Porter.

reputation as well as his own. Two dozen books followed, including his classic *Birds of North America* (1972) and *Eliot Porter's Southwest* (1985). Often termed "the Ansel Adams of color photography"—a designation he disliked—Eliot Porter reigned as the world's foremost nature photographer until his death in the fall of 1990.

When purists accused Eliot Porter of distorting nature by manipulating its colors in the dye transfer process, he would simply reply that the colors were already there. All he did was enhance or diminish them. Porter felt free to alter the colors because the essential quality of a photograph rested not with its "literalism" but with the "emotional impact" that it had on the viewer.

*Eliot Porter's black-and-white rendition of Ash Tree,
Arizona, 1958. Courtesy Jonathan Porter.*

It may seem a bit of a leap from trout hatcheries and newly released bighorn sheep to the darkrooms of Ansel Adams, Eliot Porter, and Patrick Nagatani. But perhaps the gap is not so wide after all. Whether one confronts New Mexico's landscape directly, in the Jemez Mountains or Pecos Wilderness, or indirectly, via the imagery of Adams, Porter, and Nagatani, the results are similar. In both cases, one interacts with *managed* landscape. Increased control of land and landscape has become a central aspect of New Mexican life since 1942. The wild regions of the prewar years have virtually disappeared.

◾

The second new postwar "culture" involves the culture of "big science." Although New Mexico hosted its share of astronomers, physicians, and anthropologists before World War II, big science began in earnest in the fall of 1942. That year the U.S. Army informed A. J. Connell, the headmaster of the Los Alamos Ranch School, that the school's facilities were needed for the national war effort. Construction began immediately, and the officials predicted that the proposed town of Los Alamos would eventually house perhaps two hundred scientists and their families. By 1945, however, the population had reached over five thousand and showed no signs of slowing. As the central cog in the sprawling Anglo-American Manhattan Project, the Los Alamos scientists wrestled with a momentous assignment: to produce an atomic weapon to end World War II "in the shortest possible time."

The atomic age began at 5:30 A.M., July 16, 1945, at Trinity Site, about thirty-five miles east of Socorro. The location, now part of the White Sands Missile Range, still appears on most maps. From that moment forward, New Mexico would forever be termed "the birthplace of the atomic age." Local residents knew of the existence of a mammoth bomb in July; the world learned of atomic weapons three weeks later at Hiroshima and Nagasaki. Within days, Los Alamos had achieved a worldwide reputation, the first New Mexican city to do so.

The town of Los Alamos also introduced the state to massive federal funding for scientific purposes. But would such funds continue in time of peace? After VJ-day, many officials expressed doubts that Los Alamos would survive. As the famed "first team" of scientists departed for their peacetime university jobs, pundits predicted that Los Alamos would join Shakespeare or Mogollon as simply a unique variety of New Mexico ghost town or some form of national park.

General Leslie R. Groves, the overall head of the Manhattan Project, argued vigorously for making Los Alamos permanent. He noted that the nation would never again be able to rebuild such a community. Norris Bradbury, who took over as director of the laboratory from famed scientist J. Robert Oppenheimer, felt the same way. In mid-1946, Bradbury issued his famous "go or stay" directive to wavering scientists and technical personnel. He also supervised the transition from secret wartime military base to New Mexico's first "federal city."

From 1942 to the mid-1950s, Los Alamos formed a completely federal town. The government owned everything—houses, laboratories, shops, and all else. One needed a pass to enter the gate. Of equal importance, in an isolated section of a very poor state, the government paid high wages.

The impact of these wages soon spread beyond the town to affect the entire region. Contractors, carpenters, electricians, truck drivers, merchants, restaurateurs, barbers, artists, grocers, farmers, and maids all benefited accordingly. Historian Chris Dietz has argued that the nearby Tewa-speaking pueblos of San Ildefonso, Santa Clara, and Cochiti used Los Alamos salaries to *preserve* their historic Native traditions. Pueblo leaders were able to purchase communal farm equipment, and numerous other Indians followed suit on an individual basis. A town of cultured, highly educated outsiders also provided a new outlet for Native arts and crafts. The same impact can be seen in the nearby Hispanic villages. Cordova wood-carver George Lopez supported his family in part by working at Los Alamos; in his spare time he revived, almost single-handedly, a historic Hispanic craft. The nearby predominantly Hispanic community of Española also sent its sons and daughters to work at Los Alamos. It might not be too much to suggest that a legacy of big science (or, perhaps, big technology) also found its way into the colorful, if perplexing, art of the sophisticated hydraulic lifts that adorn the Española lowriders. (The city proudly claims to be "the lowrider capital of the nation.") By the mid-1980s, Los Alamos National Laboratories employed over seven thousand people and had a budget of half a billion dollars. A decade later, the budget had more than doubled. A 1996 estimate suggested that one out of every twenty-three jobs in the region had a Los Alamos connection. A 2004 study also listed New Mexico as the second-poorest state in the Union. If it ranked that low *with* the extensive federal atomic expenditures, one can hardly imagine what it might be without them.

The culture of science reached into other areas of the state as well. Historians have shown how the establishment of Sandia National Laboratories in Albuquerque altered life in the Duke City. Like Los Alamos, Sandia brought in thousands of highly educated, sophisticated outsiders. In addition, it employed people from all ranks of life: technicians, security guards, secretaries, teachers, file clerks, and others. By the mid-1960s, Sandia employed over eight thousand. The rise of Kirtland Air Force Base, especially the closely related Special Weapons Laboratory, funneled even more federal monies into Bernalillo County. Although "Sandia" is not a widely recognized name outside of New Mexico, the mass production of nuclear weapons that occurred there from the 1950s forward made it indispensable to the national defense system.

The atomic age influenced all regions of the state. The name of Paddy Martinez is well known to all residents of Grants and Milan, for in the early 1950s the Navajo sheepherder discovered a chunk of uranium that inaugurated the biggest American mining boom since the California gold rush of 1849. Known previously as a spot to raise fine carrots, by the mid-1960s Grants basked its reputation as the "Uranium Capital of the United States." By 1980 over 40 percent of the nation's uranium was mined and milled in the Grants Uranium Belt region, and the town reached a population of 11,500. Forecasters predicted a population of one hundred thousand by the year 2000 and jested that Albuquerque would simply become "a suburb of Grants." Although private corporations financed the mining operations, federal weapons demands lay behind this boom that transformed all of west-central New Mexico into a crucial component of the postwar atomic defense system.

The Tularosa Basin underwent similar scientific transformation. Although New Mexico writer Ross Calvin once urged that the entire basin be set aside as a permanent outdoor natural laboratory, such was not to be. In the 1930s, Massachusetts scientist Robert Goddard chose nearby Roswell to test his rocket experiments, but the hamlet of Alamogordo benefited even more from the demands of the war. Afterward, the Alamogordo

Bombing Range (now White Sands Missile Range) commandeered an area larger than the state of Delaware. The largest range in the nation, it proved ideal for the postwar testing of captured V-2 rockets. By 1958 the White Sands budget approached $160 million, employing approximately 6,700 people. Steady technical demands from the Apollo program, the space shuttle program, and numerous energy contracts also helped transform nearby New Mexico Tech and New Mexico State universities into major research institutions. In 1976, Alamogordo dedicated the impressive Space Hall of Fame. It proudly called itself the "Birthplace of Atomic Energy— Home of American Rocket Research."

The Very Large Array (VLA) radio telescope on the plains of San Agustin looms as the state's most unique big science project. Operated by the National Radio Astronomy Observatory and funded by the National Science Foundation, the VLA consists of twenty-seven six-story-high radio antennas that astronomers maneuver along a dual set of railroad tracks to probe for the ultimate secrets of the universe. The average American might meet the VLA as the backdrop for science-fiction films such as *Contact* (1996), but the astrophysics community recognizes it as the world's largest telescope project and the premier instrument for probing a wide range of astronomical puzzles. Currently undergoing optic-fiber retrofitting, the VLA has contributed to scores of scientific breakthroughs. Two examples: In 1997, it provided proof, as Einstein had once predicted, that gravity could "bend" light almost like a lens. The next year, VLA scientists announced that stars emit radio signals from their outer atmosphere, a discovery that forever changed interstellar astronomy. Largely considered a success, the VLA ranks as the state's most prominent example of "pure science."

On the eastern side of New Mexico, Cannon Air Force Base in Clovis was selected in 1989 to house the nation's extensive F-111 fighter-bomber fleet. Such massive federal expenditures have produced a genuine scientific subculture. On a per capita basis, New Mexico has more scientific and technical workers than any other state. No area of New Mexico remains unaffected.

Since most of New Mexico science has involved defense measures or weapons production, the culture of big science has often carried with it a sense of moral ambiguity. On a personal level, the questions had relatively easy answers. People who were troubled about weapons work simply resigned. Some have even crusaded to encourage other federal workers to follow suit. But on a community level, the issue proved much more complex. During the late 1960s and early 1970s, antigovernment protesters blocked the entrance gates to Albuquerque's Sandia Base and staged several marches in Los Alamos proper. Angry billboards proclaiming "It [atomic weaponry] Started Here. Let's Stop It Here" and "A Mind [working on nuclear weapons] Is a Terrible Thing to Waste" periodically line the I-25 traffic corridor from Albuquerque to Santa Fe. The signs proved especially prominent during the two Iraq wars. Strangely, no group has seriously protested the open secret that the Manzano Mountains house over eight hundred nuclear warheads. "If Albuquerque were to secede from the union," one antinuclear observer noted, "we'd be the third-largest nuclear power in the world." Albuquerque's city council did not discuss potential evacuation plans until the years after the 9/11 tragedy.

The off-and-on antiwar protestors point to the dark side of New Mexico's culture of science. To establish its various bases, the federal government had to confiscate the land of about one hundred families in the Socorro region and some two hundred others near Alamogordo. Most of these pioneers left peacefully, but eighty-two-year-old John Prather, who owned land south of the Sacramento Mountains, refused to budge. In so doing, he became the symbol of crusty individual resistance to increasing federal encroachment. Fearing a scandal, the army allowed Prather to stay on his land until his death.

Other, less publicized incidents concerned public safety. On May 22, 1957, an air force B-36 bomber from Kirtland Base accidentally dropped a ten-megaton hydrogen bomb five miles south of Albuquerque, avoiding catastrophe only because the weapon was not fully armed. During the early 1970s, medical researchers concluded that Navajo uranium miners of the Four Corners area had been contracting lung cancer far above statistical norms; after almost two decades of agitation, President George H. W. Bush signed a compensation bill for them in the fall of 1990. The July 16, 1979, United Nuclear Corporation Church Rock Mill tailings pond rupture has the dubious distinction of being the worst radiation accident in all of American history. The ninety-four million gallons of radioactive liquid waste that washed into the Rio Puerco released far more radiation into the atmosphere than Pennsylvania's far better-known Three Mile Island disaster of the same year.

In 1993 *Albuquerque Tribune* journalist Eileen Welsome won a Pulitzer Prize for her investigative reporting on the eighteen Cold War citizens who were given plutonium injections (without their knowledge) as part of a long-term secret scientific experiment. Her findings later emerged in book form as *The Plutonium Files* (1999).

With the end of the Cold War in 1991, the federal government began to acknowledge—really for the first time—the serious environmental consequences of the over four decades of nuclear weapons manufacture in New Mexico. From 1990 to 2002, the government spent about $1.4 billion to clean up over 2,000 locations in Los Alamos—including the infamous "Acid Canyon" (now a nature park with hiking trails), which served as a laboratory discharge area from 1944 to the mid-1960s. Sandia National Laboratories remediated over two hundred contaminated sites and in July 2004 hosted a public community review to celebrate the official completion of twenty-five of these projects on Kirtland Air Force Base.

But environmental problems persist, and the first years of the twenty-first century have placed the state Environment Department at loggerheads with both Los Alamos and Sandia Labs over a variety of environmental concerns. For the former, the issue revolves largely around the potential migration of plutonium into the Rio Grande water supply; for the latter, the major problems involve strict adherence to the rules of handling hazardous waste materials. In January 2004, Farmington hosted a symbolic event that highlighted all these concerns. For several days, the town staged a "Healing the Uranium Legacy" gathering. During this commemoration, singers, rock bands, and various speakers voiced their concerns over the environment and the illnesses that had plagued the Navajo miners who once worked in the "yellow sand" industry.

■

Perhaps the ultimate embodiment of the ambiguity of big science in New Mexico can be seen in the twenty-year controversy over the establishment of the Waste Isolation Pilot Project (WIPP), located twenty-six miles east of Carlsbad. In 1954, scientists recommended that the ideal permanent storage area for nuclear waste would be in subterranean salt beds, and in the early 1980s, scientists selected this ten-thousand-acre area of the state as the best-possible site to store permanently the nation's low- and medium-level nuclear waste. According to theory, the region's underground salt formation had not only been stable for millennia, it would slowly "enfold" the nuclear waste (rather like plastic wrap) and thus keep it from ever entering the environment.

Proponents and opponents of the plan began to square off immediately. Drawing on pamphlets, newsletters, editorials, and speeches, each side strove valiantly to sway New Mexicans to their position. Over time, the clash pitted the more liberal north against the more conservative south. One reporter described the twenty-year dispute as the state's "longest-running soap opera."

The issues were complex but essentially boiled down to two: (1) a precise definition of the types of nuclear waste to be stored at WIPP and (2) safety concerns over the transportation routes that would bring the waste materials from such areas as Rocky Flats, Colorado, the Idaho National Engineering Laboratory, and Los Alamos. The federal government assured Carlsbad that only low- and medium-level nuclear waste—largely plutonium-contaminated clothing and equipment, etc.—most of it safe enough to be handled manually—would be sent to WIPP. The nation's slowly accumulating high-level nuclear waste—such as spent nuclear fuel rods—was scheduled to be sent only to the proposed Yucca Mountain depository in Nevada.

From the late 1970s forward, scientists from numerous disciplines placed the WIPP site under a variety of microscopes. It became perhaps the most thoroughly studied piece of real estate in the nation. Gradually the nation's geologists emerged as the most listened-to scientific experts. The majority agreed that the region had been geologically stable for aeons and would continue to be so for the indefinite future. Even so, an antinuclear astrophysicist, Charles L. Hyder, staged an eighty-two-day fast against WIPP because "you can't keep plutonium isolated in wet salt."

The transportation issue proved equally perplexing. WIPP opponents successfully forced a reconfiguration of the containers designed to haul the waste, and the state received repeated assurances of federal aid to build various urban bypasses so that waste shipments could avoid heavily populated areas. Purely on a statistical basis, scientists admitted that there would likely be five hauling accidents over WIPP's lifetime, but they insisted that the safety measures were such that none would endanger the public.

In March of 1999, WIPP finally received its first load of nuclear waste. A few protestors lined the truck route, but essentially the shipment arrived without incident. Then Department of Energy head Bill Richardson greeted the opening with relief. He viewed it as marking a major step in "cleaning up the Cold War legacy." Some observers noted the ironic justice that the state that had given birth to the atomic age had been selected to harbor the nation's first permanent nuclear waste disposal site.

Decisive though the opening of WIPP may have been, it did not end the waste disposal controversy. Watchdog committees have closely observed the nature of the shipments, and both they, the local press, and state officials have fiercely opposed any attempts to introduce higher-level waste into WIPP. Although there have been no accidents to date, the government had to formally apologize to San Ildefonso Pueblo when a 1999 shipment took an unauthorized shortcut across pueblo sacred land.

Although the controversy over WIPP simmers at a much lower level, the 1999 opening of the site marks a permanent milestone in New Mexico history. As the half-life of plutonium is twenty-four thousand years, the waste stored there will remain radioactive for the indefinite future.

◼

The abrupt end of the Cold War with the Soviet Union in 1991 heightened the latent ambiguity of life at the nation's premier weapons laboratory. Indeed, during the last fifteen years Los Alamos National Laboratory confronted a variety of embarrassing, well-publicized crises: alleged higher cancer rates for Los Alamos residents (a charge hotly denied), the pilfering of technical equipment worth millions of dollars, a credit card fraud scandal, and a criminal charge against a top-level LANL scientist, Wen Ho Lee. In December 1999, the FBI accused the Taiwanese-born Lee of delivering atomic weapons secrets to China. Because of the gravity of the accusation, Lee served nine months in solitary confinement but escaped harsher penalties by pleading guilty to a single low-level security violation. Although a number of people consider Lee an innocent victim of a paranoid security system, LANL officials maintain that if people could view the complete (classified) record, they would quickly change their minds. The issue remains contentious yet today.

If this were not bad enough, in July 2004 Los Alamos scientists could not account for two computer disks containing top-level data on nuclear weapons design. In an unprecedented move, director Pete Nanos shut down the entire lab for a week and read the approximately twelve thousand employees the riot act regarding the need to follow security rules. Long-term senator and supporter Pete Domenici wrote an open letter to the community decrying the fact that the lab's reputation as "a crown jewel of science" had been forever tarnished. After disciplinary action and tighter security regulations, the lab began to slowly return to normal. Six months later, the lab concluded that the disks had never existed in the first place.

Given these overlapping concerns—the troubles of Los Alamos, the admitted need for continual nuclear weapons stewardship, worries over damage to the environment, and—especially since September 11, 2001—fear of possible nuclear terrorism—what does the future likely hold for New Mexico's culture of big science? The question defies easy answer. Since both Los Alamos and Sandia have always conducted a certain percentage of nondefense research programs, many liberals have voiced hope that federal expenditures might shift to such areas as heat pumps, fusion power, algae farms, nuclear cleanup, nuclear safety, or cancer research. The ultimate symbol of this hope can be seen in the $57-million Clinton P. Anderson Meson facility, a cancer research institute that opened in Los Alamos in 1971. Whether this will occur or not hinges on two items: Congress's willingness to continue to fund expensive, nonmilitary-related research projects and the transferable nature of the weapons scientists' skills to assist corporate enterprise. Some hope that Sandia and Los Alamos will help create the next revolution in microtechnology and nanotechnology. Whatever the future, one thing is certain. The culture of big science and big technology has forever redefined the culture of New Mexico since 1940.

■

The third postwar new "culture" involves the culture of tourism. In 1945, the Research Division of New Mexico's Committee for Economic Development published a study of future state economic growth. Concluding that expenditures for public works projects could never provide a satisfactory economic base, the authors carefully explored the potential of agriculture, mining, oil and gas extraction, heavy manufacturing, light industries, and lumbering. Ironically, they hardly gave tourism a mention, even though prewar tourism had ranked as the state's leading source of cash income. Little has changed in the last sixty years. If one excludes the federal and state payrolls, tourism still ranks as the main source of income and employment for the state. Recent estimates put the dollar amounts at 2.2 billion; over fifty-three thousand New Mexicans are directly involved with tourism. The field is so varied that contemporary visitors can sign up for tours that range from Native American venues to UFO sightings to art gallery excursions to sites linked with Billy the Kid to atomic locations to all the venues mentioned in the Tony Hillerman novels.

Originally part of the highway department, from the late 1930s forward the state tourist bureau did its best to acquaint the nation with the wonders of New Mexico. All sections of the state joined in this crusade of self-promotion, some more effectively than others. But four sectors have parlayed their tourist appeal into a genuine international following: the Gallup Indian Ceremonial, the celebration of New Mexico skiing, "the selling of Santa Fe," and Native American gaming.

In 1922, the border town of Gallup inaugurated its first Inter-tribal Indian Ceremonial "for an exhibit of Indian ceremonials, dances, sports, handicraft and agricultural and husbandry products." The ceremonial was established, said the articles of incorporation, for "mutual benefit and not for pecuniary profit or speculation." Aided by the post–World War II highway construction boom, Gallup became far more accessible to outsiders. The fall ceremonial became the town's major attraction in the 1950s. Billing itself as "The Indian Capital of the World," Gallup entrepreneurs saw the ceremonial as the fulfillment of a nineteenth-century Navajo trader's prophecy that "tourism is the pony that they'll [the Indians will] ride out on." Throughout the 1950s and 1960s, the ceremonial put on traditional Native dances and arts displays. In addition, Gallup held conferences and speeches on Indian-related issues. By the early 1970s, the festival drew over thirty tribes, many from as far away as Mexico and Canada. The Indians utilized the Gallup gathering as a main stop on the "powwow circuit," and it became a standing joke that the ceremonial provided "an opportunity for whites to see Indians and for Indians to see Indians, too." In 1970, just to pick a single year, the four days of celebration generated $1.5 million in revenue for the Gallup area. Performances of the Buffalo Dance, Eagle Dance, *Yeibichai* dances, hoop dances, and others attracted a number of visitors, many coming from overseas.

In spite of the economic success, the ceremonial faced a variety of problems. In 1954, Gallup police arrested almost one thousand of the eleven thousand people attending for public drunkenness. The Hopi tribe boycotted the ceremonial for several years during the late 1950s, and Zuni Pueblo governors periodically had to protest against Navajo plans to move the festival to Window Rock, Arizona. In 1969, militant members of the American Indian Movement (AIM) denounced the ceremonial for exploiting Native Americans and tried to disrupt certain events. The next year, local newspapers were filled with talk about abandoning the ceremonial entirely. Eventually, however, the town forged a compromise, part of which involved moving most activities to new grounds at nearby Red Rock State Park. The local Pueblo and Navajo craftspeople strongly supported the ceremonial, for it offered a convenient and profitable outlet for their workmanship. Tourist dollars produced by the celebration of Indian life proved essential to all of Gallup, regardless of ethnic affiliations.

■

In the late 1930s, northern New Mexico boasted several small ski areas in Las Vegas, Taos, and Santa Fe. But the "ski boom" that began in the late 1950s created a series of others, such as Red River (1959), Sierra Blanca, run by the Mescalero Apache tribe (1961), and Cloudcroft (1963), all of which relied heavily on Texas and Oklahoma visitors. Albuquerque's much-debated aerial tram (1966) made the city's Sandia Peak more accessible to local skiers as well.

The central figure behind the state's postwar ski boom was Taos impresario Ernie Blake. A Swiss national, Blake (Bloch) served with Allied intelligence during World War II and arrived in the region in 1948 to manage the Santa Fe ski lift. Comparing northern New Mexico with the Alps, Blake set out on a two-year search to discover the perfect ski run. After careful surveying—including several low-level aerial flights over northern New Mexico and southern Colorado—Blake chose Twining, New Mexico, to create his Taos Ski Valley. Beginning in 1955, Blake steadily improved his area, adding chair lifts, French and Swiss chefs, boutiques, and the charm of a powerful and enigmatic personality. "Mr. Taos Ski Valley," as he was known, touted the region as "better than Switzerland" because of the dry, light snow, abundant sunshine, and lack of bitter cold. In large measure he succeeded. By the early 1970s, New Mexico's slopes had begun to attract skiers from all over the nation. Although the industry has suffered setbacks due to changing weather patterns, New Mexico still rivals Utah and Colorado for the best in inter-mountain American skiing.

The selling of Santa Fe, especially its world of crafts and fine arts, has become the most successful tourist tale of the postwar era. Although Taos and Santa Fe achieved fame as art colonies around the turn of the century, the Depression and the onset of World War II effectively brought those communities to an end. In 1945, for example, Santa Fe boasted only two art galleries, and well-known Taos artist Gustave Baumann complained to Erna Fergusson that "among the many problems that sit on my doorstep, the first one is to pay my way."

It took several decades for the art world to revive. In 1950, Albuquerque staged its first Annual All Albuquerque Artist's [sic] Exhibition. A Santa Fe art brochure of the same era felt it necessary to define such terms as *impressionism*, *abstraction*, and *expressionism* for viewers. The brochure also warned that people should not view modern art "as a series of hoaxes perpetrated on an unsuspecting public by men who wish only to gain notoriety for themselves."

New Mexico's most celebrated native-born painter for the postwar era was probably San Patricio's Peter Hurd. Working alongside his talented wife, Henriette Wyeth, Hurd captured the beauty and mystery of the twentieth-century Southwest in canvases such as *The Gate and Beyond* (1953). He also found himself in the national spotlight in 1967 when President Lyndon Johnson rejected Hurd's commissioned portrait as the "ugliest thing" he had ever seen. The Roswell Museum and Art Center contains the best collection of Hurd's work. The most famous Native American artist was Chinle-born R. C. Gorman. Gifted with great marketing ability as well as talent, Gorman moved to Taos to open his

Navajo gallery and display his skillful, if sparse, drawings of Navajo life, usually of women. Flamboyant and sophisticated, Gorman sold himself as much as his artwork and soon became a local legend.

The New Mexico artist who commandeered the widest attention in the postwar years, however, was Georgia O'Keeffe. Born in Wisconsin, O'Keeffe trained as a commercial artist and taught both in South Carolina and in Texas. In 1916, she met photographer Alfred Stieglitz, with whom her name would forever be associated. They began living together in 1918 and married in 1924. O'Keeffe fell in love with New Mexico on her first visit in 1917; she moved to Abiquiu permanently in 1949. Well before her death in Santa Fe in 1986, critics had dubbed her America's most original artist, the nation's greatest woman painter, perhaps "the greatest woman painter in the world."

Ironically, until about 1975 O'Keeffe was probably more famous nationally than in her adopted state. Dressed in a long black gown, she would often be recognized shopping in Santa Fe, but her Hispanic neighbors in Abiquiu generally marked her out as an eccentric, best left alone. (In gratitude for this, she built a fifty-thousand-dollar gymnasium for the town.) The UNM Fine Arts Museum did not stage O'Keeffe's first in-state exhibit until 1975. Not until the Santa Fe Chamber Music Festival began to use O'Keeffe reprints as popular posters in the early 1970s did New Mexicans come to appreciate her talents. As late as 1975, a reporter observed that while O'Keeffe's fame was international, she was probably one of New Mexico's least-known residents.

If local residents ignored Georgia O'Keeffe, the national art critics did not. Except for her larger-than-life images of flowers—most of which were done before she moved to New Mexico—critics invariably linked her with the southwestern landscape. They delighted in her description of the Sangre de Cristo Mountains as "miles of grey elephants" or her assessment of New Mexico's light as "the faraway nearby." Her bleached cow skulls and her numerous renditions of Pedernal Mountain ("It's *my* mountain") have confirmed that impression. Her *Black Cross, New Mexico* (1929), one of the first canvases she painted in the state, completed the identification. As a reporter noted in 1968, Georgia O'Keeffe had become the virtual symbol of the American Southwest. Founded after her death, the O'Keeffe Museum in Santa Fe attracts thousands of visitors annually.

In the 1960s, Lubbock native Forrest Fenn opened an art gallery across from the state capitol in Santa Fe, thus beginning the odyssey that would make him the Horatio Alger of the New Mexico art world. According to rumor, Fenn parlayed a $25,000 initial investment into a multi-million-dollar operation. Fenn advised potential buyers that art was "just about foolproof" as an investment. He estimated that the best pieces would increase in value from 40 to 50 percent a year and even offered refunds if they failed to appreciate. By 1980, Santa Fe contained about ninety art galleries, and Fenn Galleries claimed an annual volume of $6 million. Simultaneously, Old Town in Albuquerque had twenty-four galleries; estimates put the Albuquerque art market at $12 million a year. In 1990, Santa Fe had about two hundred galleries. It also ranked third in the nation in art, trailing only New York City and Los Angeles. Significantly, it ranked first in the category of selling art to buyers outside of the region.

What were these tourists buying? The market fluctuated, of course, but initially the steady sales came from representational western themes, especially those depicting cowboys or Indians. These proved ever popular with the Oklahoma and Texas tourists. As an *Albuquerque Tribune* reporter noted in 1970, "The demand is so great for Old West art that many contemporary artists are turning out paintings and bronzes full of buffaloes, stage coaches, cattle drives and Indians. Yet few of these busy painters have ever seen a buffalo outside a zoo." When California tourists began to replace Oklahomans and Texans, Santa Fe galleries found they could market more abstract designs. Lithographs from the famed Tamarind Institute (which moved to Albuquerque in 1970) also became quite popular.

Some visitors purchased Hispanic crafts, such as the Chimayó weavings produced by the Ortega family, wood carving, or the micaceous pottery of Felipe Ortega. The annual Santa Fe Spanish Market today attracts about fifty thousand visitors every summer. Even more popular is the city's two-day Indian Market, which claims to be the state's most-attended single event. Every August, the Indian Market attracts visitors from every corner of the globe.

The culture of tourism has provided American Indian artists with an increasing opportunity to market their work. Santa Clara artist Pablita

Velarde and her daughter, Helen Hardin, created both representational and abstract oil and earth paintings on Native themes. Choctaw Jerry Ingram's finely crafted horses and dancers also sold well. Navajo Vernon Hoskie's exquisite gold jewelry graces many a celebrity home, and the sculptures of Chiricahua Apache Allan Houser fill many tourist living rooms. Virtually every New Mexican dreams of finding a María (Martínez) of San Ildefonso black-on-black pot at a New Jersey flea market for $10.95.

◼

The most astounding tourist story of recent decades, however, involved the explosion of Indian gaming. The rise of gaming tumbled together the themes of Native American sovereignty, a vigorous antigambling crusade, a controversial governor, and the ever-volatile concern over state tax revenues. Although none of the New Mexico casinos ever approached the billion-dollar income generated by the Pequot tribe's infamous Foxwoods Resort in eastern Connecticut, they rank today as a multi-million-dollar enterprise. The approximately ten thousand state slot machines—with a daily profit each of about $150—bring in over a million dollars a day. In 2004, Native American gaming officially ranks as the third-largest industry in the state.

The story began in the early 1980s, when Acoma and Sandia pueblos reasserted their status as sovereign nations by establishing high-stakes bingo operations in crude, hastily constructed metal sheds. Four years later, on October 17, 1988, Congress passed the Indian Gaming Rights Act, which allowed federally recognized tribes to engage in certain types of gaming, provided they negotiated proper agreements with their various state governments. By the early 1990s, eleven New Mexico tribes had established such operations, in spite of a decided lack of enthusiasm from governors Gary Carruthers and Bruce King.

Then in 1994 Republican Gary Johnson assumed the governor's office and decided to take the bull by the horns. Six weeks into his term, he met with tribal leaders and signed a series of agreements. But six months later, the New Mexico Supreme Court declared these compacts null and void because Johnson had bypassed the state legislature in the process. All such compacts needed legislative approval, said the court. Later a federal judge ruled along the same lines. Johnson—once termed "the godfather of gaming in New Mexico"—found himself in deep trouble. A court ruling stated that all casinos had to close by July 27, 1996.

The sides instantly polarized. The governor of Pojoaque Pueblo called this a violation of native sovereignty and threatened to close all roads (including the heavily traveled I-25) that crossed Pojoaque lands. He also declared that the tribe was ready to use (unspecified) "extreme non-violent means" to achieve its objective. Although nine pueblos agreed to close their gaming operations on the July date—in hopes of forcing a special legislative session on the issue—Mescalero Apache president Wendell Chino refused to budge. "I don't want to tell the others what to do," he told reporters. "They have their own sovereignty." The Jicarilla Apache tribe later sided with Chino and refused to close its casino as well. Alarmists feared a repeat of a similar 1992 federal-state-tribal showdown in Arizona, where federal agents raided a casino only to find themselves captured and held hostage by tribal members. Arizona's governor had to fly in to negotiate the agents' release. If a similar situation occurred in New Mexico, Chino warned, a trigger-happy federal agent could inaugurate "another Wounded Knee massacre of Indian people."

Fortunately, a last-minute decision by U.S. District Court judge Martha Vázquez allowed the casinos to remain open during an appeal process, and the next year the tribes and the state reached a general agreement. Since states are not allowed to tax federally recognized tribes, the agreement involved "revenue sharing," whereby the tribes agreed to pay the state a certain percentage of slot machine profits. (The initial figure was pegged at 16 percent—which the tribes declared as much too high—and was lowered to between 3 and 8 percent, depending on the size of operations.)

In addition to the ongoing quarrel over financial matters, antigambling forces marshaled a sustained critique of the economics and morality of gaming. Money lost in casinos, they argued, would otherwise have been spent on taxable consumer goods. Thus, every new casino that opened ensured a drop in overall state revenues. In 1997, critics estimated that forty-five thousand New Mexicans either had a gambling problem or were related to someone who did. The only way gaming could succeed, they said, would be if it could attract a steady stream of wealthy outsiders.

All historical writing is approximate—especially so when dealing with contemporary issues—and assessing the state of Indian gaming is difficult. Santa Ana Pueblo is currently heavily in debt, San Felipe Pueblo has suffered accusations that the profits are lining certain people's pockets, Sandia Pueblo seems to have gaming affairs in balance, and the Navajo Tribal Council has repeatedly declared the whole industry a travesty on traditional Native values.

Even with this spread of opinion, by the onset of the new century it seems clear that the pro-gaming contingent has won the current battle. Signs offering aid to people with gambling problems formally dot all casino entrances, and, contrary to expectations, many of the more elaborate casinos have indeed become "destination points" for outside visitors. Over time the various state Native casinos marched steadily from rough-hewn metal sheds to smoke-filled bubble domes to state-of-the-art entertainment venues. Sandia Pueblo's new casino cost over $100 million to build. Others boast luxury hotels, soccer fields, golf courses, amphitheaters, and spacious arenas. A glance at the license plates in the parking lots shows the extent of their appeal.

The various tribes are, generally, pleased with this success. The economic boost has enabled them to build community structures and establish scholarship funds for their young people. Since the operations remain open twenty-four hours a day, the demand for workers is steady. Over twelve thousand people—the majority non-Native—are currently employed in the industry. For better or worse, during the last two decades, Indian gaming has emerged as the linchpin of the state's tourist enterprise.

But has the increased rush of tourists to New Mexico gone too far? As historian Hal Rothman has noted, tourism often entails a "devil's bargain," and many have begun to question the whole operation. If so, the state has only itself to blame.

In 1977, Santa Fe imposed a 3 percent lodgers tax on local motels, hotels, and inns. The new tax flowed into a concerted campaign to advertise the "City Different" among the moneyed, East and West Coast "high rollers." The campaign succeeded. In May 1981, *Esquire* magazine trumpeted Santa Fe as the place to be—"Great women, great weather, and plenty to do," blared the cover. The *Denver Post*, *People*, and the *Today* show picked up the chorus. Tourism quickly evolved into a year-round affair in Santa Fe. Shop owners who used to close for several months after Labor Day now began to hire extra help. Local newspapers touted tourism as a recession-proof industry.

One unforeseen dimension of increased tourism appeared when many of these moneyed visitors decided to settle permanently in Taos and Santa Fe. The arrival of a number of film and media stars drew enormous attention. Writers Neil Simon, Sam Shepard, and Judy Blume moved to Santa Fe, as did entertainers such as Goldie Hawn, Robert Redford, Lily Tomlin, Val Kilmer, Roger Miller, Amy Irving, Jessica Lange, Don Meredith, and even the duke and duchess of Bedford. Population grew from 40,000 in 1970 to 50,000 in 1980 to 56,000 in 1990 to 61,805 in 2000.

In 1988, *Megatrends* author John Naisbitt urged Santa Fe citizens to avoid industry for tourism and to continue to promote its "quality of life." But critics maintained that the rush of tourists was destroying the very thing that drew them there in the first place. Residents complain that Santa Fe has become "Aspenized," almost turned into an "Adobe Disneyland." The venerable plaza stores gradually vacated the downtown area to relocate in various suburban malls. In their stead came high-priced shops catering to the tourists, a "gallery ghetto" that ignored local citizens. Hispanics—40 percent of the town's population—virtually disappeared from the plaza, to be replaced by publicity-hungry "plaza rats." "The area's cultural integrity," complained writer John Nichols, "is just getting blown away." Touted as "an elite oasis of grandeur, fame, big money and culture," Santa Fe became the second New Mexico city to achieve a worldwide reputation. It had become "America's Salzburg." New Mexico's culture of tourism, it seems, contains many facets.

For the fourth "new culture," I want to turn to a more traditional definition: education, belles-lettres, music, and religion. Historian Ronald Davis has argued that in contemporary Texas, there has been a continual battle between indigenous culture and imported "high" culture. Such a clash also occurred in New Mexico, but to a lesser extent. In New Mexico, the indigenous traditions all utilized the imported "high culture" for their own purposes.

In 1942, the U.S. Army asked the University of California at Berkeley

Concha Ortiz y Pino de Kleven, the acknowledged grand dame of modern New Mexico. In 2005 Zimmerman Library sponsored a celebration of her career. Courtesy Center for Southwest Research, Zimmerman Library, UNM. Photographer unknown. From the Concha y Pino de Kleven Collection. Number 000-457-0017a.

to serve as a "cover" to order all equipment and pay all salaries for the scientists at Los Alamos because the modest University of New Mexico could not possibly have disguised the vast quantities of materiel and personnel needed for the Hill. This situation has changed drastically over the last six decades. Today, the state's flagship university boasts around twenty-six thousand students, several branch campuses, and international reputations in such fields as anthropology, Latin American studies, and American western history. The engineering and science departments all worked closely with the state's federal laboratories. New Mexico State University grew proportionately, and the regional colleges, such as Eastern New Mexico in Portales and Western New Mexico in Silver City, continued to serve local needs. New Mexico Highlands in Las Vegas emerged as "the Hispanic University" and continues to send many of its graduates into the political world. This educational maturity can be seen in the following incident. In the first decade of the twenty-first century, the University of Texas is bidding to take over the overall operations of Los Alamos from the University of California. In so doing, it formed an alliance with the major New Mexico universities as it prepared its official offer. Although budgetary limitations have hampered education on all levels, the state currently has a sophisticated education apparatus firmly in place.

The second area of "high culture" involves music. Although music played a major role in both traditional Indian and Spanish societies, prior to World War II few scholars had paid much attention to it. Pueblo Indian Manuel Archuleta began collecting Indian songs in the late 1940s and even formed a company to produce Native American records. "The Tom Tom Family Dancers" did not sell well, however, as many non-Native buyers complained about the "monotony" of Indian music. In truth, Native performers often had to shorten their productions for their audiences. But the market for Native American music literally exploded from 1990 to 2004. Local bands such as the powwow drum group Black Eagle, from Jemez Pueblo, and Albuquerque-based Red Earth began to garner various national music awards, such as the Grammy and the Nammy. Producer Tom Bee, who grew to maturity in Gallup and founded the pioneer Native band XIT (pronounced "exit") in the late 1960s, currently heads the music label SOAR, one that is virtually synonymous with Native music.

The revived Native sound touches many bases. XIT's song "Flight" contained hard lyrics such as "Go away white man, this is our land," but Bee has also recorded an album of Christian music. Many Native songs deal with environmental issues. Black Eagle composes lyrics in the Towa language, but Red Earth mingles Native rhythms with soul, jazz, and rock to produce what one band member termed a "tribal stew." These local Native groups believe they form the crest of an advancing wave. As Tom Bee observed of his pioneer Indian rock group, "XIT's records are still selling today because very little has changed in Native America." But the appeal extends into other areas as well. "It's time for people to tap into the true heart of Native music," said Ira Wilson of Red Earth, "and it's not New Age."

As historian Scott Meredith has shown, University of New Mexico music professor John Donald Robb almost single-handedly revived interest in the state's Hispanic musical traditions. A graduate of Harvard Law School, Robb practiced his profession for twenty years before moving to New Mexico in 1941 to begin a second career in music. Traveling throughout the state, Robb set up his recorder at New Mexican weddings, sheep camps, funerals, and campfires. He became fascinated with the blend of Hebrew, Moorish, and Gregorian chants that he found therein. In 1950, Robb drew on numerous Hispanic folk songs to compose an original opera, *The Life and Death of Little Joe*. Termed Albuquerque's "Renaissance Man," Robb also founded and directed the first UNM symphony orchestra. In 1967, the opening of the Albuquerque Civic Light Opera Association added to the city's musical scene.

With such national celebrities as the late Selena and Ricky Martin, Hispanic music now commands a multi-million-dollar audience. Locally, the traditional New Mexico *corrido*, a ballad composed about an event or a person—often more spoken than sung—has evolved into the popular *narco corrido*, hard-edged tales of the adventures of Mexican drug lords and cartels that appeal to many young people.

Several other cities, such as Roswell and Santa Fe, also began symphony orchestras, but the center of the state's postwar musical scene belonged to the "Miracle of the Desert": the Santa Fe Opera. The driving force behind the opera was John Crosby, who in 1956–57 used $200,000 of family monies to buy land north of the city and build a 470-seat wooden opera house on it.

In spite of dire predictions—"How can you sell an opera to people who have never heard one?"—Crosby persisted in his dream. To everyone's surprise, after a few years, the opera began to play to full houses. In 1967, the old opera house burned—probably the result of arson—but Crosby turned even this disaster to an advantage. The cast finished the season in the local high school gym, and the next year Crosby oversaw the creation of an entirely new opera building that sat fourteen hundred people. In 1977, the mortgage was retired, right on schedule. The role of Los Alamos citizens in this renewal has never been fully appreciated.

What began as a shoestring operation turned into the major musical institution for the entire West. Through an innovative apprentice program, Crosby brought in numerous young musicians, and a number of his "graduates" have gone on to major roles elsewhere. For years the opera tried to balance traditional offerings—*Carmen, Tosca, Madame Butterfly*—with various world premiers. Since the 1960s, the opera has proven to be one of Santa Fe's major attractions. Opening night invariably turns into a gala occasion. As Crosby reminded *New Yorker* writer Winthrop Sargeant, "Nations are not remembered for their bombers or their banking system. They are remembered for their art."

◾

The multiplicity of perspectives that has made New Mexico famous over the years is especially apparent in the realm of religion. At the end of World War II, New Mexico's religious scene was dominated by a predominantly Hispanic Catholic congregation served by Irish or French priests; a variety of traditional Native faiths, both mingled with and separate from this Catholicism; a deep-rooted German-Jewish community in Las Vegas, Las Cruces, and Santa Fe; and most of the mainline Protestant groups, led by the Presbyterians and Methodists.

Over six decades later, this religious landscape has undergone a genuine upheaval. At the dawn of the twenty-first century, the listing "no religious affiliation" forms a larger state category than any other group (about 40 percent). Roman Catholicism comes in a strong second (about 30 percent), and the Southern Baptists (over 10 percent) are now greater than all the other Protestant churches combined. The Jewish community remains at about half a percent, and "other religions," such as the Latter-day Saints, Buddhists, and Sikhs, constitute about 6 percent. Much to everyone's surprise, New Mexico has gained international publicity as a "spiritual land" that has attracted both conventional and unconventional groups in large numbers. The contemporary religious scene lies in such flux that few dare to predict its outcome.

New Mexico's spiritual roots run deep, as they stretch back to traditional Pueblo ceremonies and the Spanish Catholic *entrada* of the mid-sixteenth century. Even in the 1950s, New Mexico boasted a number of monasteries and religious conference centers. In 1955, Trappist monks established a retreat in the Pecos Mountains, but it did not thrive until 1969, when a band of Benedictine monks purchased the property and changed it drastically. The Pecos Benedictine Abbey became the only coed Catholic monastery in the states, combining a Jungian psychology with an emphasis on Catholic charismatic worship. The Benedictines also established the more traditional monastery of Christ in the Desert, near Abiquiu, with a dramatic chapel designed by architect George Nakashima. In 1947 in nearby Jemez Springs, the church established the Monastery of Via Coeli, devoted to aiding priests with personal and spiritual problems (later closed).

The Protestants have also founded two impressive conference centers in northern New Mexico: the Presbyterian Ghost Ranch and the Southern Baptist Glorieta Assembly. The former, near Abiquiu, was donated to the church by rancher Arthur N. Park, while the latter was constructed in the Pecos Mountains in the early 1950s under the leadership of Harry Stagg. In the southern region, the West Texas Bloys Camp Meeting—now over a century old—continues to influence rancher and cowboy religious life with its strongly ethical evangelical message.

The three most preeminent postwar state religious figures have probably been Catholic spokesmen Brother Mathias Barrett, Archbishop Robert F. Sanchez, and Archbishop Michael J. Sheehan. An Irish immigrant, Brother Mathias established his first house of the Little Brothers of the Good Shepherd in 1951 in Albuquerque. Dedicated to serving the needs of the desperately poor, Brother Mathias's order is now found worldwide.

Born in Socorro, the Reverend Robert F. Sanchez became New Mexico's tenth archbishop in 1974, the first native-born Hispanic to hold this post. On the national level, Sanchez was well respected for his advocacy of justice for minorities, the impoverished, and, especially, for the people of Latin America. On the local level, "the people's bishop," as his parishioners called him, was genuinely beloved. Both Protestants and Catholics respected his administrative skills, compassion, and wit. On one occasion Sanchez remarked that the Catholic Church in New Mexico had such deep roots, "we could have been saying Mass for the safety of the Pilgrims."

Given this affection, New Mexicans were stunned in early 1993 when accusations surfaced that the archbishop had been sexually involved with perhaps five different women during the 1970s and early 1980s, a story prominently featured on CBS TV's *60 Minutes* program. February and March thus provided some of the most wrenching weeks in the lengthy history of the New Mexico church. When Sanchez resigned his post on March 20, the New Mexico state house and senate recessed for thirty minutes out of respect. The next Sunday several Protestant ministers prayed for the state's Catholic populace. Just before Easter, the Pope appointed Lubbock, Texas, bishop Michael J. Sheehan to be temporary administrator of the Santa Fe archdiocese, and Sheehan also urged that Robert Sanchez's failings not overshadow "the untold amount of good" that he had accomplished during his nineteen years of leadership.

When Sheehan arrived in New Mexico, he faced perhaps the most serious challenge to New Mexican Catholicism since the Pueblo Revolt of 1680. Public outcry over priests' sexual abuse of parishioners—nation-wide but often centered on the much-publicized troubles of the Boston archdiocese—continued to mount. The Archdiocese of Santa Fe found itself caught in the same net, as it faced over 180 lawsuits against the local priests on a variety of misconduct charges. Sheehan later admitted that the archdiocese teetered on bankruptcy and he had to borrow from parish savings accounts to come up with the over $50 million needed to settle various claims.

But Sheehan refused to concede. Through aggressive action, he permanently removed twenty offenders and instituted a "zero tolerance" policy for the future. He personally apologized to all victims he could locate. Simultaneously, he began an aggressive strategy to curb Hispanic youth gang violence and calm rising interfaith tensions via strategically placed billboards that proclaimed "God Does Not Want You to Kill" and "Let Us Live Together as Sons and Daughters of God." In a special mass for his priests, he urged them to "keep their eyes on Jesus not Boston." In 2001 he worked through Catholic Charities to introduce an innovative program to curb the drug and alcohol abuse so rampant in many areas of northern New Mexico. In March 2002, Sheehan declared to the faithful that the scandals of the past now lay behind them and that the future looked bright.

In spite of Sheehan's remarkable administrative success, the religious atmosphere of New Mexico has shifted 180 degrees from the 1950s when the archbishop of Santa Fe probably possessed more cultural power than any governor. Although the Catholic faith continues to shape the individual lives of about one-third of the state's citizens, it no longer dominates the social climate. Instead, New Mexico has achieved an international reputation as a locale open to a wide variety of faith traditions. When Yogi Bhajan, founder of the Española Sikh community, died in October 2004, Governor Bill Richardson ordered that state flags be flown at half-mast in honor of "a great friend of New Mexico."

Historian Steve Fox has traced this "openness" to the historic Pueblo spiritual tradition. The Pueblo Indians have always acknowledged that spiritual power could come from a variety of sources, he noted. Thus, Pueblos could merge Catholic and Protestant traditions with their historic ceremonies. The rise of a new ecological consciousness—with both real and imagined links to the Native American past—has aided this process as well.

In the early 1970s, a Sikh community moved to the Española Valley. The ashram of about two hundred people became the group's international headquarters in 1976. The community members' white turbans, their emphasis on physical and spiritual health, and their role in local security businesses have given them a high regional profile. A mosque, Dar-al-Islam, was also established near Abiquiu, lasting from the early to the late 1980s. A small but thriving Zen center exists in Santa Fe. The New Age movement, probably best understood as an eclectic questing for spirituality, has also found a permanent home in the "City Different." At last count, Santa Fe listed ninety-five acupuncturists, making it a haven for holistic-healing practitioners from a wide variety of faith positions. In the 1990s, several Buddhist temples were established as well, and in 1991 the exiled Dalai Lama visited New Mexico to speak to overflow crowds. He found numerous parallels between Tibetan Buddhism and Native American traditions. In 2000, the Latter-day Saint community opened an impressive new temple in northeast Albuquerque to serve its rapidly growing regional constituency. At the dawn of the twenty-first century, New Mexico boasts a number of sacred sites—Chimayó, Chaco Canyon, and Tomé Hill, just to name three—that help to make it a "spiritual magnet" to outsiders. As a Sikh leader recently observed, "God lives everywhere, but his mailing address is New Mexico."

■

The six decades since the end of World War II have been good to the state's writers as they steadily moved from the provincial to the international. In the 1940s, one leading writer was Erna Fergusson, widely acknowledged as the grande dame of New Mexico letters. The first person to reach national audiences with the "three-cultures" interpretation of the state's past, Fergusson argued in the 1950s that New Mexico's experience with multiculturalism might serve as a model for a United States that now found itself thrust into a world leadership role. Drawing on her own girlhood experiences—where she heard English, Spanish, and German spoken in her family home—Fergusson argued that "the true New Mexico" had no room for prejudice. "New Mexico never had any real problems of intolerance or prejudice," she reminded an Albuquerque Kiwanis Club in 1959; "everybody got along perfectly well with everybody else." Fergusson's contemporary, Santa Fe author Dorothy L. Pillsbury, argued along equally rosy lines. She emphasized the theme of cultural harmony in numerous well-written essays. In the works of Fergusson and Pillsbury, the New Mexico story remained shrouded in romance. This would change considerably over time.

The immediate postwar literary world also included a number of historians. One of the most prolific, C. L. Sonnichsen, began his career as a professor of literature at the University of Texas at El Paso (UTEP; then Texas Western) in 1931. Within two decades, Sonnichsen had become the chief historical writer of southern New Mexican life. Calling himself a "grassroots historian," Sonnichsen sought out both old newspapers and old-timers to piece together his tales of *Alias Billy the Kid* (1955), *Mescalero Apaches* (1958), and *Tularosa: The Last of the Frontier West* (1960). But Sonnichsen was not alone. Catholic Priest Francis Stanley Crocchiola (writing as F. Stanley); Jack Rittenhouse, who established his own Stagecoach Press; and longtime state historian Myra Ellen Jenkins also added considerably to local history during the first decades after the war. So too did Marc Simmons, prolific author of over twenty books on New Mexico themes, including children's fiction, a history of Albuquerque, and the bicentennial volume on the state.

The most popular historian of New Mexico, however, was the multi-talented Fray Angélico Chávez. A Franciscan priest who served several New Mexico parishes, Chávez wrote two major works, *Missions of New Mexico, 1776* (with Eleanor B. Adams), and *Origins of New Mexico Families in the Spanish Colonial Period* (1973). Chávez probably reached the widest audience with his evocative *My Penitente Land* (1974), which compared New Mexico with central Spain in perceptive and graceful prose.

The sophistication of literature grew in step with the sophistication of historical writing. In 1960, when bookman Lawrence Clark Powell was asked to compile a "best books on New Mexico" list, he faced an embarrassment of riches. Yet the state literary renaissance had hardly begun. In 1966 playwright Mark Medoff began to teach at New Mexico State. His play *When You Comin' Back, Red Ryder?* (1973), which was set in a café in southern New Mexico, established his reputation, and his even better-known *Children of a Lesser God* reached New York, won numerous awards, and later appeared as a film. In 2004 he again reached Broadway with *Prymate.* Albuquerque playwright James (Grubb) Graebner also achieved off-Broadway success with several plays, including *The Great White Atomic Sweepstakes.*

Prior to 1960, most of the major books dealing with Native American themes, such as Oliver La Farge's *Laughing Boy* (1929), had been written by non-Indians. Shortly afterward, however, the state's Native voice began to be heard in several genres. Acoma poet Simon Ortiz collected his poems in *From Sand Creek* (1981), while Laguna Pueblo writer Leslie Marmon Silko achieved international fame with her novels *Ceremony* (1977), *Almanac of the Dead* (1991), and *Garden in the Dunes* (1999), as well as poems and short stories. Apache/Chicano poet Jimmy Santiago Baca credited poetry with (literally) saving him from a life in prison. He received the 1988 American Book Award for *Martin and Meditations in the South Valley.* In general, these were not happy voices.

Rudolfo Anaya and N. Scott Momaday probably rank as the state's most prominent ethnic writers. Born in 1937 in Pastura, a hamlet southwest of Santa Rosa, Anaya grew up in a predominantly Hispanic world—his parents never read English fluently—that he fictionalized in his classic coming-of-age novel, *Bless Me, Ultima* (1972). This poignant book launched a regionwide Chicano literary upsurge. Periodically banned by

Rudolfo Anaya, the leading figure of the Hispanic literary renaissance. Courtesy Center for Southwest Research, Zimmerman Library, UNM. Photo by Oscar Lozoya. Number 2001-012-0001.

Texas and California school districts because of its frank language and the presence of both death and magic, *Bless Me, Ultima* has never gone out of print. Today it ranks as the most widely read Hispanic novel in the world. Rudolfo and his wife, Patricia Lawless Anaya, serve as the acknowledged leaders of a burgeoning literary movement. In 2002 President George W. Bush awarded him the National Medal for the Arts.

Anaya followed this initial success with numerous other works, including *Tortuga* (1979), *Heart of Aztlan* (1981), *Alburquerque* (1992), and several ethnic mystery novels starring detective Sonny Baca. He has also written plays and children's stories. He taught for years in the English Department at the University of New Mexico until he retired to write full-time. Today he is universally acknowledged as the dean of southwestern ethnic literature. As a former UNM administrator once remarked, "Many UNM professors have written books, but Rudolfo Anaya is one of the few about whom books have been written." Over a decade later, another UNM administrator termed him one of the select few "who has changed the way we view the world."

The second-most-prominent state ethnic voice belongs to N. Scott Momaday. Born in 1934 into a predominantly Kiowa family in Oklahoma, Momaday grew up largely in Jemez Springs, New Mexico, since his parents both taught for Bureau of Indian Affairs schools there. His first novel, *A House Made of Dawn* (1969), which is set in Jemez, won the Pulitzer Prize for fiction, propelling him to a distinguished career as an English professor at the University of California and the University of Arizona. He wrote six other books, including a popular family memoir, *The Way to Rainy Mountain* (1979), and a second novel, *The Ancient Child* (1989). Like Anaya, he has also written for the theater. A mesmerizing presenter, he is much in demand as a public speaker on Native issues.

Although Anaya and Momaday hail from different cultural traditions, they share a comprehensive view of the world that contrasts sharply with that of mainstream America. Each draws deeply from the oral tradition of his people. As Anaya phrased it, "We have, along the Rio Grande corridor, one of the longest continuous traditions of storytelling, covering at least the past 12,000 years. Some of it was etched in rock; some of it is part of the oral tradition; some of it is written in books." Similarly, when speaking of the historic pain suffered by Native Americans, Momaday remarked, "Anything is bearable if you can make a story out of it." Indeed, *The Ancient Child* draws from a traditional Kiowa oral legend of a boy who changed into a bear and chased seven sisters up a butte and into a tree that carried them into the sky to form the Big Dipper.

In addition, both Anaya and Momaday write of a people who have remained linked to the land for generations. A central subtheme in *Bless Me, Ultima* revolves around the young protagonist, Tony, who is caught between the stable, farming side of his mother's family and the wild cowboy side of his father's, which traditionally roamed the Llano Estacado. So too Momaday: "The old free life of the Kiowas on the plains, the deep impulse to run and rove upon the wild earth, cannot be given up easily; perhaps it cannot be given up at all."

Both writers touch on the theme of reciprocity, the multivaried links between people, plants, animals, and the land. Most mainstream Americans (the average U.S. citizen moves five times in a lifetime) find this deep-rooted sense of place a hard one to comprehend. Southwestern Native American groups also maintain that since the animals roamed the region well before people arrived, they should be acknowledged as relatives and teachers. For example, in *Bless Me, Ultima*, the *curandera* Ultima instructs Tony to thank the plants they are busily gathering in the presence of the river: "You that grow well here in the arroyo by the dampness of the river, we lift you to make good medicine." For both writers, the southwestern landscape retains a sacred quality.

Finally, each writer has acknowledged that their best stories touch on the theme of mystery. In essence, Rudolfo Anaya spoke for both of them in a spring 2004 public address. Every sound, every deed has the potential to emerge as a story, he said, but a true story always reaches out for the transcendent, to link the reader with the sacred. A story creates a sense of mythic time—a level of understanding quite different from that shown on electric screens—that remains essential if one is to become a complete person. Thus, at its best southwestern fiction can serve as a vehicle of reintegration of self and community. By the early twenty-first century, there is no question that New Mexico writers have come of age.

In the spring of 1991, two young New Mexicans stopped for gasoline in Yakima, Washington. When the station attendant noticed their license, she asked, "What's the difference between Mexico and New Mexico?" Virtually every long-term resident has had a similar experience. Since 1969, *New Mexico Magazine* has run a regular column detailing these misunderstandings. In 1986, Richard Sandoval collected these misconceptions in a popular booklet, *One of Our Fifty Is Missing*. That same year Senator Pete Domenici introduced a tongue-in-cheek resolution into the U.S. Congress to recognize June 13, 1986, as "New Mexico Is a State Day."

Popular culture, the last of the post–World War II "cultures" I will discuss, has tried to ameliorate this situation. But until recently, even New Mexico's popular culture has grappled with problems of recognition.

From 1950 to the present day, the state's most famous citizen has been neither man nor woman. Instead, the most famous New Mexican has been a bear, a small cub that lost his mother in the 1950 El Capitan Mountain forest fire in the Lincoln National Forest. The bear in question, of course, was Smokey, who has reminded the nation for almost sixty years that "only you can prevent forest fires." Surveys showed that 95 percent of American children could correctly identify Smokey's image. No New Mexican, before or since, has done half as well.

Ironically, however, while everyone recognized Smokey, few connected the real live bear who lived out his life rather grumpily in a cage at the Washington National Zoo with the smiling cartoon figure in Levi's and the ranger hat. Even New Mexico's most famous citizen, alas, is seldom linked with the land of his birth.

The same problem of recognition lay behind the decision by Hot Springs, New Mexico, to alter its name. In early 1950, NBC impresario Ralph Edwards promised to stage his tenth-anniversary broadcast from any town that changed its name to "Truth or Consequences," the title of his radio show. The small community of Hot Springs, located on the edge of Elephant Butte Lake, elected to do so. Edwards not only kept his promise; he returned to T. or C. for over two decades to oversee an annual fiesta, well after his show had gone to media heaven. Three times various town conservatives have tried to restore the original name, but three times they failed. Ironically, although Truth or Consequences boasts New Mexico's most unusual name, few people under thirty connect it with anything other than local eccentricity.

If the state's most famous citizen is a bear and the most uniquely labeled city named for a radio show, New Mexico's most famous vegetable is, botanically, a fruit: the ubiquitous chile. Like the others, the chile's quest for national recognition is also very much a postwar phenomenon.

The 1945 state economic forecast neglected to mention chile as an important agricultural crop. As late as 1955, the major chile under production, New Mexico No. 9, proved far too *picante* for sale anywhere outside of the state. Shortly afterward, Roy Nakayama, botanist at New

Mexico State, began working with local ranchers, such as Jim Lytle of Hatch, to improve the taste and quality. Crossbreeding from both native as well as rare Peruvian chiles, Nakayama masterminded the commercial production of NuMex Big Jim in the fall of 1974. Bred to produce pods about a foot long, Big Jims also matured simultaneously, making them ideal for machine picking. On a hotness scale, with mild New Mexico 6 as 1 and Tabasco as 9, NuMex Big Jim was ranked a 3, almost ideal for the average palate. By the 1980s, New Mexico grew more acres of chile than all other states combined and the annual Hatch Chile Festival had achieved a modest national reputation. Thanks to the genius of Roy Nakayama and his colleague at NMSU, Paul Bosland, New Mexico now exports millions of pounds of chile per year, all across the land. As Mexican food is currently the second fastest growing of all ethnic cuisines (Italian is first), can the ultimate fame of the New Mexican chile be far behind?

■

Film and video probably lie at the heart of any discussion of popular culture. Interestingly, New Mexico has had a long-standing connection with the film industry. During the early years of the century, Las Vegas hosted a number of western epics. But producers soon moved on to the sunny shores of Hollywood, and for years the state wallowed in a cinematic backwater.

The first postwar film to treat New Mexico in any detail was probably *Them*, a 1954 classic about ants that had been transformed by walking across ground zero at Trinity Site. Although many of the scenes from this gem were shot in Arizona—where saguaro cacti served as the symbol of "desert"—the story was largely a New Mexican one. The first of the "mutant movies," the giant ants of *Them* brought New Mexico to the attention of the nation, although probably not in the way that the chamber of commerce would have preferred.

In 1968, Governor David Cargo—aided by novelist Max Evans— decided to ameliorate this situation. That year, he established the first state film commission in the nation. Soon New Mexican bureaucrats were badgering Hollywood producers to shoot their next films in the state. To further encourage the studios, the government built a state-owned sound stage, which it leased out at bargain basement prices. Nearby communities, such as Cerrillos, welcomed filmmakers, and state cooperation even extended to loaning state police for traffic control and letting Albuquerque schoolchildren out of class for needed crowd scenes. Whenever local stories were filmed, such as *Red Sky at Morning* and *House Made of Dawn*, the New Mexico press gave the films wide coverage. From 1968 to 1988, Hollywood shot over 150 films on location in New Mexico. Hollywood spending in the state increased steadily, from $8 million in 1983–84 to over $30 million four years later. New Mexico's film commission also served as a model for other states.

Although certain films such as *Easy Rider* contained some New Mexican scenes, the most celebrated state film was *The Milagro Beanfield War* (1986). Based on Taos writer John Nichols's novel of 1972, *Milagro* starred Sonia Braga, Freddie Fender, and Ruben Blades; Robert Redford both produced and directed it. After the citizens of Cordova turned Redford down, he moved to Truchas for the brunt of the filming, creating an artificial bean field with plastic plants as his main backdrop. Turning a 629-page book into a 123-minute movie proved challenging. While local reviewers termed *Milagro* "five star" and "the best movie ever made in the state," nationwide reaction was less enthusiastic. *Milagro* showed marvelous New Mexico scenery, but the actors' accents were off, and the film never turned the state into the much-hoped-for "Hollywood on the Rio Grande."

During the last fifteen years, however, the state has witnessed a boom in local film production. The Very Large Array has served as the backdrop for numerous movies, including *2010* (1984), *Independence Day* (1996), *Contact* (1997), and *Armageddon* (1998). The town of Cerrillos figured prominently in such epics as *The Hi-Lo Country* (1998), while El Rancho de las Golondrinas (thanks to harboring eighteenth-, nineteenth-, and twentieth-century buildings) has hosted numerous Old West settings, the most recent being Ron Howard's *The Missing* (2003). From 1968 forward, the narrow-gauge Cumbres and Toltec Scenic Railroad has figured in seventeen films, with more set to come.

The state government takes the film industry seriously. The State Investment Council provides no-interest loans to prospective filmmakers, and the New Mexico Film Office coordinates technical crews and working ranches, as well as the famed Eaves Movie Ranch, for interested producers. Because of its varied topography, New Mexico can double cinematically as "Kansas," "Old Mexico," "Dallas," and even "Los Angeles." The contemporary state goal is to create a media center with a sustainable film industry. In the words of Lisa Strout, 2004 director of the New Mexico Film Office, "We're not trying to be Hollywood. We want to be our own brand, and we're a great alternative."

◼

From 1945 to the present, New Mexican sports figures have helped bring the state into the national eye. In auto racing, the famous Unsers, Al and Bobby, became the only brothers ever to win the Indianapolis 500. In the 1980s, their sons followed them into the same profession, and in the early twenty-first century, a grandson, Al Unser, continues the family tradition. Roswell's Nancy Lopez dominated women's professional golf during the early 1980s and endeared herself to the state with her charm. A decade later, Albuquerque golfer Rosie Jones followed suit. In track, the exploits of world-class runners such as Adolph Plummer; John Baker, about whom the book *A Shining Season* (1978) was written; and Ibrahim Hussein (who won the Boston Marathon twice) commanded a wide following. The most widespread national publicity, however, came not from individual but team sports, chiefly college basketball.

From the early 1960s forward, both the UNM Lobos and the NMSU Aggies fielded increasingly competitive basketball teams. New stadiums helped: the UNM Arena (the Pit) held fifteen thousand when it was completed in 1967 (later expanded to over eighteen thousand); the Pan American Center, finished the next year, seated 13,272. Aided by lucrative television revenue, college basketball soon became the state's most popular sport, with the equivalent of one-third of the population each year attending a game. In 1978, *New Mexico Magazine* proudly proclaimed the state "the basketball capital of the world." Even the 1979–80 scandals of UNM's "Lobogate," with falsified transcripts and allegations of gambling, failed to dampen the public's enthusiasm.

Although the men's teams had mixed success during the next two decades, Lobo women's basketball flourished upon the arrival of former Eldorado High School coach Don Flanagan in 1995. Drawing largely on homegrown talent, Flanagan began to entice regular crowds of over six-teen thousand to the Pit (setting several NCAA records) and led the Lady Lobos into the NCAA tournament from 2002–05. This increased popularity had a "trickle-down" effect all across the state as basketball slowly began to edge out volleyball as the most popular girls' sport on the high school level. The annual state basketball championship finals (both boys and girls) always calls forth tremendous local support, especially in the more isolated communities, where virtually the entire town travels to support their teams.

■

From the 1950s forward a number of mass-market writers have also steadily moved New Mexico into the public eye. In 1956, Albuquerque writer Ray Hogan published his first western novel and over the next thirty-five years turned out about 125 others, many set in the state. His contemporary, Portales writer Jack Williamson, achieved an international reputation in the field of science fiction. Writer Jack Schaefer moved to New Mexico in 1954 to produce a number of works, although none matched his masterpiece, *Shane*. In 1968, Edward Abbey reached his widest audience with *Desert Solitaire*, a story of his two seasons as a ranger in Utah's Arches National Park. Abbey's *The Monkey Wrench Gang* (1975) is usually credited with inaugurating the concept of "ecoterrorism," a practice he began—allegedly chopping down billboards on Route 66—when he was a graduate student at UNM in the late 1950s. Former Albuquerque writer Lois Duncan has made New Mexico the locus of several of her juvenile fiction works, including *They Never Came Home* (1969) and *Ransom* (1984); Norman Zollinger's *Riders to Cibola* (1979) treats southern New Mexico; Judith Van Giesen is off to a good start with her Albuquerque female detective, Niel Hamel, in *Raptor* (1990), as well as her even more popular special collections librarian heroine Claire Reynier in *The Stolen Blue* (2000) and *Confidence Woman* (2002). Former Santa Fe police officer Michael McGarrity has similarly won considerable following with *Tularosa* (1996) and *Mexican Hat* (1997). So too has popular UNM history professor Virginia Scharff (writing as Virginia Swift) with her *Brown-Eyed Girl* (2000), *Bad Company* (2002), and *Bye, Bye, Love* (2004).

Yet the mystery writer most closely linked with New Mexico and the Southwest is former journalist Tony Hillerman. At the dawn of the twenty-first century, Hillerman has become one of the nation's most highly regarded mystery writers. His novels have been translated into eighteen languages and appeared as both films and made-for-TV shows. Hillerman's fictional Navajo Tribal Police detectives, Joe Leaphorn and Jim Chee, have become real people to countless readers. The Farmington Public Library, where Chee checked out books, once issued a library card in his name and mailed it to Hillerman. A 2004 election-year bumper sticker proclaimed "Jim Chee for President." Just as nineteenth-century visitors to America carried their James Fenimore Cooper or travelers to Scotland their Sir Walter Scott, so modern visitors to the Southwest arrive with copies of Hillerman stuffed in their suitcases, hoping to catch a glimpse of the legendary Leaphorn or Chee. For millions of travelers—both foreign and American—the Southwest has become "Hillerman Country."

Anthony G. Hillerman was born on May 27, 1925, in the hamlet of Sacred Heart, Oklahoma, where he grew up surrounded by Seminole and Potawatomie neighbors. When World War II broke out, he enlisted and was severely wounded. Either a grenade or mine—he still does not know which—left him with a shattered leg and temporary blindness. Of his original company of 212, only 8 survived.

Released from the army in early 1945, Hillerman took a temporary job hauling oil equipment to the Navajo Reservation in northwest New Mexico. There he saw a group of mounted Indian veterans, decked in silver, on their way to a healing ceremony, the Enemy Way, which was designed to reintegrate them back into Navajo society. Hillerman asked if he could watch and thus saw his first Navajo ceremonial. Since he too was a veteran, the Enemy Way left a deep impression on him.

Meanwhile, a reporter for the Oklahoma City *Daily Oklahoman* had read some of Hillerman's letters to his mother and asked to see him when he returned home. She urged him to become a reporter, a profession he had never dreamed of. So, drawing on the GI Bill, Hillerman entered the University of Oklahoma in Norman to major in journalism. When he graduated in 1948, he married Marie E. Unzner, a Phi Beta Kappa in microbiology who spoke five languages. She has remained his most perceptive critic and a lifelong rock of support.

Tony Hillerman engaged in his favorite pastime. Courtesy Center for Southwest Research. Zimmerman Library, UNM. Photographer unknown. From the Small Collection. Number 000-501-0002.

After graduation Hillerman took a job as a police reporter in Borger, Texas, a rough-and-tumble oil town that provided him with plenty of copy. In 1950 he switched to political reporter for United Press International in Oklahoma City and two years later was posted to Santa Fe. In 1954 he became editor of the influential *Santa Fe New Mexican*, where he remained for nine years. By then he and Marie had become parents of six children.

By all accounts, Hillerman had reached the top of his profession, but somehow he remained unsatisfied. He knew he could write descriptive prose, but he wanted to write fiction. So, at Marie's urging, he resigned his post in 1963 and moved to Albuquerque to enroll in the master's program in English at the University of New Mexico. He also served as part-time assistant to President Tom Popejoy and to his successor, William "Bud" Davis.

At UNM, Hillerman immersed himself in English literature, taking classes from such legendary teachers as Katherine Simons, Edith Buchanan, and Morris Friedman. He received his master's in 1964. As soon as he completed his master's, Hillerman switched hats. From graduate student in English (1963), he became associate professor (1964) and then professor and head of the Journalism Department (1966), which ranks as one of the most rapid rises in UNM history. In the course of his twenty-three years at UNM, Hillerman trained scores of students, including many of the key reporters for several New Mexican newspapers. In 1967 he also began working on his first novel, tentatively titled *Enemy Way*. He finished it two years later.

Hillerman first sent the manuscript of *Enemy Way* to his then literary agent, Ann Elmo, but she didn't like it. Neither did her colleagues. If you insist on rewriting it, Elmo advised, take out all that Indian stuff.

Hillerman remained unconvinced. He then asked famed mysteries editor Joan Kahn, at Harper & Row, if she would resolve the dispute. Kahn agreed and after reading the manuscript gave him the opposite advice. If he would use "more of the Indian stuff and Leaphorn," plus write a new last chapter, she promised that Harper & Row would publish it. In the revision Hillerman augmented the role of then minor character Joe Leaphorn and the now-legendary Navajo detective was born. The book appeared in 1970 under the revised title *The Blessing Way*.

The Blessing Way met with modest success. It sold more than three thousand copies and was nominated for an Edgar Allen Poe Award, given by the Mystery Writers of America. Local reviewers, however, were ecstatic. As one noted, the author "has opened a Pandora's box for himself, for no one who reads this book is going to permit him to forget that we want more." Equally important, it proved to Hillerman that he could write fiction. His second mystery, *The Fly on the Wall*, came out the next year. This non-Indian thriller drew from his experiences as a political reporter and editor in Santa Fe and pivoted on the question of journalistic ethics.

After *The Fly on the Wall*, Hillerman returned to the Native American world. Joe Leaphorn solved murders in *Dance Hall of the Dead* (1973) and *Listening Woman* (1978). *Dance Hall* won an Edgar Allen Poe Award for the best mystery of the year, and Hillerman's fan club steadily increased. By now, however, he felt restricted by the character of the middle-aged, somewhat cynical Leaphorn and introduced another, younger Navajo policeman, Jim Chee. Like Leaphorn, who had majored in anthropology at Arizona State in Tempe, Chee had been an anthropology major at the University of New Mexico. Ironically, the younger Chee was far more traditional than Leaphorn. He was training to become a *hataalíí*, a Navajo medicine man.

Chee starred in three novels of his own: *People of Darkness* (1980), *The Dark Wind* (1982), and *The Ghostway* (1984). After this, Hillerman wrote three more mysteries where the two worked together, often in a strained manner: *Skinwalkers* (1986), *A Thief of Time* (1988), and *Talking God* (1989).

The adventures of these Navajo Tribal Police detectives were praised by the national press. *Library Journal* termed *The Blessing Way* "a mystery with literary value," whereas *The New Yorker* called *Dance Hall of the Dead* "high entertainment." The *Los Angeles Times* termed his work "unique in American crime fiction." Before long, critics began to compare his later works to his earlier ones. As the *Atlantic* said of *Talking God*: "If Mr. Hillerman's latest mystery is less exciting than his best, blame the setting. Washington is a dreary place compared with New Mexico."

Indeed, some critics have argued that the landscape of the Southwest plays as crucial a role in his books as his two Navajo detectives. In *Listening Woman*, for example, he spent two pages describing the approach of a thunderstorm (for which he was criticized by a Boston reviewer who had obviously never been to the Southwest). A recent anecdote reveals his fascination with the different ways that Anglo-Americans and Natives view the land. Once he was driving through an isolated section of the Navajo Reservation marked Desolation Flats on his U.S. map. When he asked an Indian friend for its name in Navajo, he was told, "Beautiful Valley."

Critics have compared Hillerman with Arthur Conan Doyle and Agatha Christie. Imitators—the sincerest form of flattery—began to flood the market with adventures of Hispanic detectives, a Ute detective, an Albuquerque female detective, and so forth. By introducing readers to the Navajo worldview and inviting them to solve crimes by a leap of the imagination, Hillerman in essence created the genre of southwestern ethnic mystery fiction.

The central pivot of Hillerman's books rests on the uneasy intersection between the worldview of the Navajos and that of mainstream society. Leaphorn and Chee spend a great deal of time trying to understand the ways of the *bilagaána* (white people), especially their greed and their willingness to kill one another. In *The Ghostway*, Hosteen Joe witnesses a murder in front of the Shiprock Economy Wash-O-Mat. "'The driver was Navajo,' he thought, 'but this was white man's business'"(3).

Some of the dilemmas are metaphysical: traditional Navajos have no concept of revenge. The idea of an "eye for an eye" is totally foreign to them. They also have a decided aversion to entering a building where someone has died, even going so far as to destroy a hogan where a death occurred. A person of wealth is feared rather than revered; he might have used witchcraft to gain his possessions. The ultimate goal of life is the prosperity of the tribe, not the individual. In the Navajo emergence myth, the Holy People gave a name to evil: they termed it "the way to make money."

In the immediate post–World War II years, Albuquerque writer Erna Fergusson pointed with pride to the cultural harmony of New Mexico and how each group had "selectively borrowed" from the others in the realms of technology (pickup trucks), holidays (Thanksgiving, July Fourth, Cinco de Mayo), and foods (corn, beans, squash, chile, soft drinks). Out of necessity, Fergusson suggested, the cultures of the Southwest had learned to tolerate one another.

Hillerman is far less didactic, but he is much in her camp. Unlike Fergusson, he never preaches. He is primarily a storyteller. Still, it is a dull reader who finishes one of his novels without a great sense of appreciation for the complicated cultural interactions of the American Southwest.

Hillerman's mysteries all end well. Leaphorn and/or Chee always solve the crime. Justice, often a Native American justice, prevails. In various interviews Hillerman has stated that one of his purposes in writing has been to present the Navajos and other Indians as "good, normal and solid human beings." All the Native peoples in his books have a right to the tree of life.

This ecumenical theme can be seen in Hillerman's concentration on the Navajo concept of *hózhó*, or harmony with one's surroundings. Navajos who fall out of harmony need ceremonies, such as the Nightway, the Enemy Way, or the Blessing Way, to restore them to wholeness. In *Talking God*, the seriously ill Agnes Tso requests a *Yeibichai* ceremony. The Yeibichai will not cure her—she is dying of liver cancer—but it will help her come to terms with her condition. Both ritual and myth are needed. As the singer in the Nightway ceremony says:

> *In the house made of dawn*
> *in the house made of sunset light*
> *in the house made of rain cloud*
> *with beauty before me, I walk*
> *with beauty behind me, I walk*
> *with beauty all around me, I walk. . . .*

In a larger sense, Hillerman's books provide the same sense of harmony for their readers. Leaphorn and Chee are always successful. The disharmony caused by evil is resolved. When readers finish the books, they too have been restored to a sense of hózhó.

Victory. Justice. Evil overcome. The triumph of faith, reason, and the "Navajo way." Harmony. Wholeness. Hózhó. All set against the complex cultures and overpowering landscape of the American Southwest. By melding these ingredients in a mystery format, Tony Hillerman provides a genuine sense of enchantment for millions of readers, all across the globe.

■

The rise of the new post–World War II "cultures" of landscape, science, tourism, high culture, and popular culture have transformed modern New Mexico. In many and subtle ways, they have intersected with the famed "heroic triad" of the Native American, Hispanic, and Anglo-pioneer worlds. Few would disagree that the charm and uniqueness of New Mexico can be traced to the interaction of its various cultures. Now the question is: which cultures?

PART THREE

Atomic New Mexico

INTRODUCTION

I had been at the University of New Mexico about a decade when I began to shift my research focus to regional concerns. By the early 1980s, my first book—a revised version of my dissertation—had (finally) been accepted for publication, and I found myself thoroughly sick of the subject. I needed a new area of research, and I needed it badly. By chance I watched a Jon Else documentary on PBS titled "The Day After Trinity," in which the narrator observed that just prior to the Trinity blast in July of 1945, General Leslie R. Groves had phoned the governor of New Mexico to alert him that it might be necessary to evacuate the central part of the state. This, I thought, would make a fine article for the *New Mexico Historical Review*. So began my research on the story of the Trinity Site. My friends Jack Reed and Mel Merritt graciously placed me in contact with a number of people who had had firsthand involvement with the Manhattan Project. To my luck, a number of project veterans had returned to New Mexico after retirement. One interview led to another, and soon I found myself completely captivated by the story of the early atomic era.

My interviews ranged across the lot. I spoke with such well-known figures as Frank Oppenheimer, Hans Bethe, Edward Teller, and Louis Hempelmann. I also talked at length with George Marchi, the Los Alamos chef, and a woman who had been at UNM as an anthropology student and—because she hailed from a radical New York family—had been tapped by army security to work as a waitress at La Posada to watch for possible Soviet spies. Engineer Robert Henderson, photographer Berlyn Brixner, and former Special Engineer Detachment member MacAllister Hull also provided insights. What began as a quest for a twenty-page article evolved into a lifelong fascination that eventually resulted in two books and numerous essays. The story of the early atomic age simply would not let me go.

The Manhattan Project, of course, stretched across the entire nation. Columbia University inaugurated many of the earliest scientific experiments, and the wooded area of eastern Tennessee (now Oak Ridge National Laboratory) has the dubious distinction of being the first lands that General Leslie R. Groves condemned for a project location. The unused football stadium at the University of Chicago became the venue for Enrico Fermi's pathbreaking controlled nuclear reaction experiment on December 2, 1942. The windswept plain north of the Columbia River in eastern Washington (now Hanford) housed the gigantic operation that produced the plutonium for the Trinity and Nagasaki weapons. The University of California, Berkeley, oversaw the entire Los Alamos operations, and so on.

Even though the Manhattan Project reached from coast to coast, the state of New Mexico has always claimed center stage in the public mind. Oak Ridge and Hanford rightly claim regional prominence, but Los Alamos is recognized around the world. For reasons that are not always clear, the "atomic firsts" in New Mexico seem to have taken precedence over the others:

- Los Alamos as the world's first secret weapons laboratory
- Trinity Site as the site of the world's first atomic detonation
- Albuquerque's Sandia Laboratories as the first "assembly line" to produce nuclear weapons
- The WIPP site near Carlsbad as the nation's first permanent burial grounds for low- and medium-level nuclear wastes, etc.

From the selection of Site Y in 1942 to the 1950s uranium boom in the Grants area to the establishment of WIPP, the story of modern New Mexico has ever been intertwined with the emergence of atomic America.[1]

This section consists of three atomic-themed chapters: "Cutting the Gordian Knot: How Leslie R. Groves and Norris Bradbury Made the Los Alamos Scientific Laboratory Permanent, 1945–48," "New Mexico's Forgotten Nuclear Tests: Projects Gnome (1961) and Gasbuggy (1967)," and "The History of Atomic Photography."

CHAPTER FIVE

Cutting the Gordian Knot

How Leslie R. Groves and
Norris Bradbury Made the
Los Alamos Scientific Laboratory
Permanent, 1945-48

On August 6, 1945, President Harry S Truman took to the airwaves to announce the Allied atomic bombing of Hiroshima. Dorothy McKibben, famed manager of the 109 East Palace Avenue Manhattan Project office in Santa Fe, listened to the president with her fifteen-year-old son, Kevin. "That's our bomb, Kevin," she said; "it was made in Los Alamos." Schooled in the secrecy of the time, the startled boy replied, "But he shouldn't be telling it."[1]

Like the McKibben family, most New Mexicans were simultaneously bewildered and enthralled when they first heard the news. For a small, out-of-the-way state, New Mexico had made major contributions to the costly victory over the Axis powers. The nationalized New Mexico National Guard unit, posted to the Philippines in the fall of 1941, fell to the Japanese invaders immediately after Pearl Harbor. Most of them participated in the infamous Bataan Death March. Held captive for over three years in horrific conditions, only about half of the original contingent of two thousand returned alive.[2]

During the conflict, a number of regional writers, cartoonists, and artists helped forge national public opinion. Through his regular newspaper columns, Ernie Pyle, who lived on south Girard Avenue in Albuquerque, emerged as the voice of the average GI. Many local readers turned to his column first whenever they picked up the morning paper. Two collections of his essays, *Here Is Your War* (1943) and *Brave Men* (1944), reached best-seller status.[3] Alamogordo-born cartoonist Bill Mauldin gained equal fame for his sardonic depiction of the lives of GIs Willie and Joe in "Stars and Stripes." The compilation of his wartime cartoons, *Up Front* (1945), has lost none of its power over the years.[4] Although not as widely recognized, nearby El Paso native Tom Lea ranked with the best of the combat artists. His classic painting *The Thousand Mile Stare* captured the experience of thousands of combat veterans.[5] Finally, the efforts of the scientists and technicians at Site Y, as the secret Los Alamos Scientific Laboratory (LASL) was then known, brought the war to its abrupt conclusion.

Even after sixty years, Los Alamos retains its rank as the most prominent of all the Manhattan Project installations. Originally intended to house perhaps one hundred scientists and their families, by 1945 the population of "the Hill" reached about five thousand, with no end in sight. During the spring and summer of 1945, a steady stream of cars and trucks crawled over the narrow two-lane roads from Los Alamos to Trinity Site, about thirty miles east of Socorro, where scientists had erected the nation's largest outdoor laboratory. There on the morning of July 16, 1945, they detonated the world's first atomic bomb.[6] Shortly thereafter, on the island of Tinian in the south Pacific, navy commander William "Deke" Parsons lay on his stomach to personally arm the complex uranium weapon (only after takeoff) as the B-29 *Enola Gay* started its fateful rendezvous with the industrial city of Hiroshima.[7] The second B-29, *Bock's Car*, dropped the Nagasaki bomb three days later. Thus, from start to finish, New Mexican involvement with World War II proved extensive; the efforts at Los Alamos and Trinity Site proved decisive.

But with the surrender of Japan on August 14, 1945, the situation abruptly changed. The war was over. Victory lay at hand. What would become of New Mexico's two major wartime installations, Trinity Site and Los Alamos?

In the heady days after the surrender, a number of people suggested that both sites be turned into some form of national park. Trinity Site and Site Y could be frozen in time as permanent monuments to the onset of the atomic age.

Indeed, on the day after Truman's announcement on Hiroshima, the Alamogordo Chamber of Commerce nominated Trinity Site for possible inclusion in the national park system. Newton B. Drury, director of the National Park Service, accepted the idea. Soon the Park Service drew up elaborate plans for a New Mexican national monument at Trinity. The venue would contain a paved pathway to the heart of the fenced-in area of Ground Zero, where the ball of fire had touched the earth. Visitors could also drive about seven miles to one of the three wood-and-earthen command posts, possibly via a fenced-in right-of-way. The proposed visitor's center would display numerous artifacts of early atomic history, probably flanked by a B-29 (perhaps even the *Enola Gay* itself).[8]

Postwar LASL officials proved very cooperative. In July of 1946, they agreed to give the Park Service any items it desired, including the lead-lined tanks and the massive container termed "Jumbo" (both from Trinity), a variety of photographs, and the names of all the participants. LASL scientists also agreed to help erect a shelter over part of the green-gray glass, "trinitite" (formed when the ball of fire touched the earth), so as to protect it from the incessant wind. Virtually everyone agreed that Trinity Site merited national park status for its role in the Manhattan Project.[9]

A number of voices called for a similar park status for Los Alamos itself. They argued that the ramshackle buildings on the mesa should similarly be frozen in time. Los Alamos might then serve as the Williamsburg of the atomic age or, in a harsher interpretation, a monument of man's inhumanity to man.

One has to make a distinction here between national plans for future atomic research and the *place* where such research would likely take place. No one in 1945 dreamed the United States should turn its back on nuclear energy. As physicist John von Neumann testified in subsequent U.S. Senate hearings, for the first time in history science had produced something that required immediate intervention on the part of the government. Edward Teller gloomily predicted that unless future wars could be eliminated, people would live in a world "in which safety no longer exists."[10] The question, then, was not should the government desert the field of atomic research, but should the field of atomic research desert the mesas of northern New Mexico?

In the fall of 1945, the aspects of northern New Mexico that had initially made Los Alamos so attractive all seemed to be drawbacks. The isolation from major urban centers (primarily for security reasons) now loomed as both unnecessary and provincial. How could the government attract top-level scientists to such an out-of-the-way location in times of peace?

Several voices suggested that the nation should transfer future atomic research elsewhere. Only two days after Hiroshima, Army Air Corps General Carl "Tooey" Spaatz argued that since the atomic bomb had emerged as essentially an air weapon, the postwar weapons program should be relocated to Palm Springs or Victorville, California. The nearby California desert would serve as an ideal proving ground for further Trinity Site–type tests.[11]

About two weeks after the Nagasaki bomb, General Thomas Ferrell wrote Manhattan Project director General Leslie R. Groves with a similar recommendation. He argued that the laboratory's functions should be relocated to a place where "first class scientists will not flee in peacetime." He recommended Berkeley, Chicago, or "the East." He too leaned toward Pasadena because of its proximity to the potential testing grounds of the California desert.[12]

These arguments made a good deal of sense at the time. Since virtually all the Los Alamos scientists had hailed from university environments, it seemed logical to transfer future nuclear research to some form of similar university setting. Wartime Los Alamos always had a temporary feel to it. Excluding the thirty or so Ranch School buildings, few of the hastily erected structures reflected any sense of permanence. The Quonset huts, flimsy four-plex apartments, small prefabricated homes,

General Leslie R. Groves's badge photo in wartime Los Alamos. Courtesy Los Alamos National Laboratories.

multistory dormitories for the Women's Army Corps (WACs) and Special Engineer Detachment (SED) single people, as well as the densely packed laboratory buildings in the Technical Area, all reflected the urgency of wartime lab construction.

From the beginning General Groves frankly considered Site Y as temporary. He once told General George Marshall, "These scientists will like anything you build for them. Put up some barracks. They will think they are pioneers out here in the Far West."[13] Virtually the only area of Los Alamos life where Groves did not scrimp involved food. A beefy man who enjoyed eating, he always felt that abundant food made for contented workers. Thus, he insisted that bargain, wholesome meals be available at all LASL mess halls throughout the war.

The presence of so many obviously temporary structures produced a sense of uneasiness that hung over the Hill for almost three years after Hiroshima. On August 6, 1945, a Los Alamos spokesman admitted that he had no guarantee that the project would continue there. Two months later, Groves stated that while the laboratory would stay where it was "for quite a while," any question of its permanency would ultimately rest with Congress.[14]

During the immediate postwar era, people discussed a number of possible options for the future of the Hill. A high-ranking laboratory official—carefully unnamed in all the secondary accounts—vigorously advocated some form of museum status for Site Y. An official report in 1946 formally acknowledged that "one school of thought suggested the Laboratory should become a monument."[15] Canadian Kathleen Mark, who arrived in 1944, recalled that in the postwar era, "the future of Los Alamos was always uncertain."[16]

Although there is a current movement—headed by the Atomic Heritage Foundation of Washington, D.C.—to incorporate various Manhattan Project sites into the national park system, at the moment neither Trinity Site nor Los Alamos appears on a list of contemporary national parks. The early attempts to monumentize each area collapsed for a variety of reasons. Since Trinity Site lies in the northwest corner of the White Sands Missile Range, army base commanders were understandably reluctant to deal with thousands of "atomic tourists." Moreover, LASL safety experts worried about radiation exposure to Park Service rangers and visitors in the vicinity of Ground Zero. After rattlesnakes invaded the various deserted command bunkers, the army leveled them as well. Consequently, there was not a lot to see at Trinity Site. Within a few years, the once-popular idea of establishing a national park at Trinity had quietly faded away. As a Park Service official noted in 1947, there was "no rush" to create such a monument.[17]

The events that allowed Los Alamos to dodge national park status proved even more complex. For better or worse, the fact that the nation's premier scientific weapons laboratory remains in northern New Mexico can be traced to two overlapping themes that occurred during the 1945–48 era. The first involved a series of major decisions by Leslie R. Groves, who for sixteen long months after Hiroshima and Nagasaki carried on as

General Leslie R. Groves addressing the crowd at Los Alamos,
1945. Photographer Unknown. Courtesy Palace of the Governors
(MNM/DCA). Neg. no. 30423.

lame-duck commander of the Manhattan Project. He did not officially
relinquish his authority to the newly created Atomic Energy Commission
(AEC) until January 1, 1947.

The second involved the vigorous responses that newly appointed
LASL director Norris Bradbury made to Groves's decisions. By acting
decisively within an atmosphere of overwhelming atomic uncertainty,
Groves and Bradbury effectively presented the newly created AEC with
"semi *fait accomplis*."[18] Although the question was not officially settled
until 1948, Groves's and Bradbury's decisions meant that Los Alamos
would achieve international fame not as a "must-see" national park but
as the premier nuclear weapons laboratory in the world.

With President Truman's announcement regarding Hiroshima, the secret of Los Alamos was officially out of the bag. Three days later, in response to a request from the North American News Alliance, lab director J. Robert Oppenheimer issued a formal statement. It said that the laboratory collectively believed that the Hiroshima weapon might shorten the war, that the use of the bomb would force nations to realize the necessity of avoiding future wars, and that in the hands of statesmen, science in general, and atomic power in particular, might bridge the gap between cultures.[19]

Ironically, two of the "cultures" that needed bridging lay very close at home: the army, which ran Site Y, and the scientists who put the weapons together. From the onset of the Manhattan Project, the two groups held each other at arm's length. There were many causes for this, of course, but the chief one lay in a fundamental clash of disciplines. For the scientists, advances emerged largely through the free sharing of scientific data; for the military, and for Groves in particular, the nation's atomic information had to remain under the strictest secrecy. Groves won the first round, and security on the Hill during the war proved all-pervasive. All mail on the Hill was censored. No one could travel farther than seventy-five miles without special permission. Diaries were forbidden and cameras allowed only to record family events. Army intelligence (G-2) agents staffed hotels and restaurants in Santa Fe and Albuquerque. Top-level figures such as Oppenheimer and Enrico Fermi traveled with full-time bodyguards. Others, such as Niels Bohr, were secretly tailed.

But after Truman's announcement, many scientists considered such security excessive. Only the technical matters needed classification, they argued. The consequences of the atomic bomb had become obvious to the entire world. Competent researchers around the globe should eventually be able to duplicate the Allies' efforts.

The scientists had a point. Within weeks after Hiroshima, virtually every thinking person realized the potential of this new weapon. In a famous editorial, *New York Times* reporter Hanson W. Baldwin observed, "Yesterday we clinched victory in the Pacific, but we sowed the whirlwind."[20] Writer Dorothy Thompson similarly noted that if Switzerland possessed the bomb and the Soviet Union did not, Switzerland would easily rank as the more powerful nation. The popular University of Chicago

Round Table discussion on NBC radio for August 12, 1945, pondered the question: "Is the atomic bomb good or bad for the world?"[21] After surveying the literature of the postwar era, historian Paul Boyer has concluded that "most Americans instantly recognized that this new weapon had fundamentally altered both traditional warfare and conventional morality."[22]

The scientists at LASL also recognized that they held a form of fundamental knowledge that no other group possessed. Before 1945, perhaps two thousand people in the world truly realized the nature of atomic energy. Appalled by the wild misinformation spread by the postwar press and conscious of their duty as citizens, in the fall of 1945 a group of younger scientists at Los Alamos organized the Association of Los Alamos Scientists (ALAS) to correct this situation. They hoped to enlighten officials in Washington, as well as local residents, as to the nature of the new atomic world. Yet under existing army regulations, they felt restricted in what they could say.[23]

The key to the future control of the atom, of course, lay with Congress and the president. During the last months of the war, Hill scientists spent endless hours arguing about how best to harness their awesome creation. The best-selling book of the day—Wendell L. Willkie's *One World* (1943)— argued that any future thinking "must be world-wide." Combined with their natural international orientation, Willkie's idealistic views, in essence, became the LASL scientists' position.[24] Only some form of international control, probably under the supervision of the fledgling United Nations, could ensure the peace of the world.

In his August 6 statement, the president informed the nation that a new agency (what would become the AEC) would have complete control over atomic energy matters. From his desk in the New War Building in Washington, Groves believed that Truman might call a special session of Congress to create the organization. When this did not occur, he surely would have agreed with an Oppenheimer memo of August 20, 1945, that suggested that the new organization would emerge within sixty days.[25]

But postwar national politics played by its own set of rules. True, the first atomic legislation was introduced into Congress in early October, but the so-called May-Johnson bill (named after its sponsors Representative Andrew J. May and Senator Edwin Johnson) ran into immediate political trouble. LASL scientists were outraged that the legislation appeared to place all atomic items under military control. They argued that such oversight would drastically restrict atomic research and would seriously hinder any attempt to achieve international supervision of the atom.[26] Dismay over the May-Johnson bill may well have helped spur the creation of the Association of Los Alamos Scientists.

In December 1946, Connecticut senator Brien McMahon introduced a substitute measure. His bill placed its emphasis on the as-yet-unknown potential of the *peaceful* atom. Section Six of this bill, however, plus a number of other clauses, seemed to virtually *exclude* the military from the whole process.

The rhetoric on these measures soon reached the boiling point. Physicist Harold Urey of Columbia termed the May-Johnson bill a "Communist bill or a Nazi bill." McMahon himself cast the dispute as a black-and-white "military vs. civilian" issue.[27]

The U.S. military, which had expected to place the secretary of the navy and the secretary of war on the AEC, suddenly found itself wrong-footed.[28] Groves spent many hours testifying before Congress and when he refused to reveal some top-secret classified information found himself attacked by newspapermen for possessing data that eluded his civilian superiors—the secretary of war and the president. The widely publicized simultaneous hearings over the failure of intelligence at Pearl Harbor did not increase the nation's confidence in military oversight. Consequently, Groves became increasingly frustrated with every *Washington Post* morning headline. Convinced that the nation needed more and improved atomic weapons, he found himself stymied at every turn by the vagaries of the political situation.

As with the best of democratic discourse, Congress eventually reached a compromise on the Atomic Energy Act. The new AEC would indeed be under civilian auspices, but after an amendment by Senator Arthur Vandenberg it would also contain the integral Military Liaison Committee. On August 1, 1946, Truman signed the bill, with the AEC to take control on the first of the new year.

During the same period, the United States introduced its plan to internationalize the atom to the fledgling United Nations. Oppenheimer wrote most of the document that elder statesman Bernard Baruch presented to the UN, all amid great publicity. The United States hoped to create an international agency that would have control over all nuclear activity, including the power to inspect and the power to punish. When this regulatory body was firmly in place, the United States would dismantle its own atomic weapons.

But the Soviet Union—which was frantically working to develop a weapon of its own—presented an alternative plan. They denounced the idea of UN inspection as a violation of sovereignty and demanded that the United States destroy its atomic stockpile *before* any serious negotiations could begin. Although the UNAEC limped into place—followed in 1957 by the more powerful International Atomic Energy Agency—no international body has been able to halt the spread of nuclear weapons. The Soviet Union detonated its first atomic bomb in 1949, and the arms race suddenly took a new turn.

Both the Los Alamos scientists and the army's General Groves found themselves increasingly frustrated by this sixteen-month period of atomic stagnation. Although they might view each other from the opposite side of the political fence, they both shared a wartime heritage of crisp, decisive actions. The direct chain of command that Groves had utilized so well to run the Manhattan Project—where his word was virtual law—had distinct echoes in the laboratory's steady technical advances toward an atomic weapon. But during late 1945, the question of atomic energy seemed bogged down in a morass of congressional wrangling. The age of atomic uncertainty had begun.

Psychologists tell us that the most frustrating of all mental states—for individuals as well as organizations—involves uncertainty. Yet that was the atmosphere that surrounded both Groves and Bradbury for well over a year. The new AEC—in whatever form it finally emerged—would have the mandate to control the nation's atomic future. Neither Groves nor Bradbury wished to hamstring its operations before it assumed command, but both felt that something had to be done immediately.

In the frustrating days of December 1945, Groves decided to act. The May-Johnson bill (which he supported) had stalled, and the UN General Assembly, which would debate the scheme for international nuclear control (which he opposed), had yet to meet. With the approval of the secretary of war, Groves had kept crucial Manhattan Project contractors busy with construction for the last four months. In addition, he had instructed Oak Ridge and Hanford to continue production of fissionable materials and carefully laid plans to develop a stockpile of weapons.[29]

Since he had helped select the original site, Groves remained partial to Los Alamos. In November he had warned a Senate committee that the nation's weapons laboratory should remain where it was. The United States could never reassemble a similar laboratory, he said, except in time of war. Moreover, he noted, the nation had already invested about $75 million in the project.[30] So, on January 4, 1946, Groves informed Bradbury that—even though he might be committing the AEC to something it would later disapprove of—he was ready to take the bull by the horns. Convinced that "we should not count on atomic bomb development being stopped in the foreseeable future," Groves informed the new director of Los Alamos that the Los Alamos Scientific Laboratory should remain where it was. As no viable alternative had emerged, the present site still offered the best-possible location.

In many ways Groves viewed the situation from the perspective of a construction engineer (which he was). If the new AEC elected to move the lab elsewhere, it would consume about two years in so doing. It would take six months to plan the move, twelve months to build the new location, and another six months for the actual move itself. With this January 4, 1946, letter, Groves cut the Gordian knot of atomic uncertainty. As he put it, "The only solution, therefore, is to stay at Los Alamos for at least the next few years, and to improve the existing facilities to such a degree as is necessary."[31]

The next day Groves informed the public of his decision. He went out of his way to express appreciation to the state of New Mexico and the city of Santa Fe for all their previous cooperation. He assured them that while he could not say definitely, he felt confident that the work of Site Y would continue there for a long time.[32]

Groves may well have had security in mind when he made his decision. By keeping the lab on the isolated mesas of New Mexico—rather than moving it to a crowded, urban university environment—he could more easily guard the nation's atomic secrets. In May of 1946, he informed Los Alamos that the number of people involved in the actual construction of, or even knowledge of, atomic weapons should be kept to an absolute minimum.[33] Although various congressmen and military figures arrived to tour LASL that spring, none learned the exact nature of the atomic stockpile. In September 1946, physicist John Manley wrote to Groves that this transitional period had become "a greater challenge to your wisdom and understanding" than the actual Manhattan Project itself.[34]

The atomic uncertainty in Washington and New York reverberated throughout Los Alamos as well. The first three years after the war proved exceptionally difficult for LASL scientists and their wives. Since they had completed their main assignment, the lab floundered as it searched for a new raison d'être. When Oppenheimer turned in his resignation as director on October 15, 1945, the first phase of atomic history drew to an abrupt close.

The man who replaced Oppenheimer was Norris Bradbury, a naval commander who had been on leave from the Department of Physics at Stanford for the duration. Oppenheimer had personally recommended Bradbury, and Groves, who wanted a young director who might view this new assignment as an opportunity, agreed.[35] When he received the formal offer, Bradbury reluctantly accepted the position for a six-month period or until the AEC took command, should this occur earlier. Eventually the six months stretched into twenty-five years. Not until 1970 did Norris Bradbury relinquish the reins of Los Alamos to his successor, Harold Agrew.

Today, the Bradbury years at Los Alamos (1945–70) have become somewhat controversial. From the viewpoint of the Hill, Norris Bradbury is regarded as the lab's number-one citizen. Not only did he direct LASL for a quarter of a century, he continued to live there until his death in 1997. In 1993 he witnessed the dedication of the Bradbury Science Museum in his honor. An unassuming, no-nonsense administrator, he earned a well-deserved reputation for efficiency and fairness. As long-term Los Alamos scientist Louis Rosen remarked, "Robert Oppenheimer was the founder of the Laboratory, but Norris Bradbury was its savior."[36]

During his years as director, LASL weapons designers created forty-nine of the fifty-six atomic bombs that eventually became part of the U.S. arsenal. Virtually all the major advances in weapons technology, including the hydrogen bomb, occurred under his watch. A firm believer in the doctrine of nuclear deterrence, Bradbury insisted that the U.S. nuclear stockpile supplied the key to maintaining peace during the Cold

War era.[37] Even so, he often stated that the goal of the laboratory was to create something that he hoped would never be used. He always maintained that he was trying to put himself out of business.

But as contemporary concerns over long-term environmental and health issues mount, Bradbury's reputation has been somewhat sullied. Most of the nation's aboveground nuclear tests at the Nevada Test Site (NTS) occurred while he was director, and they exposed virtually every American of that generation to radioactive fallout. The largely Latter-day Saint "downwinders" of Nevada, Utah, and Arizona suffered terribly from a number of tests. Although the AEC insisted at the time that the aboveground tests posed no danger, there is evidence that Bradbury instructed his family members to remain "upwind" of all atomic testing.[38] In 1994 former secretary of interior Stewart Udall publicly blamed him for encouraging NTS testing in spite of the dangers. Three years later, Greg Mello of Santa Fe's Los Alamos Study Project observed, "Norris knew it was dangerous and, to my knowledge, did nothing to stop it."[39]

In spite of this controversy, virtually everyone agrees that without Bradbury, Los Alamos would not exist where it is today. The decisions he made, both before and in response to Groves's January 4, 1946, letter, helped shape the course of New Mexican history.

■

Even before he assumed official command, Bradbury had convened the LASL Coordinating Council on October 1, 1945. There he laid out the problems at hand. In a thoughtful and balanced assessment, he argued that given the atmosphere of uncertainty, the best plan for LASL would be to (a) maintain the best project possible to hand over to the new agency, whenever Congress established it, and (b) to continue weapons research so as to stockpile the Fat Man plutonium bombs up to fifteen. (This was, perhaps, the first recorded statement regarding a stockpile.) In defense of this action, he noted that "the mere possession of weapons does not bring about war." He also recommended that the much smaller lab should become a largely civilian-run institution. But to do this, he said, he would have to offer salaries comparable to those in industry or in the academy. He also urged increased research on the peacetime uses of nuclear energy. His most perceptive comment: "For myself, I feel that

Norris Bradbury about the time he took over as director of Los Alamos. Courtesy Los Alamos National Laboratories.

the bear which we have caught by the tail is so formidable that there is a strong obligation upon us to find out how to let go or hang on."[40]

Bradbury also moved quickly to reduce the all-pervasive military atmosphere on the Hill. On November 3, 1945, he wrote Groves for permission to end censorship of mail and to allow friends and relatives to visit all locations except for the Technical Area. Although the nation had glimpsed its first views of Los Alamos in October, it was not until December that much of LASL security had been lifted. Still, Los Alamos remained a closed community until 1957.

Bradbury also pushed Groves to clarify the lines of authority over LASL technical operations. As director, he told the general, *he*, not the army, had to assume full responsibility for Technical Area security. He also insisted that he be given full command over all post problems, especially those involving housing conditions. He needed this authority, he said, because as early as November 1945 it had become clear to him that the project would remain in place for another twelve to eighteen months, at least.[41] From November 23 forward, all teletypes and telegrams from the lab were marked "signed Bradbury."[42]

It is hard to overestimate Bradbury's problems during the pre-AEC era of Los Alamos. Virtually all the scientists considered their job finished. Although they could not begin teaching until the forthcoming spring term, the majority anticipated an immediate return to the classroom. To their delight, they had a number of offers to choose from. Since science had emerged from the war with increased prestige, relatively new institutions such as the University of Oklahoma, which had never previously done work with nuclear physics, were eager to build up their programs in this area. Thus, Hill scientists faced a buyers' market. Somewhat naively, Bradbury even invited university and industry representatives to talk to lab members about future employment.[43] Groves once visited Los Alamos to urge people to stay, but to little effect.

The vast LASL support staff was eager to leave as well. Most of the Special Engineer Detachment—enlisted men with some college physics or chemistry (a few even had PhDs)—hoped to complete their educations. The WACs—who had performed many essential lab functions—were being similarly discharged. Group leaders at the lab found themselves so short staffed that they began stealing workers from their colleagues, a practice that Bradbury had to stop.

On August 7, 1946, David Hawkins complained to Bradbury that the lab "has functioned entirely without direction" for over a year.[44] Historians Richard Hewlett and Francis Duncan have termed the lab's activities during this period "spiritless make work."[45] Those assessments, however, may be overly harsh. The first years of the postwar era provided a canvas on which Bradbury tested a variety of options for a possible peacetime LASL identity.

Accordingly, he tried a number of approaches. The first involved the creation of a Los Alamos university. Only four days after Nagasaki, explosives expert George Kistiakowsky wrote a memo stating that the lab should now change its emphasis from "practical developments" to a study of scientific "fundamentals."[46] What better way to explore such fundamentals than through a series of undergraduate and graduate-level classes? So, from September 1945 to June 1946, LASL set up a miniature university. Indeed, perhaps one purpose of the postwar lab would be to serve as a scientific university on the Hill.

The instructors for the fledgling Los Alamos "university" just happened to be the best in the world. G. S. Kistiakowsky taught thermodynamics; J. W. Kennedy, radiochemistry; Hans Bethe, electromagnetic theory; John Manley and Victor Weisskopf, nuclear physics; Enrico Fermi, neutron physics; R. S. Peierls, hydrodynamics; and Edward Teller, elementary quantum mechanics.

Stellar though the instructors may have been, the Los Alamos university was a bit of a flop. It operated for nine months, but the classes were often scheduled at awkward times, and the auditors almost doubled those officially enrolled. (Of the 279 who enrolled, only 134 actually earned official credit.)[47] Although the lab would maintain a teaching function for the next half century, it never evolved into a genuine "New Mexico scientific university."

Along similar lines, Bradbury also tried to forge links with various regional universities. In May 1946, he informed Groves that he planned to extend invitations to all universities and colleges within a thousand-mile radius to gather at LASL to explore the prospect of their sending graduate students to work on basic problems in nuclear physics and chemistry. The lab would be ideal for this, he noted, since few universities had extensive laboratories and most of them were overloaded with students.[48]

The universities eagerly responded, and fifteen representatives met on the Hill in mid-June to discuss the matter. The hoped-for links were considered vital, both to reduce potential competition with the major universities and to ensure a continual supply of graduate students to replace the present generation of atomic scientists. Although the discussion proved frank and open, no extensive long-term LASL-university alliance ever emerged. The universities argued that they needed to retain control over the research that their students conducted if they officially awarded them advanced degrees. They also expressed concern over LASL's meager library facilities. The chief dilemma, however, lay with research on classified subjects, especially those unlikely ever to be declassified. All universities placed their PhD dissertations on open library shelves; awarding an advanced degree implied that anyone could read the results. Once again, concern over secrecy clashed with the traditional mission of the university, and again the former proved victorious.

Thus, the proposed lab-university links never moved much past the initial discussions. Although Los Alamos would, over the years, invite selected graduate students to work on various projects, because of security concerns the laboratory has never evolved into an integral part of regional university graduate programs.[49] (As an example of why this failed, under the direction of Hans Bethe, the scientists also wrote up the famed Los Alamos Technical Series, most of which remain classified today.)

Along with these false starts, a temporary new laboratory focus arrived almost by accident. In late 1945, the U.S. Navy argued that it needed to assess the potential impact of atomic weapons on ships. Thus, it requested a test series in the south Pacific. LASL learned of this plan—termed Crossroads—in December 1945 and soon allocated about one-eighth of its staff—about 150 scientists—to the project.[50] The precise timing of the tests—late June and July of 1946—all hinged on having sufficient LASL scientists to man the various experiments. Norris Bradbury informed the navy that because so many scientists and technicians were leaving, any test would be difficult by summer and likely impossible after September.

The Crossroads nuclear explosions of 1946 remain problematic to this day. In spite of the navy's stated purpose, many observers felt that the real goal was to demonstrate the power of atomic weapons to the world. Nearby ships were loaded with photographers and newsmen from around the globe, and the publicity proved extensive. Since failure would have been terribly embarrassing, the navy insisted that Los Alamos supply them with three proven (Trinity-type, implosion) weapons. Although all detonated as planned, the June 30 air-dropped Able missed its target by a considerable distance and the July 25 Baker (detonated underwater) contaminated a large number of nearby ships. Truman canceled the proposed third shot, Charlie.[51]

The Crossroads tests at Bikini produced numerous scientific reports, startling photographs, a telling memoir by radiation safety specialist David Bradley, *No Place to Hide* (1948), and a revealing swimsuit. But they hardly fulfilled the ostensible purpose. It is difficult to find a more banal observation than that given by Admiral W. H. P. Blandy afterward: "We know now . . . that with ships closely grouped, one atomic bomb exploded either from the air or at comparatively shallow depth underwater can sink several ships."[52]

Ironically, Crossroads bolstered the future of Los Alamos almost more than it did the U.S. Navy. The tests kept LASL in the public eye and proved to those who remained on the Hill that they could successfully complete a project, in spite of the fact that the highly celebrated "First Team" of scientists had departed for university environments. It was on the cusp of the tests (May 15, 1946) that Bradbury wrote the first letter that mentioned the permanence of Los Alamos.

By late 1946, then, Bradbury had created a new mission for the laboratory: LASL would oversee the "scientific management" (now termed "stewardship") of the nation's atomic weapons, it would provide for all future weapons design, it would oversee future atomic testing, and it would engage in basic research into peaceful uses of the fissioned atom.

One thing LASL would not do, however, was *assemble* the weapons. This task was given to Sandia Base in Albuquerque. Everyone acknowledged that new weapons demanded further testing. In October 1946, Bradbury allowed the Trinity Site area to return to its former role as grazing land "subject to its return to us in case of another shot."[53]

Perhaps the most difficult problem that Bradbury faced in the initial postwar era involved the ever-present dilemma of keeping staff morale high. After the news of Hiroshima, army-civilian tensions—which had been kept within bounds during wartime—began to take on a new intensity. From the fall of 1945 to the spring of 1946, grumbling rose to a crescendo. The catalyst came with the infamous water crisis of January–February 1946.

The haste with which the original lab was built can be clearly seen in the laying of the Guaje Canyon pipeline, the main water supply line to the Hill. Already secondhand when it was installed, the army laid most of it aboveground, assuming that a heavy snowfall would provide sufficient insulation. This occurred during the war years, but the winter of 1946 brought little snow and freezing temperatures that reached minus ten degrees Fahrenheit. As a result, four hundred feet of the line

Norris Bradbury, second director of Los Alamos, 1945–70. Courtesy Los Alamos National Laboratories.

froze solid, and suddenly the Hill found itself completely without water. Showers, toilets, and taps came to a standstill. The army rushed thirteen tanker trucks into action and began to haul four hundred thousand gallons every twenty-four hours. Housewives lined up daily with buckets.[54] Except for about three days of exceptionally icy road conditions, the army trucks met their goal of supplying the town with one hundred gallons per person per day. Still, as François Ulam recalled, "It [the water] was treated with liberal amounts of chlorine, but it tasted of gasoline, diesel fuel, or whatever else the truck had been hauling previously."[55]

Army colonel A. W. Betts wrote daily memos to all LASL division leaders on this matter. In one he complained of "innumerable difficulties" that the army faced in repairing the rickety line. The daily water reports ended on February 23, but the army continued to haul water by truck for several days afterward.[56] The new permanent water line was not installed until late in the following summer.

The water crisis proved a catalyst as far as civilian morale was concerned. Several families considered it the last straw and decided to leave immediately. Mass meetings gathered to denounce the hapless army officers. Wild rumors circulated that the army had sent soldiers to thaw the pipes by lighting matches under them. Another rumor stated that General Groves had said that he didn't give a tinker's damn about the scientists, but he wanted to be absolutely certain that the Technical Area wouldn't burn down. Visitors reported to Groves in Washington that Los Alamos lay in shambles.[57] The "great exodus" of the scientists from the Hill increased rapidly, and by spring of 1946 Los Alamos had dropped to little more than a thousand employees.[58]

Once again, Bradbury responded with alacrity. In mid-May 1946 he issued his famous "go-or-stay" order. If anyone left before September 1, 1946, the lab would pay their full moving expenses. But afterward, people were on their own. This decision also helped slice the Gordian knot of atomic uncertainty. Scientists and technicians who remained at LASL had committed themselves to the multifaceted new agenda.

Another area that Bradbury had to oversee after the war involved the lab's outreach to neighboring communities, especially nearby Santa Fe. Citizens of the "City Different" had been content to ask few questions during the conflict. But now they were burning with curiosity. Hill scientists proved generous with their time. Edward Teller spoke in Taos, and Cyril Smith talked to the Lions Club of Santa Fe. After army secrecy was removed in December 1945, the Laboratory of Anthropology in Santa Fe hosted a gathering of top-level scientists. It proved so popular that loudspeakers were set up to accommodate those who could not gain entrance. Afterward, scores of Santa Feans invited various Hill scientists to cocktail parties and dinner engagements. In a gesture of response, a number of Los Alamos wives decided to invite Santa Feans, including several "rich old ladies who lived behind adobe walls in lovely adobe houses," to come to the Hill for a "progressive dinner."[59]

Dorothy McKibben helped the invitees fill out the proper bureaucratic forms and arranged for car pools, since LASL security refused to allow chauffeurs in.[60] But then the water crisis struck and everything had to be canceled. "Santa Fe is stricken," McKibben reported. The next day, with the army supplying water by truck, the Hill wives tried again, and several dozen Santa Feans received their first glimpse of Site Y. They recognized the old Ranch School buildings, of course, but they were stunned by the appearance of the thirty-seven army-green technical buildings, the bleak dormitories, and the approximately three hundred housing facilities. Although they dined at various homes, as Alice Kimball Smith recalled, the guests "were so shocked by their sight of near squalor with barrack-like buildings covering their favorite mesa that I don't think they noticed what they were eating."[61]

Perhaps the key component that Bradbury faced in the morale department involved the question of housing. As historian Craig Martin has noted, "Griping about housing became part of the Los Alamos experience from the very first."[62] Even Bradbury marveled that the future success of the nation's premier scientific laboratory essentially pivoted on the relatively mundane matter of adequate housing.

From 1945 through 1947 Bradbury devoted a great deal of time to this issue. He sent a construction group to visit Hanford, Washington, to examine wartime housing there and inquired if any of the structures could be adapted to Site Y conditions. He later ordered one hundred one- or two-bedroom prefabricated houses (Pasco houses) shipped from the Hanford Site.[63] In early 1946, he enlisted the McKee Company to begin construction on the western area, the second permanent housing project on the Hill. Who got which government-owned home depended on a complex formula linked to family size and importance of lab position. Group leaders always had a crucial say in who received housing priority.[64] A number of these houses were ready for occupancy by January of 1947.[65] In addition, Bradbury hired a community planner who created a scheme for expansion that included community facilities such as a drugstore, food store, barbershop, beauty parlor, bowling alley, and chapel. Because the army remained in official control, Bradbury always kept Groves informed on all housing matters. All through his lame-duck days, Groves retained an interest in housing issues. Ever conscious of expense, he banned such "luxuries" as garages, carports, or master bedrooms. He even discouraged the proposed beauty parlor and drugstore. After negotiations with the secretary of war, he decided that $10,000 would be the maximum paid for lab housing. All construction bids had to come in under that sum.[66]

Under Bradbury's urging, the housing program began to accelerate. On April 14, 1946, George L. Williams of the Tech Maintenance Group revealed an elaborate scheme to convert the lab to a permanent basis. He recommended that there be a gradual shift "from the present hodge-podge of shabby temporary technical buildings" to solid, stable structures. He also recommended starting from scratch so that all the major laboratory buildings were situated on a new section of the mesa. By starting afresh, he argued, the government could build "a truly beautiful and impressive laboratory in the grand manner." He then devised a four-year program to bring this about.

Williams's plan touched many bases, ranging from the mundane to the philosophical. Any new, permanent laboratory would have to include such items as adequate parking, a cafeteria, a library, an archive, and conference rooms that seated over twenty people (one of Oppenheimer's constant complaints). In addition, the lab would have to clean up numerous scrap heaps and collect debris scattered alongside the road. It would also need to mend countless (literal) fences and construct miles of new roads across the mesa tops.

Everyone agreed that the proposed new laboratory buildings had to be constructed with creativity in mind. It was important that the scientists have frequent access to one another, for this constant interaction, it was widely believed, had allowed the Manhattan Project to succeed in spite of the odds. All new construction, of course, had to be clearly seen as "permanent."[67]

These various programs and construction schemes were moving full tilt when the first nine-member delegation of AEC officials arrived on the Hill on November 14, 1946.[68] During their three-day stay, Bradbury rolled out the red carpet. While politely reassuring AEC officials that the nation's atomic future lay in *their* hands, he presented Los Alamos in the best-possible light. Officially, the AEC took over on January 1, 1947, but as the Senate did not officially confirm the appointees until April, the delay proved even longer. The AEC did not really come on track until spring 1947, when yet another delegation visited the Hill to again assess the situation.

But time proved on Bradbury's side. When the AEC finally did assume control, it faced a ramshackle but still growing laboratory that had its future plans firmly in place.

Bradbury remained frank and honest throughout the discussions. The old laboratory would have to be entirely scrapped. Since the crowded Tech Area buildings were bounded by the canyon on one side and the town site on the other, they could be neither modified nor expanded. Many were already a fire hazard. Although never revealed to the public, several Tech Area buildings were also so contaminated with radioactivity that people could barely work there in safety. But the new laboratory would take care of all these problems.

By 1947, then, the lab had clearly stabilized. Housing remained tight, but building continued at a rapid pace. Morale continued to improve. Although most of the "First Team" of enlightened liberal physicists had departed, many agreed to return on a consulting basis. Moreover, the government had already sunk about $75 million into Los Alamos. The new, multifaceted vision for LASL had emerged.[69] With this increased stability, the magnificent scenery and the relative isolation of the mesas began to loom as positive aspects once again.[70]

■

To illustrate the key roles that Groves and Bradbury played in this scenario, it may be helpful to pose a contrafactual question. What if the AEC had been created in November 1945, as initially planned? Had the commissioners first arrived on the Hill in late 1945, rather than late 1946, they would have confronted the following: a raw, unproven director; a major water crisis on the horizon; collapsing morale; a steady exodus of first-rank scientists; and bitter civilian antagonism toward the army. In short, they would have met virtual social chaos. All this would have been compounded by the University of California's indecision as to whether it wished to continue to oversee the nation's nuclear weapons complex. (This was partially resolved when Z Division of Los Alamos—which was charged with the manufacture and assembly of weapons—transferred to Sandia Base in Albuquerque, eventually to be managed by Western Electric.)[71] Had the AEC officials arrived in the fall of 1945, they might well have decided to relocate the major laboratory functions elsewhere—

*Formal portrait of
General Leslie R. Groves,
one of World War II's
most controversial leaders.
Courtesy Los Alamos
National Laboratories.*

either to southern California or to the urban East Coast, near the nation's most prestigious universities. Los Alamos could indeed have become a national park or assumed the role of Williamsburg West.

Still, even with the generally favorable climate of early 1947, the final decision on the permanence of Los Alamos had to wait an additional year. In early 1948, after several extensive studies, the AEC officially decided "to make Los Alamos a permanent laboratory and permanent community."[72] That year the AEC officially launched a $100-million program to create an entirely new laboratory along with needed supporting facilities. Fiscal years 1949 and 1950 saw the beginning of two large permanent buildings—the first of an "adequate, permanent type Laboratory group" on the South Mesa site. These structures came complete with new power and steam plants to ensure that they would always have adequate electricity.[73] A proper water line now stretched from the Rio Grande Valley to the Hill. Construction also began on an impressive new bridge to arch Los Alamos Canyon. A 1949 consultant declared Los Alamos the finest government laboratory in the nation.[74] That same year, a reporter described Los Alamos as "the most important point on the map of the United States, except for Washington."[75] There would never again be any talk of relocating the laboratory elsewhere.

For better or worse, then, the decisions that Leslie R. Groves and Norris Bradbury made from late 1945 to 1948—during the era of atomic uncertainty—forever shaped the course of New Mexico's atomic future. Together they helped forge a revived purpose for postwar Los Alamos, one that the newly formed Atomic Energy Commission could readily agree to. With this, the town that a 1950 observer once termed "the world's newest and strangest city" became a permanent part of the northern New Mexico landscape.[76]

New Mexico's
Forgotten Nuclear Tests

Projects Gnome (1961) and

Gasbuggy (1967)

On July 16, 1945, scientists from the Manhattan Project detonated an atomic device at Trinity Site, in the northwest corner of the Alamogordo Bombing Range in central New Mexico. The select group of eyewitnesses watched in awe as the mushroom cloud rose to forty thousand feet and slowly drifted north-northeast over the Chupadera Mesa toward Oklahoma and Kansas. With this, the state of New Mexico entered history as "the birthplace of the Atomic Age."[1]

Five days after the explosion, Stafford Warren, the physician in charge of health safety for the Manhattan Project, wrote to the overall head—General Leslie R. Groves. In this lengthy missive, Warren cautioned Groves that central New Mexico was far too populated for further nuclear explosions. He recommended that any future tests be held in a location with a radius of at least 150 miles without people.[2]

Unfortunately, the newly formed Atomic Energy Commission (AEC) could discover no location that fit this requirement. Consequently, the government compromised. In December 1950, President Harry S Truman announced that the Nevada Test Site (NTS)—sixty-five miles northwest of Las Vegas—would serve as America's premier continental nuclear testing ground. In January 1951, the AEC began aboveground atomic testing at the NTS. By 1958, Nevada had witnessed over one hundred such explosions.[3]

At various times, however, the AEC selected other "off-site" areas to detonate underground nuclear devices. During the 1960s, they chose two locations in New Mexico. The first was Gnome (1961), about twenty-five miles southeast of Carlsbad; the second was Gasbuggy (1967), about fifty-five miles east of Farmington.

Each of New Mexico's three nuclear detonations proved groundbreaking in every sense of the term. The Trinity test, of course, inaugurated the atomic age. Project Gnome was widely praised as the first "atoms for peace" nuclear explosion, a test designed to harness the power of the atom for peaceful purposes. In a similar fashion, Gasbuggy gained publicity as the first joint U.S. government–private industry (El Paso Natural Gas) effort to use nuclear explosions to improve the production of natural gas fields, inaugurating a partnership that everyone expected to continue. With these tests, New Mexico joined Alaska as the only state outside Nevada where the government has detonated nuclear bombs in three separate locations.[4]

The dubious prominence of New Mexico in this regard points to the important role that the state has played in postwar nuclear history. It also points to a variety of ecological dilemmas that have resulted from these nuclear experiments. All three explosions released man-made radionuclides into the atmosphere and drove them deep into the surface of the earth. Although the AEC and its successor agency, the Department of Energy (DOE), have cleaned up each site on several occasions, radioactive trace elements from these explosions still remain. Government monitors continue to visit each site on a regular basis to measure surface contamination and to ensure that the underground radiation has not migrated into the water table. Consequently, the saga of these three nuclear tests is not just limited to the New Mexican past; it affects the New Mexico future as well.

Trinity

One can best understand the Gnome and Gasbuggy events by starting with an overview of Trinity. In the spring of 1944, a small team from the secret city of Los Alamos (Site Y) began the search for a suitable location to test the plutonium weapon under construction in the Manhattan Project. The test location needed to be relatively flat, with basically good weather, isolated from any center of population, and close enough to Los Alamos to facilitate transportation. At one time scientists considered eight locations—including the Malpais region south of Grants—but eventually decided on the Jornada del Muerto high desert that lies to the east of Socorro. One reason for the choice lay in the fact that the federal government had already confiscated much of this land for the Alamogordo Bombing Range.[5] It proved relatively uncomplicated to transfer the northwest corner to the Manhattan Project.

Construction began in November 1944, and within months workers had erected the world's first gigantic outdoor laboratory. Miles of roads, a base camp, and thousands of feet of wire appeared almost overnight. Three earth-and-concrete bunkers and numerous unmanned posts surrounded Ground Zero, where scientists hauled the atomic device to the top of a one-hundred-foot steel tower. After a night of violent rain and a two-hour postponement, head meteorologist Jack Hubbard gave the clearance for a five thirty detonation.

The power of the fissioned atom proved greater than anyone had ever imagined. The blast was heard in three states and could have been seen from another planet. Where the ball of fire touched the earth, it fused the sand into a greenish gray, radioactive glass—later termed "atomsite" or "trinitite." The mushroom cloud broke into three parts, with the brunt moving slowly east over the continent, spreading radioactivity over an area as large as Australia. Three weeks later, at Hiroshima and Nagasaki, the world at large similarly learned about the power of the fissioned atom.

Afterward, federal and state officials hoped to turn New Mexico's Trinity Site into a national monument. The *Albuquerque Journal* argued that such a monument would long keep the state in the public eye.[6] Unsolvable dilemmas regarding surface radiation, plus the fact that

Trinity Site lay within the renamed White Sands Missile Range, pre-
vented this from occurring. In 1965, however, the National Park Service
declared Trinity Site a National Historic Landmark, and a decade later
they designated it a National Historic Site. Twice a year, in spring and fall,
the army opens the Trinity area for visitors. Although Los Alamos has
thrice cleaned up the region and buried the trinitite (in steel barrels),
army officials still limit on-site visits to about three hours. Even today,
however, the Department of Defense Environmental Restoration
Program maintains responsibility for cleaning up the region.[7]

During the summer of 2005, as the Allies commemorated the sixtieth
anniversary of the end of World War II, Albuquerque hosted an international gathering of Manhattan Project veterans, antinuclear protesters,
and news media figures. The army opened Trinity Site for a July 16, 2005,
sixtieth-anniversary visit that drew several thousand spectators. As the
international news coverage of this event showed, Trinity Site, New
Mexico, has earned a secure niche in the national memory of the World
War II years.

Plowshare

The second and third New Mexico nuclear detonations proved quite
different from the Trinity Site explosion. Neither Gnome nor Gasbuggy
formed part of the nation's military effort. Rather, they were keystones
in President Dwight D. Eisenhower's Plowshare Program, an attempt to
harness the destructive power of the atom for purposes of peace.
Although front-page stories at the time, Gnome and Gasbuggy are virtually forgotten today, even by many local residents. The modest historic
markers placed at the sites reflect this oblivion as well as the dashed
hopes surrounding each detonation.

During the early 1950s, the AEC first conceived the idea of using underground nuclear explosions for large-scale construction projects. Aerial photographs of the 1952 hydrogen bomb tests at Eniwetok Atoll in the South
Pacific showed that the explosion had created a huge crater, which might,
conceivably, be turned into a harbor. Moreover, such fission explosions
released far fewer radionuclides into the atmosphere than conventional
atomic bombs, although A-bombs were used to "trigger" the hydrogen

devices. Viewed purely in economic terms, this meant that thermonuclear bombs might be able to move large amounts of earth at very little expense, perhaps as low as twenty cents per cubic yard.[8]

The Suez crisis of 1956 brought this concern into sharp focus. After Egyptian president Gamal Nasser closed the Suez Canal by sinking ships in the waterway, Harold Brown, director of the Lawrence Radiation Laboratory (LRL), suggested that the West could cut a new canal across Israel by using controlled nuclear explosions. A French engineer published the first book on the subject that same year. In 1957, the 1.7-kiloton shot called Ranier at the NTS was fully contained underground. The confluence of these events led LRL physicist Herbert York to gather scientists from Los Alamos, Sandia National Laboratories, and the LRL in the secret Livermore Conference to discuss the matter. Thus was born the concept of "geographical engineering" via underground nuclear detonations.[9]

The idea caught on in both the scientific and engineering communities. The second conference on the theme was held in San Francisco in 1959 and open to the public, while the third, in Davis, California, five years later, evoked even greater response.[10] The last large symposium on engineering with nuclear explosives was held in Las Vegas, Nevada, in January 1970. By that time, however, the concept had fallen into disrepute.[11]

The overall name for programs such as this emerged in 1957 as "Project Plowshare." The term derived from the famous passage in Isaiah, chapter two, verse four: "And they shall beat their swords into plowshares, and their spears into pruning hooks; nation shall not lift up sword against nation; neither shall they learn war any more." President Eisenhower always gave Plowshare his strongest support.

During the late 1950s, the government did yeoman work to popularize the Plowshare concept. The U.S. Post Office issued a variety of stamps and first-day covers to celebrate the "Atoms for Peace" program. New York sculptor Moissaye Marans created a fourteen-and-a-half-foot statue to symbolize the spirit of the venture: a stylized Old Testament figure standing on a plow, holding a broken sword in his hands. The sculpture won several awards and was widely praised.[12]

The Atoms for Peace program bolstered the late 1950s optimism regarding the future of the nuclear world. Scientists spoke of utilizing underground explosions to cut canals, dig harbors, redirect the flow of

These first-day covers (1955) illustrated the widespread hope that the atom could be turned to peaceful purposes—the driving force behind the Plowshare Program. Collection of the author.

rivers, build dams, and enhance underground aquifers. Mining engineers hoped that nuclear blasts might reveal new ways to extract oil from tar sands and shale and increase natural gas from low-production fields.[13] Other scientists dreamed of using nuclear explosions for weather control, space travel, or even a nuclear-powered aircraft. The respected scientific press joined this chorus. Gerald W. Johnson and Harold Brown suggested in *Scientific American* that the nation was "on the verge of a new period of 'geographical engineering.'"[14] Writing in *Physics Today*, David B. Lambert argued that while blast radiation could never be completely eliminated from these cratering explosions, it could be "controlled to the extent that radioactive hazards need not be an obstacle to the industrial exploitation of this technique."[15]

The most prominent spokesman for this position was Manhattan Project veteran Edward Teller. An enthusiastic promoter, Teller's assurances were often quoted by the national press. On one occasion, Teller stated, "I can say, not with certainty but with quite a bit of hope, that we can make nuclear explosives so clean that the worry about radioactivity in its peaceful applications may disappear completely."[16] On another, he promised that nuclear engineering could "change the earth's surface to suit us."[17]

Some historians have viewed the scientists' enthusiasm for Plowshare programs as just a facade for the continued testing of nuclear weapons.[18] This cynical view, however, fails to acknowledge the dreams of many Manhattan pioneers, who, from the 1940s forward, had hoped that the positive aspects of the subatomic world would eventually outweigh the theme of nuclear destruction. Physicists Joseph Rotblat, J. Robert Oppenheimer, and Edward Teller had all expressed such views. Alice Kimball Smith, who had lived in Los Alamos during the war, similarly recalled that the hopes for peaceful applications of atomic power formed a central part of many wartime Los Alamos conversations.[19]

Still, the AEC courted public approval for their "Atoms for Peace" idea for another very pragmatic reason. By the late 1950s, popular fears concerning fallout dangers from aboveground atomic testing were running at full tide. Groups ranging from the Nevada League of Women Voters to British philosopher Bertrand Russell to Nobel laureate Linus Pauling had begun to call for an immediate halt to all aboveground testing. In 1956, Democratic Party candidate Adlai Stevenson made this a major issue of his presidential campaign. A number of international scientists who attended the influential traveling Pugwash gatherings took this consensus back to their respective governments.[20] Consequently, on November 1, 1958, the United States, the USSR, and Great Britain began a voluntary moratorium on aboveground nuclear testing. At the Geneva talks on this matter, President Eisenhower tried (unsuccessfully) to have Plowshare detonations, which were intended to be open to all observers, exempted from the moratorium. Soviet spokesmen protested, however, arguing that any nuclear explosion could have military applications.

The 1958 test ban agreement brought the AEC's Plowshare plans to an abrupt halt. All such projects went back to the drawing board, where they remained until 1961. That year, the Soviets broke the ban and renewed their nuclear tests. Immediately President John F. Kennedy announced that America would resume its aboveground testing as well. After two more years of testing, Soviet premier Nikita Khrushchev and President Kennedy signed the 1963 treaty that banned all atmospheric and oceanic explosions. Henceforth, the only nuclear experiments allowed would be those detonated beneath the earth's surface.

The 1958–61 test ban had major consequences for several states, especially Alaska and New Mexico. The three-year gap allowed Alaskan Natives, university scientists, and antinuclear activists to quash a proposed Plowshare program (Chariot) that would have drawn on three to four underground nuclear explosions to create a harbor in northwest Alaska near Point Hope.[21] With Chariot in disfavor, the AEC turned its attention to Gnome as the first Plowshare test. And Gnome was scheduled for New Mexico.

Gnome

During the Plowshare years, New Mexico had a strong friend in Washington in the person of Democratic senator Clinton P. Anderson. Born in South Dakota, young Anderson had studied journalism at the University of Wisconsin before tuberculosis drove him to New Mexico. After a close brush with death, he recovered to become a respected businessman in the fields of journalism and insurance. Anderson felt that New Mexico had saved his life, and while in Congress he worked hard to bring federal largesse to his adopted home state. After brief service as Harry S Truman's secretary of agriculture, Anderson sought appointment on the Joint Congressional Committee on Atomic Energy. He served on that crucial body from 1951 until 1972. Thus, Anderson found himself in an ideal position to direct numerous AEC funds toward New Mexico. In 1961, he estimated that two-fifths of all federal spending in the state had some form of atomic connection.[22] Just before the 1961 Gnome detonation, Anderson credited atomic energy as "the keystone of the research and development structure" of New Mexico.[23] Anderson especially encouraged the matchup of Plowshare, Gnome, and the town of Carlsbad.

In 1961, Carlsbad contained about twenty-six thousand people and ranked as the sixth-largest city in the state. The local economy revolved largely around the mining of potash for fertilizer and the twenty thousand acres of irrigated cotton, alfalfa, maize, barley, castor beans, and pasture grass from the impounded Pecos River. Tourism was also vital to the region, for the famed Carlsbad Caverns had been part of the national park system since 1923 and an official national park since 1930. On November 24, 1961, the ten-millionth visitor passed through the caverns. At the time, Carlsbad Caverns formed New Mexico's most popular tourist attraction.[24]

When the AEC first approached Carlsbad officials in the summer of 1958 for a possible July 1959 Plowshare test, they met with mixed local response. The city newspaper, the *Current-Argus*, welcomed the idea as an economic boon for the region.[25] "Nuclear Emphasis Shifts from Geneva to Carlsbad" blared one headline.[26]

But other area residents expressed doubt. Farmers feared that radioactive fallout might damage their crops, while Park Service officials and motel owners expressed concern that the proposed ten-kiloton Gnome shot might collapse the famed caverns. The strongest reservations came from the potash mine owners and miners, who feared similar damage to the mine shafts.

The AEC recognized the validity of these objections and convened a panel of experts, recommended by the National Academy of Sciences, to study the matter. The panel reviewed the local geography, gathered seismic data from the NTS, and concluded in February 1959 that Gnome would cause no damage to crops (it would be contained underground).

They similarly concluded that the proposed test would not be powerful enough to damage either the potash mines or the caverns.

Although potash industry executives had been AEC guests to the NTS to witness several 1958 detonations, they remained skeptical. Their lawyers approached both Lloyd's of London and the Nuclear Energy Property Insurance Association to underwrite the risk of mine collapse.[27] After Clinton Anderson helped arrange a compromise, however, most of the local businessmen fell into line.[28]

The 1958 moratorium on testing temporarily shelved the initial Gnome plans, but the AEC utilized the interim to detonate other, non-nuclear blasts in preparation for its eventual lifting.[29] Thus, when nuclear testing did resume in 1961, Gnome was ready for rapid deployment.[30] With Chariot in Alaska now canceled, the AEC turned the spotlight on Carlsbad as the pioneer Plowshare experiment. Gnome was billed as the world's first atomic blast for wholly peaceful purposes.[31]

On October 23, 1961, President Kennedy gave the official go-ahead. When Carlsbad citizens heard the news, the *Current-Argus* noted, they became "quietly jubilant."[32] As shot time grew closer, anticipation and rhetoric both intensified. New Mexico's sole congressman, Thomas G. Morris, observed that as Alamogordo had become the symbol of the beginning of the A-bomb, so would Carlsbad symbolize the beginning of peaceful uses of nuclear explosives.[33] The *Current-Argus* predicted that in the future, Carlsbad would be known not only as the home of Carlsbad Caverns but also as the home of Project Gnome.[34]

The underground blast was scheduled for December 10, 1961, and the AEC handled all preparations with considerable skill. They arranged a series of talks at Carlsbad High School the evening before, where prominent local citizens and Edward Teller spoke of the "miracle of the decade."[35]

On the next morning, buses took visitors to the designated observer area, 4.5 miles from surface ground zero. Loudspeakers broadcast the countdown to the immediate vicinity, and Carlsbad radio picked up the transmission for those sitting in their own vehicles on State Road 37, Potash Road. Visitors were told to bring binoculars, but scientists expected little, if any, visual impact. Scaled down to 3.1 kilotons, the nuclear device rested at 1,184 feet underground, at the end of a 1,116-foot button-hook tunnel that was expected to seal itself off after the explosion.

As a further precaution, the six potash companies, one within five miles of Gnome, ordered all their miners to the surface during the shot. At the last minute, the AEC agreed to reimburse the potash industry for the shutdown loss.[36] National Park Service officials also kept visitors out of Carlsbad Caverns during blast time. Originally scheduled for 8:00 A.M., meteorologists postponed the detonation twice as surface winds over ground zero would have brought any unexpected fallout toward Carlsbad.

The list of national media and foreign visitors attending Gnome proved impressive. Seventy-one news media officials were there, including representatives from ABC, CBS, *Life*, *Time*, the *New York Times*, *US News and World Report*, and UPI. Official UN representatives also attended, as well as nine international visitors. The Soviets were invited to observe but declined the invitation.[37]

The press gave considerable publicity to the four announced goals of Gnome. First, they hoped to learn how nuclear explosions in the Carlsbad area salt beds differed from those detonated in tuff, the chief rock strata of the NTS. The scientists believed that different rock strata coupled energy into seismic waves in different patterns. They needed such seismic data for a salt bed explosion. One aspect of this, a theme virtually ignored by the popular press but clear to all those in the nuclear industry, was that such seismic data would allow Americans to detect any secret nuclear test that the Soviets might detonate in their own salt beds. Second, LRL and Los Alamos scientists set up an elaborate neutron wheel in the tunnel to make neutron cross-section measurements to aid nuclear reactor development. Third, scientists also set up experiments to investigate the possibility of recovering radioisotopes from the blast. These would be used for future scientific and industrial applications. Last, the aspect of Gnome that received the greatest publicity lay with the hope that the blast would create a vast reservoir of heat that would be gradually released over an extended period.[38] If the salt beds indeed retained the heat as expected, then workers could pump water into the newly formed cavity, extract the energy as steam, and turn it into electricity.[39] Locals also hoped that the Gnome blast would create underground reservoirs or aquifers for water storage, flood control, and the recharging of water-bearing strata.[40] Consequently, Project Gnome embodied a number of both local and national expectations.

At noon on December 10, 1961, LRL scientists detonated Gnome as the first Plowshare explosion. It was also the first continental nuclear explosion outside of the Nevada Test Site since Trinity. The 3.1-kiloton blast performed as expected. It produced extremely high temperatures and created an underground cavity of approximately 960,000 cubic feet. The cavity was about 75 feet high and about 150 feet in diameter, and newsmen likened it to an underground eight-story building as wide as the base of the U.S. Capitol. All previous cavities from NTS shots had collapsed almost immediately, but the surface of Gnome remained intact. Scientists expected it to remain so for years.

Five months later, when the radiation had decayed to safe levels, a number of scientists entered the Gnome cavity to view the situation firsthand (a practice that would not be allowed today). Sandia National Laboratories scientist Wendell Weart recalled the striking color of the walls, for the shot's gamma rays had transformed them from dull gray into deep shades of blue, yellow, and black. The radioactivity in the cavity had largely been trapped by the melted salt and rock that lay at the bottom. Still, the extreme heat—one hundred degrees Fahrenheit with 60 percent humidity—made all visits necessarily brief.[41]

On the first anniversary of the Gnome blast, the AEC briefly escorted U.S. news media into the cavity. The resulting photographs, especially those of men standing on the Gnome rubble, proved startling.[42] Scientists continued to study the Gnome cavity for several years.

If the underground nuclear explosion at Gnome had gone as expected, the crowd of visitors would have observed little. Initially, scientists had estimated that anyone standing at the Gnome control point would not see or detect anything unless he or she possessed scientific instruments.[43] Edward Teller repeated this belief at his high school talk. "I hope all of us observers will be disappointed," he said. "If everything goes right, we will see nothing." Later he added as an afterthought: "I think there might be a little cloud of dust if the ground jumps."[44]

But Gnome visitors saw more than they bargained for. Over surface ground zero, the earth heaved about four feet and most people felt a "thump." The shock sent a blanket of dust swirling across the site, and the seismic wave cracked a filling station wall at Malaga, twelve miles away. It also knocked cans off a shelf in nearby Loving. One rancher remarked of the shock: "That shook up your rattlesnakes."[45] The planned experiment with conventional explosives at surface ground zero, designed to calibrate the shock to the atmosphere with the seismic effects of the detonation underground, went off unexpectedly, at the exact same time as the nuclear blast. This sent a premature fireball and cloud of smoke into the air. Since the image of the mushroom cloud had become familiar to most Americans by 1961, many visitors involuntarily ducked.[46] The ground shock also jiggled many stationary automatic cameras, blurring a large number of the official images.

The chief miscalculation, however, appeared two to three minutes after detonation, when a plume of what seemed to be gray smoke emerged from the elevator shaft, about 340 meters southwest of surface ground zero. This plume, which turned out not to be smoke but radioactive steam, continued in earnest for about thirty minutes. Observers could still detect small amounts of steam at the shaft the next day. The release of this unexpected radioactivity also damaged numerous photographs. *Life*'s images were all below par.

Contrary to expectations, the steam produced by the heat of the blast had breached the self-sealing shaft through an unnoticed fault line and had escaped to the surface via the elevator shaft. The "vented" cloud moved slowly in a north-northwest direction toward the town of Artesia. When radiation levels reached about two milliroentgens per hour, state police halted all traffic between the control point and Carlsbad for almost three hours. Most of the approximately three hundred observers who had witnessed the blast and now were on their way home had to return to the control point. Officials later washed down the seven cars that had driven into the region.[47] The AEC also purchased animal feed for several months for those Artesia ranchers whose fields lay in the direct path of the fallout.[48]

Over time, the unexpected venting of this radioactive steam produced two regional anecdotes. The first involved Edward Teller. According to legend, someone pointed to the white cloud and asked Teller what it was. In his thick Hungarian accent, Teller responded: "Vy, that looks like steam."[49] Since Teller observed the actual blast from a helicopter, which did not land until later, this story probably derives from a postshot question-and-answer session held at the Carlsbad observation point. There Teller was indeed asked: "What kind of vapor is that?" His laconic response: "White vapor." With retelling, this anecdote has become enhanced.[50]

The second anecdote involves the residents of nearby Artesia. According to this story, radiation monitors stationed near the mouth of the Rio Grande subsequently detected increased radioactivity in the waters there. Artesians claimed that this unexpected increase came primarily from the Gnome cloud, which had dropped radionuclides into the Pecos River, whence they eventually made their way down the Rio Grande.[51] Monitors on the lower Rio Grande may indeed have detected increased radioactivity. But the origin of the radionuclides is far more likely to have come from worldwide, aboveground testing than from the minute amounts of radiation vented at Gnome.

In spite of these setbacks, immediate reaction to Gnome remained upbeat. As they plugged the radioactive steam leak with blast furnace clay, scientists claimed that they could salvage perhaps 70 percent of the data. The neutron wheels were initially believed lost but were later recovered and sent to the LRL and Los Alamos for analysis. Scientists also declared the isotope creation experiments worthwhile and even spoke optimistically about recovering virtually intact images from the fogged camera film.[52] Ronald E. Rawson of the LRL spoke of "some disappointments and also some very exciting results," while George Cowan of the Los Alamos Scientific Laboratory termed it a "qualified success."[53] The chief seismologist for the U.S. Coast and Geodesic Survey said that the extensive shock waves "flabbergasted everybody," for they were picked up in Finland, Sweden, and Japan. The seismological data probably proved the most valuable.[54] Gary W. Higgins of LRL put it this way: "Gnome has been an extremely successful experiment and has laid the groundwork for several additional and valuable projects."[55] Phil O. Randolph of LRL, however, pointed out that it might be years before the long-range objectives could be accomplished.[56]

Aside from the radioactive steam cloud, the largest disappointment came with the lack of any hoped-for underground heat reservoir that might be turned into a power source. Postshot drilling discovered that no such reservoir had been created by the blast.[57] In 1965, LRL issued a "final report" on Gnome that tried to sum up the results in neutral language. Still, the disappointment was obvious.[58] The cancellation of a second experiment planned for the same location—Project Coach—reflects this lack of accomplishment.[59]

*Scientist standing in the underground cavern created by
Gnome. AEC photo. Courtesy of the Los Alamos National
Laboratory Archives.*

For six years after the test, Gnome remained on what the AEC termed
"standby status." Officials erected a fence around the region to keep out
livestock and set up a plaque that detailed the historic importance of the
site. All drilling or mining in the region was prohibited forever.

Their experiments finished in 1968, the AEC prepared to return the
680-acre Gnome site to the Bureau of Land Management. Consequently,
workers removed all contaminated materials and facilities and plugged
all drill holes, save two kept open for purposes of monitoring. Workers
reinserted some of the contaminated debris into the 1,200-foot entry
shaft and sealed it. They also shipped contaminated equipment to the

NTS for storage. All was done according to 1968 AEC criteria for surface radiological contamination. Radiation monitors continued to visit the site on a regular basis.

A 1972 monitoring crew discovered that some previously buried material northeast of the access shaft had become slightly exposed, and the DOE paid closer attention to that section for the next five years. In 1977, the DOE contracted with Reynolds Electrical and Engineering Co., Inc., and Fenix and Scisson, Inc., to decontaminate the Gnome site. In 1977, DOE guidelines had been altered from the 1968 dose rate measurements to soil contamination limits, two noninterchangeable systems of data collection.[60] Two years later, this $2 million project began in earnest. Workers reactivated power lines, improved roads to the Gnome site, and cleaned the area water wells. About twenty-five workers took contaminated surface soil and salt, crushed and slurried it, and then pumped the mixture into the Gnome cavity, filling it to approximately 80 percent capacity. Workers placed other Gnome waste into barrels for shipment to low-level storage facilities at the NTS. When they finally returned the land to the custody of the BLM in 1980, the DOE placed no restrictions on surface use. Today cattle forage over the site, which also abounds with wildlife. The region boasts one of the highest raptor concentrations in the world. Five area ranchers also benefit from the Gnome well, drilled by the AEC in 1961, which was made operational in 1982.

The site of Project Gnome, however, is still surveyed on an annual basis. A 1991 visit found that while underground tritium and cesium levels exceeded EPA standards, the contamination remained confined to the site. "There are no certainties in life," one official noted, "but from the hydrological reports I've read it's not going to get into the drinking water."[61] In 1995, ecologist Jim Kenney led a team of New Mexico Environmental Evaluators to survey Gnome yet again. Although the team made no major recommendations, they agreed that "additional work" would be necessary to see if any contamination existed at greater soil depths or outside the survey area.[62]

As scientists and technicians from DOE contractor Westinghouse prepared the Gnome area for the highly anticipated opening of the Waste Isolation Pilot Plant (WIPP), they occasionally discovered trace isotopes of plutonium and americium in the region. These radionuclides had not leaked from any WIPP waste. Instead, they derived from either the plume of steam raised by Gnome or from a well-known Gnome waste burial site.[63] Although the radiation from Gnome is still measurable, scientists believe that it has been unable to enter the region's ecosystem. The current consensus is that it is not harmful to either wildlife or human activity.[64]

Gasbuggy

Over two hundred weapons-related and Plowshare explosions occurred during the six years from Gnome to Gasbuggy, the third and final New Mexico nuclear detonation of December 10, 1967. But Gasbuggy was also hailed at the time as a "pioneering" nuclear project. It was touted as the first joint federal government–private industry venture of the Plowshare Program. The private industry was El Paso Natural Gas, and the goal was to draw on underground nuclear detonations to improve gas flows from low-production natural gas fields.[65]

Gas companies had relied on the technique of hydraulic fracturing of low-yield fields for years. In "tight," or low-flow, rock strata, field workers would inject explosives, such as nitroglycerin, to create cavities that would improve gas flow. In fact, El Paso Natural Gas had often used nitroglycerin to enhance their San Juan Basin fields in the Farmington area. Such conventional fracturing utilized between one thousand and twenty-five hundred quarts of explosive per blast. If successful, these fractures might increase gas production 10 percent over a twenty-year period, the usual lifetime of such a field. The hoped-for nuclear fracturing experiment at Gasbuggy was set at a high level, twenty-six kilotons, slightly larger than the blasts at Hiroshima and Nagasaki combined. It became the equivalent of 12.5 million quarts of nitroglycerin. Scientists hoped that this fracture would capture, perhaps, 70 percent of all gas in the area.[66]

The acknowledged national energy crisis of the late 1960s fueled the urgency of the program. If the nuclear-fracturing technique at Gasbuggy proved successful, one report suggested, it could be used in similar low-permeability natural gas fields all through the mountain West. Some Bureau of Mines officials even predicted that Gasbuggy-type explosions might double the nation's gas reserves.[67] Officials cautioned, however, that the final results of this nuclear experiment might not be known for several years.

In June 1965, the assistant secretary of the interior informed New Mexico congressman Joseph M. Montoya and Governor Jack Campbell that the AEC had decided to test a ten-kiloton device in the state's gas fields.[68] The site chosen for the nuclear fracturing of low-yield fields lay on El Paso Natural Gas properties in a pine-covered forest in the San Juan Basin of the Carson National Forest, just west of the Jicarilla Apache Reservation. The closest community of any size was Farmington, then a town of about twenty-three thousand, fifty-five air miles to the west. The hamlet of Dulce, with five hundred people, lay fifteen miles to the northeast. Navajo Dam was about fifty miles to the northwest.

A visitor to the Gasbuggy installation in 1967 would have discovered a typical Four Corners mining venture. Work crews drilled several exploratory holes and then a very large (18.5-inch diameter) hole 4,240 feet into the Lewis Shale formation. They used extremely large pipes, which proved difficult to handle, to house the nuclear device. AEC officials placed seismic recording devices in Dulce, Baca, Farmington, El Vado Dam, and Navajo Dam. New Mexico State Police also made plans to close all roads in the vicinity at zero hour. As a final precaution, El Paso Natural Gas workers physically cut apart all gas pipelines within a five-mile radius of Gasbuggy ground zero.

In general, the numerous state, federal, and tribal agencies involved worked together well. The Jicarilla Apache tribe, which derived much of its revenue from oil and gas production, approved the experiment. The state of New Mexico built a $100,000 all-weather road through the Jicarilla Reservation to the site. Congress approved the funds, and the secretary of the interior, Stuart Udall, signed all necessary documents. The AEC, the U.S. Department of the Interior's Bureau of Mines, LRL staff, and El Paso Natural Gas had all studied this concept for over six years. Both Washington and private companies had their fingers crossed that such nuclear stimulation might be the answer to the nation's energy woes.

As with previous Plowshare shots, the AEC welcomed all publicity for this venture. They supplied speakers to the Farmington Elks Club, which hosted a popular two-day preshot symposium in September. Local residents heard numerous lectures from top government officials. Fred

The Gasbuggy experiment resembled a conventional drilling operation. AEC photo. Courtesy of the Los Alamos National Laboratory Archives.

Holzer of the LRL, author of an extensive preshot report, spoke there, as did several other scientists. Discussion ranged over the origin of Plowshare, the purpose of Gasbuggy, possible ground motion at the time of the blast, and, especially, safety measures. The speakers all emphasized safety, although not always in the most eloquent form. As scientist Roland F. Beers phrased it: "Nearly all centers of population within the expected area of human perception will be instrumented."[69]

The AEC also staged a major symposium for the news media at the Albuquerque Civic Auditorium on Saturday, December 9. New Mexico's lieutenant governor, Lee Francis, welcomed the various dignitaries, including about three hundred top-level visitors from government and industry. The group later boarded chartered buses to Farmington for another Dedication Day program on Sunday.

By this time, however, the story of Plowshare underground explosions had lost its media glamour.[70] The *Farmington Times* might hail Gasbuggy as the top state story of the year, but this did not translate to the national stage. The national media were conspicuous by their absence at the Gasbuggy shot. Interestingly, opposition to the test was similarly absent. No group made any legal attempt to prevent either the detonation or the later flaring of the radioactive gas. Contemporary criticism seemed limited to a crank letter from California and a more balanced one from W. A. Boyle, president of the United Mine Workers of America. Boyle called the explosion a "mad proposal" that would release "dangerous amounts of radioactivity into the earth's atmosphere."[71] Earlier concerns that Gasbuggy might cause the collapse of Navajo Dam or El Vado Dam had apparently been satisfied.

As with Gnome, the AEC encouraged the local public to attend the detonation. The thirty-minute countdown was broadcast over a public address system for nearby listeners. All went as planned, and at 12:30 P.M., Sunday, December 10, 1967, Gasbuggy exploded. The blast created an underground cavity 160 feet in diameter, which soon collapsed to form a zone or chimney about the size of a half-block-square, thirty-five-story building.

The ground at surface ground zero rumbled but did not collapse. The only surface damage came with a few minor cracks in the dirt access road, a bent axle to a cable reel, and modest damage to some electrical equipment at the control point. Nearby gas wells, some as close as twenty-six hundred feet to surface ground zero, experienced no structural damage.[72]

In fact, in spite of all the publicity, Gasbuggy proved to be quite without drama. As Al Kendrick of Aztec recalled in 1995, "We didn't hear anything. There was a shock wave that was visible. The vegetation moved as the shock wave came in our direction. We were primarily looking for something to erupt in the air."[73]

About eight hours after detonation, monitors detected small amounts of xenon and krypton at the head of the firing cable. Radioactive gas had somehow found its way up the cable to the surface. Within an hour and a half, these cables were sealed off. Eight hours later, all but a small area adjacent to the well had been opened to normal activity.

As soon as possible, officials tried to assess the consequences of Gasbuggy. The reentry drill holes brought some additional radiation to the surface, but this too was carefully monitored. The flaring of the gas from the subsequently drilled test wells also released radionuclides into the air. By January 10, 1968, El Paso Natural Gas workers had completed their reentry drilling. Then the testing began.

Unfortunately, the results of the tests did not bear out earlier hopes. Prior gas pressure in the Gasbuggy reservoir was about 1,050 pounds per square inch (psi), but after the shot, the pressure registered at only 950 psi. Hopes existed, however, that the pressure would soon rise to normal or above. Fred Holzer's preliminary postshot report was pessimistic,[74] but he admitted that his views were not shared by all El Paso Natural Gas people. The AEC cautioned that everything needed to be further analyzed over the next years.[75]

The professional scientific journals expressed similar caution about the results. In October 1973, the *Journal of Petroleum Technology* ran an extensive article on the Gasbuggy experiment. They listed as the crucial question the extent to which the blast had fractured the rocks beyond the "chimney." They concluded that Gasbuggy had extended only about 220 feet beyond the chimney, a relatively small distance indeed.[76] Further experiments of nuclear fracturing at Rulison, Colorado (September 10, 1969, forty-three kilotons), and Rio Blanco, Colorado (simultaneous detonations of thirty-three-kiloton devices, May 17, 1973), also proved disappointing. One finds at the time such phrases as "unique experiment" and "technical success," but this was just whistling in the dark.[77] Although the Gasbuggy experiment increased the San Juan Basin gas by a modest amount, the gain never approximated earlier expectations.

In addition, of course, the gas in the vicinity of the blast had become radioactive. While El Paso Natural Gas spokesmen argued that this radioactive gas could be easily mixed with other gas and thus diluted to totally safe levels, by 1970 public opinion had begun to shift. The anxiety over strontium-90, opposition to fallout from the NTS, and later (1979) the accident at Three Mile Island had made Americans aware of the dangers of radioactivity. No amount of public relations from the El Paso Gas Company could have convinced New Mexico citizens to let radioactive gas, no matter at what level, into their homes.[78] DOE hydrologist Kevin Leary put it succinctly in 1995: "They tried to stimulate gas flow by fracturing the sandstone. It didn't work."[79]

Although there was little release of radionuclides at the time of the shot, when El Paso Natural Gas workers returned to drill the cavity, they did release additional radioactivity into the air, especially in flow tests one and two, conducted on January 12–13, 1968. The flaring of the gas produced several radionuclides, chiefly xenon-133, with a 5.3-day half-life, and also low levels of tritium.[80]

The release was deemed acceptable, and except for a hastily erected fence, the area soon returned to its chief preshot use—hunting. Locals jested that the deer there were easy to bag because they glowed in the dark. Concern remained on a jocular level until 1972. That year the DOE instituted a hydraulic monitoring program that has continued to the present. In August and September 1978, the El Paso Gas Company, which had completed testing two years earlier, cleaned up the site by plugging surface holes and removing all surface features. The large tank filled with tritium-contaminated liquid was reinserted into the earth and the hole capped. Workers placed other low-level or impossible-to-determine waste into barrels. Afterward they sealed, labeled, and externally steam-cleaned the containers before shipping them to the NTS for storage. Careful monitoring of all personnel engaged in the cleanup revealed no overexposure. The DOE decided to allow one well to remain open as part of a long-term monitoring program.[81] Officials placed a small stone marker at the site to detail its historical significance and then left.

In the late 1980s, the DOE office in Nevada made a series of surface-monitoring missions to examine all non-NTS sites that had been used for underground nuclear tests. Concern for long-term hydrologic monitoring also sent teams to Gasbuggy in both 1986 and 1994 to examine the possible migration of the radionuclides.

The teams found that most of the radiation was still contained in the underground cavity, 90 percent locked in the fused rock glass. Only the drilling of the cavity and the firing of gas for test purposes had brought radionuclides to the surface. These releases had both been well documented and, according to records, controlled. The team found no soil or water samples that exceeded DOE site restoration criteria, nor did they uncover any waste barrels at the site. The only man-made isotope they found was cesium-137, which proved detectable in certain forest litter piles.

As for the vital question of possible groundwater contamination, the team was optimistic. They estimated that water in the Ojo Alamo sandstone moved at 0.04 feet per year. By the time it reached the San Juan River, about fifty miles away, the tritium, strontium-90, and cesium-137 would have all decayed to levels well below guidelines.[82]

Conclusion

The sites of New Mexico's three nuclear explosions today are all commemorated with modest markers. But their legacy extends far beyond the brief messages inscribed on these brass plaques. Although the Trinity test produced no controversy at the time, its inevitable aftermath in Hiroshima and Nagasaki has inaugurated a discussion of tactics and morality among historians and the general populace that shows little likelihood of disappearing.[83]

The Plowshare experiments of Gnome and Gasbuggy were, perhaps, an attempt to compensate for this tragic loss of life at Hiroshima and Nagasaki. Unfortunately, they proved terribly disappointing. As one 1978 book on Plowshare phrased it: "Experts still cannot agree whether nuclear explosives employed for peaceful ends many eventually result in damage of greater weight than the gains they provide."[84]

The most enduring legacy of New Mexico's nuclear detonations, however, rests with the impact on the environment. All the blasts produced radionuclides that contaminated both air and soil to varying degrees. Although the federal government has cleaned up each site on several occasions, residues still remain.[85] There is no water at Trinity, but officials routinely monitor nearby Chupadera Mesa and test the wells in both Rio Arriba and Eddy counties to see if underground aquifers reflect migration of radioactive materials. Such monitoring, as one spokesman at Gnome noted in 1978, "will be continued indefinitely."[86] Perhaps this is the ultimate legacy of New Mexico's three atomic detonations.

CHAPTER SEVEN

The History *of*
Atomic Photography

*W*hen the scientists from Los Alamos triggered the Trinity Site nuclear explosion on July 16, 1945, they also created a variety of scientific/technical subfields. One of these involved photography, for the blast not only introduced a startling new breed of high-speed cameras, it also inaugurated a subdiscipline that would eventually march around the world: atomic photography.

This specialty began in 1943 with G—later M—Division, the optics group, under the initial direction of Julian E. Mack. It was considerably enhanced when El Paso native Berlyn Brixner joined as the main photographer. Brixner had been working in Albuquerque as a photogrammetric engineer with the Soil Conservation Service when he received a phone call from his childhood friend David Hawkins, who was already living on the Hill. When Brixner drove up for an interview, Julian Mack showed him the plans—still theoretical, as nothing had been built—for a revolutionary high-speed camera and asked if he thought he could operate it. When Brixner said yes, Mack hired him immediately.

While working on the Manhattan Project from 1943 to 1945, Brixner participated in a variety of photographic breakthroughs. The group designed and constructed numerous specialized cameras (often shielded in armor) to record high-explosive blasts and a stereoscopic camera to record the imploding hemispheres that formed the heart of the plutonium weapon under construction. Brixner was also instrumental in creating a high-speed rotating mirror camera designed to capture every aspect of the anticipated mushroom cloud. He also maintained that it was his strong opposition to the Malpais area south of Grants—the lava flows there would hamper photography, he said—that proved crucial in the eventual selection of the Jornada del Muerto as the site for the eventual Trinity test.

After the war ended, Brixner remained on the Hill to head the optics division. For over three decades he worked at the cutting edge of atomic photography. Part of the crew that photographed the aboveground blasts at Bikini atoll, Eniwetok, and the Nevada Test Site (NTS), he also helped invent several new cameras and lenses. Working closely with physicist Edward Teller, Brixner helped develop cameras that used revolving mirrors to provide ten thousand pictures per second, later raised to three million pictures per second. Although he retired in 1978, Brixner lived in Los Alamos for many years.

In the spring of 1945, the main assignment of the optics group was to provide a "complete photographic record coverage" of all aspects of the Trinity test. Of course, there would be no possibility of rehearsal or "retake." Mack and his staff of fourteen set up fifty-five cameras, most of them motion picture cameras because hand operation was not deemed fast enough. The M crew also built four concrete bunkers for the cameras, two (manned) at ten thousand feet from ground zero and two (remote operated) only eight hundred yards away. Remnants of the latter can still be seen by visitors to Trinity Site.[1]

At T minus thirty seconds, the automatic cameras began to roll. Brixner and his assistant, Ralph Conrad, who were stationed at the north ten thousand bunker, oversaw both handheld and turret-mounted cameras there. After the blast, they tried to follow the upward path of the mushroom cloud as best they could. They were busy filming when the radiation monitors shouted that everyone needed to leave immediately (the cloud had broken into three parts and the central portion drifted directly over

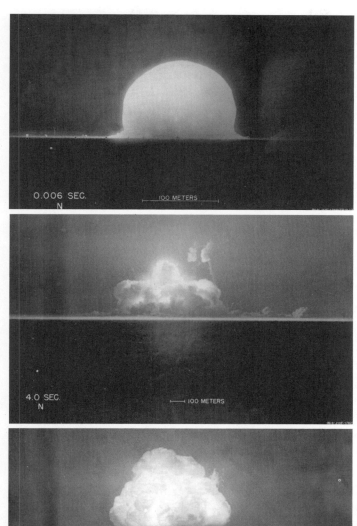

0.006 SEC.
N   100 METERS

4.0 SEC.
N   100 METERS

9.0 SEC.
N   100 METERS

Berlyn Brixner's striking images of the Trinity fireball on July 16, 1945. Courtesy of Los Alamos National Laboratory.

north ten thousand). So they grabbed their film and hastily jumped onto the retreating trucks.

Brixner sent the film to Wendover Army Air Base in Utah for development, and the results were shown at the next colloquium at Los Alamos. General Leslie R. Groves requested that the footage be duplicated for newsreel release, and eventually clips from the Trinity blast received worldwide distribution. Photographers Esther Samra and Rachael Fermi have calculated that Mack and Brixner's cameras made over one hundred thousand exposures of the Trinity blast,[2] making it the most photographed event in the world up until that time. As Brixner later confessed, "Even I was amazed that I had made such spectacular pictures."[3] Although Brixner's Trinity Site photographs are widely recognized today, it was not until the late 1980s that he began to receive credit for them. Berlyn Brixner thus has the dubious distinction of ranking as the world's first atomic photographer.

But others took photos at Trinity Site as well. Lab employees E. Wallace and L. D. P. King provided most of the extensive black-and-white photographic record of the construction of Trinity and the arming of the "Gadget" (the code name for the bomb) atop the one-hundred-foot steel tower at Ground Zero. Julian Mack shot numerous images as well. Just prior to the July 16 blast, Special Engineer Detachment member Jack Aeby purchased a roll of the relatively new color film, and he took the lone color photographs of the Trinity mushroom cloud.[4]

Three weeks later, Sergeant George Caron, tail gunner for the *Enola Gay*, joined this select crew. As B-29 pilot Paul Tibbets banked the plane, Caron shot several photographs of the awesome cloud that rose over the now-devastated city of Hiroshima. Los Alamos physicist Robert Serber had originally been scheduled to fly aboard the observation plane on August 9 for the Nagasaki bombing run, primarily to record the blast with a new Fastax camera, one that he alone knew how to operate. But when the plane came up one parachute short, Serber found himself bumped from this assignment. Thus, the main images of the Nagasaki cloud derive from bombardier Charles Levy, who took a series of snapshots with his own personal camera.[5]

Hiroshima photographer Yoshito Matsushige entered this select circle through more tragic circumstances. A Hiroshima native, in August 1945 he was serving both as a reporter for the Japanese army and as a photographer for the *Chugoku Shimbun* newspaper. Matsushige and his wife were eating breakfast about 2.7 kilometers from the epicenter when the bomb detonated. Grabbing his tiny six-by-six-inch Mamiya viewfinder camera and two rolls of black-and-white film (twelve exposures to the roll), Matsushige hopped on his bicycle and raced to army headquarters. Stunned by the death and devastation that surrounded him, he was only able to click the shutter on five scenes that day: a police station housing a temporary medical treatment operation, the backs of several female students seeking aid, two shots of his now-destroyed home, and an injured soldier overseeing the distribution of food. These images remain as the sole known photographs of Hiroshima on August 6, 1945.

Years later, Matsushige was asked why he didn't use up all his twenty-four shots. He confessed that he was too overwhelmed by the horrors surrounding him. "I couldn't take pictures of so many terrible scenes," he said.[6] In fact, his tears fogged his viewfinder on several shots. The power of Matsushige's five images hinges on knowing their precise context. They are not well recognized in the States.

After Hiroshima and Nagasaki, the list of atomic photographers began to grow exponentially. Numerous cameramen accompanied the U.S. forces of occupation to Japan. Shortly after the surrender, Robert Serber visited both destroyed cities and recorded a number of powerful images of the destruction. To satisfy the demands of American newsmen, General Groves opened Trinity Site to the national media. As the ground was still highly radioactive, visitors were allowed to remain only twenty minutes. Lab physician Louis Hempelmann had to caution photographers that their film might be ruined if they overstayed their time.[7]

The Crossroads blasts at Bikini in the spring of 1946 opened the door of atomic photography even wider. Designed to demonstrate the power of the fissioned atom to the world, the United States invited hundreds of international lensmen and reporters to attend. The ensuing coverage of shots Able (an air drop on ships) and Baker (an underwater blast) filled newspapers and magazines from Moscow to Dublin and from Rome to Paris. *Life* covered the event thoroughly for American readers.[8] The next year, a special photographic group, the 1352nd, of the newly formed U.S. Air Force, borrowed from the latest Hollywood technology to systematically

The underwater Crossroads/Baker blast of 1946 produced a
tower of radioactive water over a mile and a half high. This
image of the mushroom cloud was published around the world.
Courtesy of the Los Alamos National Laboratory.

record the hundreds of aboveground blasts that would follow. They closed shop in 1969.

Indeed, from the late 1940s forward, the mushroom cloud became a familiar visual artifact for Cold War America. Art historian Peter B. Hales has argued that the central icon of the postwar atomic culture was the "mushroom cloud rising above the lush tropical atolls of the South Pacific or the wastelands of the Great American Desert."[9] Historian Jon Hunner, whose father worked in the nuclear industry during the 1960s, grew to maturity surrounded by photographs of atomic blasts on his living room walls. He assumed that other children had similar images on theirs as well.[10] For over three decades, the mushroom cloud became the ultimate symbol of "atomic kitsch."

Ironically, in the hands of talented professionals, these mushroom cloud images could often be "beautiful." Yet they almost always filled a viewer with a vague sense of discomfort that the "beauty" could never quite dispel. Moreover, the ubiquitous cloud images often concealed as much as they revealed. It was not until the fall of 1952, for example, that *Life* printed the first photographs of the burned corpses and devastation of the two destroyed Japanese cities. The ultimate concealment, of course, extended to the nation's burgeoning nuclear weapons industry. From uranium-mining operations to nuclear processing plants, from weapons laboratories to assembly sites, from missile silos to sophisticated air force delivery systems, the nation's nuclear complex lay well below the public radar. In truth, it had become virtually "invisible."

In 1981 California-born photographer Robert Del Tredici began researching the nation's nuclear weapons complex. Dismayed by the hidden nature thereof, he set about tracking it down and in the process crossed paths with several other photographers who were documenting various other aspects of the nuclear industry. In 1986 he organized the Atomic Photographers Guild. The official mandate made their purpose clear: to "reveal all aspects of [the nuclear age], making it visually accessible."[11]

The Atomic Photographers Guild proved international from the start. It included pioneers Brixner and Matsushige; several Russian, German, and Japanese lensmen; and crusading American photographers such as Carol Gallagher, Mark Ruwedel, and Paul Shabroom. Formal membership hovered around thirty.

Many of the guild members had either published books on the theme and/or exhibited in such museums as the Museum of Modern Art, the Metropolitan Museum of Art, and the Los Angeles County Museum of Art. Still, they discovered that their new guild raised their profile considerably. A year after the founding, they held a show at the international exhibition at the New York Open Center in conjunction with the first Global Radiation Victims Conference. The next year, they showed again at the Palais de Congrès in Montreal, this time to coordinate with the annual Congress of the International Physicians for the Prevention of Nuclear War.

Their third, and by far the most publicized, show opened in Berlin in 1990. After traveling throughout Germany, it moved to Copenhagen. (The show continued to travel in Germany for another five years.) An elaborate catalog, *Bombensicher* (1991), accompanied this exhibition. A big San Francisco show titled "Nuclear Matters" followed shortly thereafter.

The photographs shown ranged from Brixner's "bubble" imagery of the Trinity Site explosion to Matsushige's less well-known five Hiroshima shots to Russian photographer Igor Kostin's image of a bewildered guard at Chernobyl. The photographers also displayed shots of grieving Navajo mining families; the Church Rock, New Mexico, radiation spill; a Montana missile silo; and angry Middletown, Pennsylvania, residents at a hearing on the proposed cleanup of the nuclear generation station at Three Mile Island.[12]

In their latest group showing, the Atomic Photographers Guild displayed their images at the Photographers Workshop Gallery in Toronto in early 2001. The exhibit traveled to the Art Gallery of Peterborough, Ontario, the "Diefenbunker" nuclear fallout bastion outside Ottawa, and the Anna Leonowens Gallery in Halifax, Nova Scotia. A catalog, *Visibility and Invisibility in the Nuclear Era*, accompanied these exhibitions.[13]

The end of the Cold War in 1991 served to whet public interest in atomic photography. The new openness by both the United States and the former Soviet Union allowed access to hundreds of previously restricted documents and images. In addition, the nation's belated acknowledgment that its Cold War nuclear complex had damaged the lives of tens of thousands of industry workers, uranium miners, and citizens living near weapons production and testing sites produced a number of photographic reformers. James Crnkovich, for example, spent over a decade photographing whatever he could find of nuclear culture—from Great Plains missile silos, nuclear factories, and protest movements to diners, pizza parlors, car washes, and other commercial establishments with the word *atomic* in their name. Similarly, Barbara Norfleet turned her photographic attention to the Savannah River Plant of South Carolina and the people who had lost their property to it. A number of nonguild lensmen have joined the bandwagon as well. Russian Galina Moskaleva photographed a chilling set of images in the "Children Who Have Had Thyroid Operations from the Chernobyl Disaster" series in June 1996. In a related vein, Navajo Reservation photographer Milton Snow took several images of Navajos working in the uranium mines during the 1950s. A generation later,

Douglas Brugge of the Tufts School of Public Health created an exhibit, a video, and a book of images on the plight of the Navajo uranium miners.[14] The list could be extended.

During the last two decades, the following seven books of atomic photography have probably reached the greatest audience. Taken together, they represent the first concerted effort to reveal—both in documentary and artistic formats—the implications of the nation's nuclear subculture.

The most prolific atomic photographer is guild founder Robert Del Tredici. Born in California in 1938 and trained for eight years in a seminary run by Sulpicians, Del Tredici was drawn into the nuclear world with the 1978 near meltdown of the reactor at Three Mile Island in southeastern Pennsylvania. Over the next year, he made a dozen trips into the region and spent hundreds of hours interviewing residents and taking photographs. The Sierra Club published his work as *The People of Three Mile Island* in 1980.[15] It was subsequently expanded and translated into German by 2001 as *Die Menschen von Harrisburg*.

Buoyed by the success of this volume, Del Tredici spent the next six years exploring the darker corners of the nation's nuclear weapons establishment. This second collection of interviews and images appeared in 1987 under the title *At Work in the Fields of the Bomb*.[16] Del Tredici's approach is straightforward. Whether shooting bomb factories or people, the artist gives us bold images of Navajo uranium miners; plutonium plant workers; Leroy Mathieson, the Texas Catholic bishop who urged his parishioners to leaver their jobs at the Pantex nuclear weapons final assembly plant outside of Amarillo; Paul Tibbets, the man in charge of dropping the first atomic bombs; Admiral Hyman Rickover, inventor of the nuclear submarine; Edward Teller, the "father" of the H-bomb; and Dr. Alice Stewart, one of the world's leading authorities on the biological impact of low-level ionizing radiation. Under Del Tredici's lens, many of the faces of the atomic pioneers, victims, and activists stare back at us as if we had suddenly opened a friend's family album.

When Del Tredici moves overseas, his images assume even greater power. (He is married to a Japanese woman, Setsumi Katagiri, whom he met as an interpreter while interviewing *hibakusha*, or A-bomb survivors in Nagasaki.) In Japan, he presents an image of aged hibakusha and a handful of the very paper cranes folded by twelve-year-old radiation victim Sadako Sasaki. He closes the volume with a photo taken in Swedish Lapland of a large commercial meat locker full of reindeer carcasses too radioactively contaminated (by cesium-137 from the Chernobyl cloud) for human consumption.

In addition to his black-and-white photographs, Del Tredici has included over sixty pages of interviews and field notes. He is as open here as he is with his photographs. When Edward Teller says that one of Del Tredici's questions makes "no sense," he reports it as stated. From discussions with Sam Cohen, "father" of the neutron bomb, to an interview with Yoshito Matsushige, Del Tredici keeps a distanced point of view in both image and text.

Still, only a Neanderthal could miss the meaning of his message. The photographer has "constructed" his photos so that the viewer comes up against the irony of the nuclear world at every turn. The two Pantex public relations men stand in front of a replica of the Nagasaki atomic bomb ("Fat Man") as nonchalantly as if they were posing in front of the Washington Monument. The frozen smile of the attractive Goodyear sales representative beside a Pershing II missile reentry nose cone forms an image not soon forgotten. Although Del Tredici's photos seem at first glance to be "straightforward," on a closer inspection they are ever laced with irony.

In the early 1990s, *At Work in the Fields of the Bomb* caught the attention of the recently elected Bill Clinton administration. Under the direction of Secretary of Energy Hazel O'Leary, the government inaugurated an "openness initiative" regarding the previously submerged nuclear complex. Not only did the DOE open their files to public inspection, as part of their initiative they contracted with Del Tredici in 1993 to photograph the extensive—but not well-known—cleanup process. Del Tredici jumped at the chance to revisit the weapons site he had earlier haunted as a lone freelancer. Now he could rephotograph the complex as someone "from headquarters."

Del Tredici's efforts in this regard emerged in the form of three government reports on the present (*Closing the Circle on the Splitting of the Atom*), the past (*Linking Legacies*), and the future (*From Cleanup to Stewardship*). Overall, his work provided the first photographic depiction of "the second half" of the nuclear cycle: "dealing with the waste and contamination from

A Goodyear sales representative displays Goodyear's contribution to the Pershing II missile system at the U.S. Army Weapons Bazaar, Sheraton Hotel, Washington, D.C., October 15, 1986. Photo by Robert Del Tredici.

nuclear weapons production."[17] With these documents, the nation's nuclear complex began to take on visual form. Still, as Del Tredici once observed, "the closer you get to nuclear weapons, the harder it is to see them."[18]

Since Del Tredici has taught most of his career in Montreal, it was inevitable that he would turn his attention to the Canadian nuclear industry as well. Working with mathematician and scientist Dr. Gordon Edwards, he created a photographic exhibition for the Confederation Art Center on Prince Edward Island titled "The Nuclear Map of Canada Project" that documented, in his familiar style, the Canadian uranium mining, milling, and enrichment industry; Canada's nuclear reactors; and the ever-present reality of radioactive waste disposal. Informative and provocative as these images may have been, the heart of Del Tredici's exhibit consisted of a gigantic (six-by-four-foot) map depicting all the known nuclear facilities in Canada. The first of its kind, the map has seen wide distribution.[19]

Peter Goin, who teaches photography at the University of Nevada, Reno, uses a similar approach. Goin, however, shoots largely in color, and he usually excludes people from his photos. His book *Nuclear Landscapes* (1991) begins with a shot of the monument at Trinity Site and closes with images of nuclear ruins on Bikini and Eniwetok atolls.[20] The heart of the volume, however, lies with Goin's photographic rendition of the Nevada Test Site and the Hanford Nuclear Reservation in Washington State.

The NTS is bleak under the best of conditions, but Goin's artful images accentuate the washed-out majesty of Nevada's vast endless space. His shot of Yucca Flats, where numerous aboveground tests were conducted until 1963, is almost serene. That of Jackass Flats, equally tranquil, was taken from the top of Yucca Mountain, doubly ironic because Yucca Mountain looms as the probable disposal site for the nation's high-level nuclear waste. The image of Sedan Crater, a gigantic crater from a Plowshare underground explosion, is truly awesome. The numerous shots of abandoned structures such as distorted railroad trestles, a collapsed hangar, and the ruins of an artificially constructed NTS "Doom Town" house might under a different set of circumstances be viewed as remnants of a southwestern ghost town.

Goin treats the high desert surrounding Hanford in a similar fashion. From tree stumps of an abandoned orchard, lost when the Manhattan Project confiscated the area for a plutonium production facility, to decommissioned reactors, the viewer wanders through strange juxtapositions of empty space and rusted-out machinery. The "burial ground" area—home of several underground storage tanks filled with thousands of gallons of high-level liquid nuclear wastes—looks strangely placid. Only a glance at the captions alerts the viewer to the real meaning of this nuclear landscape. Like Del Tredici, Goin has loaded his camera with as much irony as film. The contrasts between the captions and the landscapes seldom miss their mark.

As a long introductory essay by Eugenia Parry Janis to *Nuclear Enchantment* shows, University of New Mexico photographer Patrick Nagatani is cut from a far different piece of cloth.[21] In *Nuclear Enchantment*, the Chicago-born Japanese American artist has carefully constructed each of his forty photographic nuclear images so that they serve as atomic metaphors rather than as a straightforward documentary. He achieves this effect through the manipulation of color (especially the sky), collage techniques, and the frequent appearance of his vast collection of model military airplanes. No viewer would ever take Nagatani's images for "realistic" photographs, but no viewer could miss their meaning, either.

Nagatani's varied imagery remains complex. One needs Eugenia Parry Janis's explanation that the figures of carp in his photo of the Jackpile Mine uranium tailings at Laguna Pueblo reflect a traditional Japanese celebration of life. Similarly, the viewer needs to know that the striped figures dominating the foreground of the Missile Park at White Sands Missile Range in Alamogordo are *koshare*, or Tewa ritual clowns. But even without this explanation, most New Mexicans would recognize the floating green bits in Nagatani's Trinity Site photo as pieces of trinitite, the radioactive fused sand created by the 1945 ball of nuclear fire. Most New Mexicans would also recognize the meaning of the three dead Vaughn roadrunners lying next to a truck hauling nuclear waste to the WIPP site near Carlsbad. And no citizen of the modern era could miss the implications of Nagatani's final shot, a father and child (Nagatani and his son) standing under an umbrella amid a downpour of sinister black rain.

Nagatani's manipulation of color is masterful. The sky above the Navajo tract homes situated next to abandoned uranium mill tailings in Shiprock looms as an eerie red, while the air in an elementary school classroom full of students discussing radon gas has turned a sickly green. The Lysistrata image of the National Atomic Museum in Albuquerque might be described as "millennial red," while the background of the uranium mine near Mount Taylor emerges as an uncomfortable yellow. The most telling color manipulation, however, rests with Nagatani's photo of snow falling in the contaminated Mortandad Canyon in Los Alamos. Because the ground is "hot," it melts the snow and remains strangely green throughout this otherwise peaceful winter scene. While Nagatani's images have been constructed in a way that Del Tredici's and Goin's have not, all the photographers have developed their images in the same bath of irony.

Carole Gallagher's *American Ground Zero: The Secret Nuclear War* strikes a different chord.[22] A native New Yorker, Gallagher was spurred to investigate the plight of the "downwinders" of Utah and northern Arizona by the nuclear disaster at Three Mile Island. What she thought would be a brief months-long assignment became a decade-long, all-consuming commitment. She interviewed one thousand people living east of the Nevada Test Site, in an area once described by the Atomic Energy Commission as "virtually uninhabitable desert terrain."[23] From the early 1950s to the test ban treaty of 1963, the Atomic Energy Commission set off a hundred aboveground atomic explosions—almost one a month for ten years—and the prevailing winds carried the brunt of the radioactive fallout away from Las Vegas and inexorably over these largely Mormon hamlets and villages. By the late 1950s, a number of the one hundred thousand "virtual inhabitants" had noticed increased local sheep and cattle deaths and, even more terrifying, a much higher-than-normal rate of mental retardation, solid cancers, and childhood leukemias. Author Terry Tempest Williams has written poignantly of her own family as a "clan of one-breasted women."[24]

The Atomic Energy Commission, however, assured everyone that all needs were being carefully considered. Now, over forty years later, there is no question that this aboveground testing, plus the accidental "venting" of several underground NTS explosions, has brought deep misery to the people who lived in this region. In 1988, Congress finally acknowledged responsibility and awarded modest compensation to the victims.

Over thirty publishers rejected Gallagher's book of photographs and interviews until MIT Press took a chance and discovered, to its delight, that the first print run of ten thousand sold out immediately. Gallagher's photographic style bears some resemblance to Del Tredici's. She presents a series of full-face, black-and-white portraits of NTS workers, atomic veterans, and downwinders, interspersed with the Nevada/Utah landscape. Scattered photos taken by Dorothea Lange in the early 1950s offer a tranquil "before" to Gallagher's painful "after." The images are intimately linked to the texts—usually interviews—that flank the facing pages. The tragedies that swept over their lives spurred the downwinders to bitter eloquence:

> Josephine Simkins, "I feel like we were really used, and I'll never trust our government again"; Elmer Pickett, "They done to us what the Russians couldn't do"; Glenna Orton, "I'm just a person. I'm just as important as anyone in Las Vegas or New York"; Frances Spendlove, "I don't believe anything the government says"; Delayne Evans, " I love the country and I love my government but I think they sure done us wrong."[25]

The combination of Gallagher's stark black-and-white portraits, plus the power of the tragic texts, leaves the reader with deep weariness of heart.

While Gallagher occasionally draws on irony, her book hinges largely on rage. In a 1993 newspaper interview, she used terms such as *holocaust* and *original sin* to describe the situation of the downwinders.[26] She is unsparing in her criticism of the hierarchy of the Latter-day Saint (Mormon) church, the Atomic Energy Commission, and the U.S. Government. The artist's skillful juxtapositions of family-style photographs (although many of the "family" are obviously very ill) with the straightforward texts bring the point home. Although Gallagher closes her volume with several irenic shots of St. George, Utah, and its surrounding landscape, her positive images are far too few to change the melancholy tenor of this study. *American Ground Zero* forms one of the most uncompromising books of the post–World War II generation.

Gallagher's rage over the government's duplicity and the Latter-day Saints' silence contrasts sharply with the photographs compiled by Esther Samra and Rachael Fermi in *Picturing the Bomb* (1995). Drawing on recently opened photographic archives as well as family connections (Rachael is physicist Enrico Fermi's granddaughter), they have gathered a vast array of images of the 1943–45 era that have never been seen before. Although General Groves did not actually prohibit cameras at Los Alamos, he did insist that people record only family gatherings, such as hikes, picnics, and various parties. Thus, the images in *Picturing the Bomb* reflect neither rage nor irony; instead they display the "ordinariness" of life on the various Manhattan Project sites: a Girl Scout troop on its way to a meeting at Oak Ridge; the segregated toilets and housing units of eastern Tennessee; Kim and Kathy Manley, about three and six, respectively, dressed in their Los Alamos Sunday best; two-year-old Peter Oppenheimer chomping on one of his father's pipes; three-year-old Paul Teller astride his father's shoulders; physicist Niels Bohr skiing on Sawyer's Hill outside of Los Alamos, etc.

But not all is tranquil in this compilation. The peaceful family snapshots contrast sharply with altogether different images of utter destruction taken by Robert Serber on his August 1945 visits to Hiroshima and Nagasaki. One of the strengths of documentary photography lies with juxtaposition, and the viewer finds it here in spades.[27]

The latest contribution to the evolving subfield of atomic photography emerged in 2003. That year Peter Kuran assembled the film footage from a top-secret team of Hollywood lensmen who had been assigned to photograph the various aboveground nuclear tests. Drawing on the latest Hollywood equipment, the teams completed their assignments, showed the films to a few top-level government officials, and filed the footage away. Kuran's DVD *Hollywood's Top Secret Film Studio* makes the startling blast images available for the first time.

Michael Light's *100 Suns, 1945–1967* (2003), moves along a similar trajectory. Drawing from the recently opened collections of archival photos at Los Alamos and other national repositories, Light has assembled a large-format, coffee table volume composed of one hundred mushroom clouds, both black-and-white and in color. The book contains virtually no text. The "suns" range from the Trinity Site shot to various NTS explosions bearing such ordinary names as Zucchini, Fox, Hood, and Climax. Several Indian nations lent their names—Zuni, Apache, Cherokee—as well. To view these strangely beautiful "100 suns" in a single sitting is a draining experience. The brief statistical and photographic information tucked into the final pages takes a backseat to the power of the images. There is no question where Light stands on this issue. His concluding comment: "May no further detonation photographs be made, ever."[28]

From 1945 forward, the all-too-familiar image of the mushroom cloud came to symbolize—and simultaneously obfuscate—the evolving atomic age. Yet until the late 1980s, much of the nation's vast nuclear complex lay hidden from public view. Through their exhibits and books, the members of the Atomic Photographers Guild—along with their sympathetic colleagues—have produced a quiet revolution. They have opened the eyes of the nation to a hitherto invisible subculture, one that has so far cost the United States in excess of $5.5 trillion.[29]

The story of the origin and consequences of the atomic age, of course, has been told many times before.[30] But nuclear issues remain complicated. Nonexperts can easily get lost when confronted with shifting radiation statistics and disagreements among experts over issues of public safety. But the atomic photographers' exhibitions and photographs have proven far more accessible to the ordinary person. *Everyone* can respond to them. Thus, the images created by atomic photographers have, in some sense, *democratized* the nuclear age. As famed photographer Ansel Adams once observed: people trust photographs.

As the power of the visual media grows with each generation, so too will the power of these atomic images. It seems likely that these atomic photographs will be to future generations what the photos of Jacob Riis were to the 1890s, or those of Lewis Hine to the Progressive Era, or those of the Farm Security Administration to the Great Depression—they will become the key visual documents for their generation.

PART FOUR

Mysteries

INTRODUCTION

॰॰

From sixteenth-century Spanish explorer Francisco de Coronado's quest
for the elusive "Seven Cities of Cibola" to the forced excitement of contemporary Indian casino advertisements, the lure of sudden wealth has
ever fueled the regional imagination. Newspaperman Thomas Penfield
once counted eighty-one Southwest buried treasure tales—six in what is
now New Mexico—but he overlooked the vanished Indian turquoise
mines, the lost Sanchez and Juan Mondragon mines, and the missing
treasure of Santa Fe madame María Toulos. Another observer has discovered over twenty-five legends that speak of lost or buried New Mexican
treasure. Virtually every area of the state has its own saga.[1]

The most notorious of these stories involves prospector Ova "Doc"
Noss, who early in the century claimed to have found a vast treasure of
buried gold bars—along with twenty-seven skeletons—in a cave in
Victorio Peak in the San Andreas Mountains southeast of Las Cruces.
This rugged area currently forms part of the White Sands Missile Range,
and the presence of the U.S. military has decidedly complicated efforts
to substantiate Noss's claims. In 1977, the army reluctantly allowed a
well-publicized search of Victorio Peak by a Florida-based salvage company, which failed to discover anything. Searchers claimed, however,

that they were hampered by bad weather and simply needed more time. Harsher critics have even accused the army of looting the treasure for its own purposes.

Legends of lost Spanish treasure form a central part of New Mexico folklore. Thus, they are often told to Hispanic children as an integral part of their heritage. Historian Michael Welsh has observed that these persistent tales of "treasure lost and never found" serve well as a means of moral instruction. In countless ways, they speak to the harsh boundaries of the New Mexico landscape, the dangers of untrammeled greed, and the enduring power of mystery itself.[2] Perhaps the ultimate treasure lies in the retelling of the story to the next generation.

■

The omnipresent spiritual dimension of the New Mexican past has produced its own share of mysterious events. A recent list of national sacred sites included eighteen New Mexico locations, the majority of which consisted of natural features sacred to the Pueblo or Navajo Indians.[3] The first regional Euro-American religious mystery dates from the early seventeenth century. Although the mystical nun Maria de Agreda never left her Spanish convent, several people claimed to have seen her ministering to American Indians in the area during the 1620s. Today Maria de Agreda is revered as the "Blue Lady" of the American Southwest.[4]

Similar mystery tales lie at the heart of many northern New Mexico folk traditions. One story speaks of the wooden santo of San Ysidro, who left his mantelpiece one spring evening to plow the fields for a good but poor farmer who had been injured. The farmer's family discovered what happened only when they noticed that the santo's feet were coated with mud. The sacred earth of the Sanctuario de Chimayó has been credited with healings for over two centuries. Flanked by discarded crutches and votive offerings, Chimayó has gained a reputation as the "American Lourdes."

But northern New Mexico folktales can reflect a darker side as well. A selfish woman danced with a handsome stranger at a ball until she noticed he had cloven feet. The fierce winds are often said to echo the mournful sounds of La Llorona, the Weeping Woman, who is doomed to wander eternally, searching for her two lost children.[5]

Ever since the 1930s, the legend of the "miraculous staircase" in the Loretto Chapel in Santa Fe has increasingly caught the national eye. In the late nineteenth century, New Mexico archbishop Jean Baptiste Lamy invited the Sisters of Loretto to come to the state, and, eventually, they contracted to build a French-style chapel for their services. As construction neared completion, the sisters were horrified to discover that the architect had left insufficient room for stairs to reach the choir loft at the upper level of the chapel. But then a mysterious man appeared who built a graceful staircase—complete with two 360-degree complete turns—and disappeared before they could pay him. For the faithful, the carpenter was clearly St. Joseph. As the legend grew, the staircase became a "must-see" venue for Santa Fe's increasing post–World War II tourist industry.

In the 1980s, Santa Fe historian Mary Jane Cook became fascinated with this tale. In 1994 she visited a small museum near Alamogordo and discovered that a French homesteader, François-Jean (Frenchy) Rochas— who had been murdered in 1896—had left behind a vast array of sophisticated carpenter's tools. Intrigued, she tracked down his obituary in the January 6, 1896, *Santa Fe New Mexican*, which declared: "He built the handsome staircase in the Loretto Chapel."[6] For some, this discovery has soured the image of the historian, who now appears as a grinch of the first order. But it seems to have had minimal impact on the appeal of the intricately carved staircase, now shown as a private rather than a religious venue. Tapping this publicity, the Alamogordo chamber of commerce has begun to advertise the ruins of Frenchy's cabin in the Dog Canyon area of Oliver Lee Memorial State Park as a potential tourist attraction. Local legends of mystery can cut in a number of ways.

■

Even in the more skeptical post–World War II era, New Mexico continues to foster its share of mysteries. Stories of bizarre cattle mutilations on isolated northern ranches have been common for at least three decades.[7] Legendary tales of a mythical, quasi-alien creature, *chupacabra*, or "goat sucker," may push it back even further. During the late 1970s, the state spent about $50,000 to investigate the phenomenon but with no definitive results. Possible culprits included various satanic cults and even UFOs. Many ranchers feel there is some form of governmental cover-up involved.

On April 24, 1964, Socorro policeman Lonnie Zamora became an unwilling part of one of the more prominent of these mysteries. Chasing a speeding car, he was sidetracked by a sudden explosion, and when he drove to investigate, he claimed to see an oval-shaped object—surrounded by two adults—that took off suddenly, leaving burned vegetation and distinct tracks in the spring mud. The surrounding publicity of this UFO encounter forever changed Zamora's life.[8]

The most persistent (and perplexing) modern New Mexican mystery clearly revolves around the question of what happened in Roswell on July 3, 1947. Was the scattered debris that rancher W. W. "Max" Brazel found on his ranch a crashed weather balloon—as the U.S. Air Force continues to insist in several lengthy reports—or was it clear evidence of contact from outer space? On the fiftieth anniversary of the alleged crash, the city of Roswell hosted a gala national celebration that drew thousands of visitors to the region. Their now-annual UFO festivities continue to have wide appeal, and visitors can today visit several UFO museums and even camp out at the alleged crash site.[9]

In the following section, I will explore three of these local mysteries: "Francis Schlatter: The Spiritual Healer of the Southwest," "The Tolar, New Mexico, Munitions Train Explosion, November 30, 1944," and "The Saga of Chaco Canyon's 'Threatening Rock,' ca. 550 B.C.E.–January 22, 1941." Modern New Mexico does not lack for tales of wonder.

Francis Schlatter

The Spiritual Healer
of the Southwest

$\mathcal{T}$he Photographic Division of the Library of Congress contains several stereo-cards of a remarkable scene. It was the fall of 1895, and over a thousand people were lined up in Denver to be touched by a German immigrant who bore a startling resemblance to the standard pictures of Jesus. They would walk up a wooden platform, grasp the hands of the man—he would then offer a short prayer—and they would walk away. Many testified to miraculous cures. Moreover, the man took no payment for any of this. "I have no use for money," he said. Whenever people thanked him, he replied, "Don't thank me; thank the Heavenly Father. Put your faith in him, not in me. I have no power but what he gives me through my faith. He will give you the same." The man was Francis Schlatter, "The New Mexico Messiah," "The Healer," "El Gran Hombre," and his is one of the most remarkable stories of the Southwest during the 1890s.[1]

Francis Schlatter, ca. 1895.
Photographer unknown.
Courtesy of the Palace of the
Governors (MNM/DCA).
Neg. no. 132505.

Francis Schlatter was born on April 29, 1856, in the French province of Alsace-Lorraine. His parents were German peasants, and he quit school at fourteen to learn the trade of shoemaker. Born a Roman Catholic, he remained one throughout his life. When his parents died, he emigrated to America, where he arrived around 1884. He spent several years in New York City and in Jamesport, Long Island, working both as a cobbler and as a fireman on the local steamboats. In the fall of 1892 he arrived in Denver and set up shop, first on Stout Street and later on Downing Avenue.[2]

While working at this trade in Denver, he cured a friend by letter. With this he began to feel that "The Father" had chosen him to perform great deeds of healing. First, however, he would have to be tested. So, in

July of 1893 he left Denver in the rain, with only three dollars in his pocket, and began to wander across the western United States. He had no itinerary but simply followed the voice of The Father.

His wanderings took almost two years. From Denver he walked through Kansas, stopping at Clay Center, Topeka, and Lawrence. At Kansas City, he turned south and eventually entered Indian Territory. When he came to Hot Springs, Arkansas, he was arrested for vagrancy, given fifty lashes, and thrown in jail for five months. When he was released, he traveled through Texas, where he was again arrested, at Throckmorton, and spent three more days in jail. From there he went to El Paso, across the desert to Yuma, and finally to San Diego. He began healing in the San Diego area during July 1894 (where he was robbed by a fellow wanderer). Then he journeyed to San Francisco, eventually crossed the Mojave, and spent a few months herding sheep with some Navajo Indians around Flagstaff, Arizona. Since he had little money, he either begged food or did without. Although friendly railroad men offered him rides on occasion, he walked most of the way, usually barefoot. His fellow itinerants poked fun at "that crazy shoemaker," as they called him, but they were also somewhat in awe of him.[3]

He arrived at Pajarito, New Mexico, a hamlet near present-day Los Lunas, around July 9, 1895. Drawing on the *curandero* tradition of the little Spanish village, he began healing there in earnest. Stories of numerous cures soon reached Albuquerque, and the *Albuquerque Morning Democrat* sent reporters down to investigate. There they were met with incredible tales of healing. These would have been instantly dismissed had not hundreds of people vouched for their truth. Jesús María Vásques, who had been blind for three years, was touched by Schlatter and now could see. Juliana Sedillo, who for sixteen years could not use her arms, was now off working in the fields, and so on. Andreas Romero, an elderly, prominent citizen of nearby Peralta, confirmed the stories. "The work of this man is something inexplicable and wonderful," he said. "There is something in his touch which seems to heal the sick. What you have heard of him is true to the letter. I cannot explain it myself; no one can; yet we know some remarkable cures have been effected."[4]

When the *Albuquerque Morning Democrat* broke the story, the issue sold out immediately. "El Sanador" became the sole topic of conversation on every street corner. Small boys swore they saw him on top of a nearby mountain, and several citizens believed that he had literally dropped from the clouds.

In addition to his healing, the mystery surrounding Schlatter deepened when he confessed to reporters that The Father had instructed him to fast and that he had eaten nothing for over ten days. The people with whom he was living vouched for this. "Food is not necessary to him who has the proper faith in my Master," he said.[5] Stranger still, Schlatter bore an uncanny resemblance to the standard representations of Jesus. The *Democrat* reporter gulped as his gaze moved from Schlatter to an inexpensive print of Christ on the wall behind him. "As one looked from the flesh to the presentment [on the wall]," he noted, "the likeness was startling. Every line and touch to be found in the picture were found in the man."[6]

From Peralta, Schlatter walked to Los Lunas, where crowds from Isleta Pueblo gathered around him. Seated in a small home, he touched scores of people, and while many noticed no change, others claimed that they experienced immediate improvement. Rumors spread through Valencia County that Christ had returned to their midst. Several Albuquerqueans urged Schlatter to come to their city, and he arrived on July 20. His fame had preceded him. When he began healing in Old Town the following day, he was met by a huge crowd. Here, however, he met his first opposition. "The Catholic Church does not sanction or approve of such proceedings," said Albuquerque priest Father Mandalari. "He is a fraud from beginning to end," remarked Frank A. Hubbell. He is a "humbug of the first water," said another official. A prominent judge stated he should probably be locked up under the vagrancy act.[7] Yet none of the local police would have dared to try to arrest him, so convinced were the people of his power.[8] "The train of wagons which never seems to end," noted the *Democrat*, "prove better than argument the implicit faith the people have in the strange man."[9]

Numerous people claimed to have been healed, and in spite of careful scrutiny, no one was able to detect fraud in any of the reported cures: black railroad worker Charles Stamp could suddenly walk on his crushed foot; Peter Maguire found himself cured of his rheumatism; Mrs. C. J. Roentgen could now hear better; C. G. Lott could suddenly move his paralyzed arm.[10] For those who sensed no improvement, Schlatter simply

Francis Schlatter in Albuquerque. Photo by Mrs. Albright's Art Parlor. Courtesy of the Palace of the Governors (MNM/DCA). Neg. no. 51264.

said that more treatments were necessary.[11] Moreover, he took no payment for any of his work. When money was occasionally forced on him, he later distributed it to the poor.

The mysterious cobbler took no credit for any cures. When four members of Zuni Pueblo, carrying an ill comrade, approached, they threw themselves at his feet. Schlatter protested, "Don't prostrate yourselves to me. I want none to kneel to me." Whenever he was questioned about his power, he said that he was only a poor shoemaker who was simply doing the bidding of his Master. When asked to account for the cures, he replied, "My work speaks for itself."[12] Although he initially faced a good deal of skepticism in Albuquerque, several former scoffers became believers when family members claimed to have benefited from his touch.[13]

Albuquerqueans were astounded when he ended a lengthy fast by eating a gigantic meal and seemingly felt no ill aftereffects.[14] They were even more astounded when he informed Reverend Charles Bovard that he was Jesus returned for a second life on earth. He did not volunteer this information but, when asked directly, replied in the affirmative.[15] By the middle of August, Schlatter's fame had spread throughout the Rocky Mountain West.

A number of Coloradans sought him out for healing as well. Blind Denver fireman Henry Haverstein claimed improvement after being touched, and Edward L. Fox, a former Denver Alderman who had accompanied Haverstein, asked Schlatter if he would come to Colorado. Schlatter agreed and made plans to leave on August 21. How long will you be in Denver? a reporter asked him. Not over two months, was the reply. Where will you go then? No one knows but The Father, said Schlatter. "Probably I will disappear and no one will know where I am." Will you return ever? "Yes," he said, "but not in the form that I have now."[16] As a gesture of gratitude, the mercantile firm of Grunsfeld Brothers presented him with a fresh change of clothes. All told, he had been in Albuquerque about two months.

A crowd gathered at the railway station to see him off, and many wept openly when he boarded the train. When it stopped at Bernalillo, Cerrillos, Lamy, Las Vegas, and on up the line on its way north, people crowded the platforms for a glimpse or a word. At times Schlatter stayed inside, but whenever he emerged from the coach, he told the crowds that it was not necessary that he touch them. The Father would cure them of their ills, he said, because their coming to the station served as proof of their faith.[17] "Last night," noted a *Democrat* reporter, "the curtain dropped on a drama which will claim a place in the history of the Territory of New Mexico."[18]

In Denver, Schlatter rested for several weeks at the home of E. L. Fox. During that time, Fox had a special platform built behind his house so that the crowds could come up single file and be touched. On September 16, Schlatter again began healing. He would start at 9:00 A.M. and continue until five in the evening. Although he usually insisted that people remain in line, at times he would walk among the crowd to touch invalids who could not mount the ramp. The audience ranged from those who arrived in elegant carriages to the desperately poor. He made no distinction. One Denver reporter estimated that on average six people passed him every minute. The September 17 crowd approached a thousand.[19]

The endless lines thronged the Fox home for almost two months. As people filed by, Schlatter would simply grasp their hands and offer a brief prayer. Once, however, he clasped a woman's hands for two solid hours, after which she collapsed.[20] He also began to bless handkerchiefs that the faithful thrust toward him. When one man noted with embarrassment that his was soiled, Schlatter replied, "So also are the souls of all of us, but what matters it?"[21] To all he stressed that the healing was gradual but that it came through faith alone. "If only you beliefe," he said in heavily accented English, "or less soon, just as you beliefe will you get well."[22]

Denver was as amazed as Albuquerque had been. The streetcars thronged with the faithful, the scoffers, and the merely curious. The lines began to form before dawn, and during the day small boys moved among them selling iced drinks, popcorn, and sandwiches.[23] Some entrepreneurs arrived early in order to sell their places in line to latecomers. When an official of the Union Pacific Railroad felt himself cured of deafness, he offered his employees free trips to Denver. Special trains were also run from Albuquerque and Omaha. "The work of this man of faith," remarked one reporter, "is one of the greatest sensations in Denver for years."[24]

From Denver, Schlatter's reputation spread across the nation. In mid-October a skeptical reporter from Chicago arrived to survey the situation. To his surprise, he found that the majority who claimed to be healed were not especially active churchgoers.[25] No one could explain the phenomenon.

Colorado's physicians and clergymen found themselves equally baffled. Later the state medical board would be accused of driving him out of town because he took away from their business, a charge they hotly denied. On Sunday, September 22, Denver's clergymen devoted their sermons to the theme "Divine Healing." The next Thursday several clerics met to discuss Schlatter in more detail. The consensus: he was a mild but harmless lunatic.[26]

A print of Schlatter engaged in an act of healing (probably in Denver). Photographer unknown. Courtesy of the Palace of the Governors (MNM/DCA). Neg. no. 49733.

FRANCIS SCHLATTER
EN EL ACTO DE CURAR

COPYRIGHT 1895

But the scorn from the physicians and clerics proved no match for the testimonials of miraculous cures. So many people tried to withdraw their children from the Colorado Springs State Institute for the Deaf and Blind that the officials sought (unsuccessfully) to have Schlatter visit their institution. Despite persistent scoffing, many of the cures were verified by outsiders. Several people signed affidavits, while other cases were attested to by skeptical reporters. "'Faith moveth mountains,'" remarked Joseph Emerson Smith, who covered the story for the *Denver Post*. "Now, after 46 years, I am still unable to account otherwise for the healings I saw."[27]

In October two rascals tried to make money from this excitement by selling handkerchiefs (supposedly blessed by Schlatter) as far away as the East Coast. The federal government indicted them for using the mails to defraud, and it had plans to call Schlatter as a witness against them. Before any action could be taken, however, Schlatter disappeared.[28] On the morning of November 14, 1895, Fox and his wife went in to wake the healer, only to find a note pinned to the pillow of his cot: "Mr. Fox—My mission is finished. Father takes me away. Goodbye. [signed] Francis Schlatter."[29]

The Denver papers then launched a hunt for Schlatter as if he were public enemy number one. Sightings were reported in every area of the state and in Kansas City and Omaha. The hundreds of people who had come to see him voiced their disappointment, and souvenir hunters tore down the fence surrounding Fox's house. The federal government quickly dropped the handkerchief fraud case, but it was too late. The Healer had disappeared from Denver forever.

While Coloradans frantically searched for him, Schlatter rode Butte, a big white horse that he had been given, south into New Mexico. In mid-December he was spotted in the Santa Fe area, and he spent time healing in Peña Blanca, Santo Domingo, and Bernalillo. Several prominent citizens urged him to return to Albuquerque, but he refused to commit himself. He would go where The Father wished, he said. When word of his whereabouts spread, numerous packages and letters were sent to him care of the postmaster of Santa Fe. "Suffering humanity outside of New Mexico," remarked a Santa Fe editor, "is trying hard to definitely locate Schlatter, the healer."[30]

Early in January, Schlatter quietly appeared at the Morley ranch in Datil, New Mexico. There he met a sympathetic listener in Mrs. Ada Morley, who gladly housed him for the winter months. "The Father has directed me to a safe retreat," he told her. "I must restore my spiritual powers in seclusion and prayer." For three months Schlatter stayed in an upstairs room at the Morley household, venturing out only when the coast was clear. During that time he alternately rested and exercised by swinging a large copper rod over his head, as a drum major might swing a baton. He said that The Father had told him this was necessary or he would lose his power. He and Mrs. Morley had long conversations during the winter and, with his permission, she copied them down in a book

The famous copper rod utilized by Francis Schlatter to bolster his spiritual strength. Photo by Arthur Taylor. Courtesy of the Palace of the Governors (MNM/DCA). Neg. no. 67152.

later published under the title *The Life of the Harp in the Hand of the Harper* (Denver, 1897). Only three copies of this volume are still extant.[31]

Historians owe a great debt of gratitude to Mrs. Morley, for this little book provides the main source for Schlatter's ideas and social attitudes. Here he elaborated on his views of The Father, his impressions of the truth of reincarnation, his criticism of American society, and his vision of the coming of the new Jerusalem.

When spring arrived, Schlatter informed his hostess that it was time for him to leave. Word had leaked out as to his whereabouts, and people were beginning to seek his aid at the ranch. After bidding Mrs. Morley goodbye, he headed south. He was spotted near Silver City on April 8, but he appeared to be avoiding settled areas.[32] He crossed the line into Mexico a few days later.

For over twenty years afterward, imposters claiming to be Schlatter appeared intermittently across the nation. Chicago; New York City; Canton, Ohio; central Nebraska; Los Angeles; Long Beach; and St. Louis all produced healers who said they were he. But there was a key difference between Schlatter and his imposters: they almost always took money.[33]

Schlatter himself lived only about a year after he left the Morley ranch. His death occurred sometime in 1897 in Chihuahua, Old Mexico. Rumors of his death spread in the spring of 1897, but they were discounted by his followers. His passing was reported in 1901 by H. F. Gray, a Los Angeles doctor, and this was confirmed five years later by archaeologist Edgar L. Hewett. Hewett tells it this way: In the spring of 1906 he was surveying the eastern slope of the Sierra Madres, near Casas Grandes, about 150 miles south of the American border. Here he heard the story of Schlatter's death from his Mexican guide. Several years earlier the guide had one day found a white horse standing by a man he assumed was sleeping. When he ran to get the village authorities, they discovered the man was dead. *Francis Schlatter* was written on the flyleaf of the Bible in the saddlebags, and a large copper rod lay nearby. After Hewett donated a check to the village educational fund, the *jefe político* of Casas Grandes gave him the rod. Hewett, in turn, donated it to the Museum of New Mexico, where it rests today.[34] Thus, while much of the western United States was actively seeking Schlatter, the healer had quietly passed away in a tiny Mexican village.

The Schlatter legend, however, refused to disappear. In 1968, a spiritual healing organization republished Harry B. Magill's 1896 biography of Schlatter in paperback. Two decades later, Norman Cleaveland gathered together the major primary sources on the healer, concentrating on the role of his Datil grandmother, Ada Morley.[35] Contemporary medium Vernon Overlee—who specializes in spiritual healing—professes to manifest the spirit of Francis Schlatter at many of his séances.[36] For over a century numerous people have drawn on this remarkable story for their own purposes.

But the mysterious saga of Francis Schlatter can best be understood by placing it firmly within the context of America in the 1890s, a decade that can justly be hailed as an "age of transition" for national life. American culture in the 1890s underwent major shifts in two areas, especially (1) the relationship between rich and poor and (2) discoveries in the world of medicine.

Historians agree that the "Gay Nineties" hardly deserve their sobriquet. A far better nickname would be the "Grim Nineties," for the depression that lasted from 1893 to 1897—without any governmental intervention—may well have been the nation's worst.[37] The violent strikes at Homestead, Pennsylvania (1892), and Pullman, Illinois (1894), were just the most spectacular of thousands of smaller labor-management conflicts. The election of 1896, which pitted Democrat and Populist William Jennings Bryan against Republican William McKinley, saw America split along lines of poor against rich. The nation was more divided on economic grounds in 1896 than in any other election, with the possible exception of 1936. In 1892 Episcopal priest John J. McCook, an expert on the matter, estimated that there were perhaps fifty thousand unemployed men roaming the land. One of these gentlemen of the road, Connecticut Fatty, told McCook that there were only two truly happy people in the world: the millionaire and the bum.[38] During the 1890s, it seemed, there were plenty of both.

Francis Schlatter was very much a part of this milieu. He denounced American society for its love of money and for its injustice to the working classes. "The moneyed few," he said, "are the bloodsucking parasites on the common people." Moreover, he interpreted the message of Jesus of Nazareth as utopian socialism.

"Never forget," he told Mrs. Morley, "I was a workingman. It's a devilish system! It's the cursed institution and those who uphold it will reap their reward. If they sow the wind they will reap the whirlwind. That is the law from on high. Have they clothed the naked, fed the hungry? Have they housed the homeless? Have they protected the widow and orphan?

"There has been no peace since Adam. Is not 6,000 years enough? How long must they suffer? But the day cometh when the promise for thousands of years shall be fulfilled. He will show the world unmistakably that He is the Lord their God and they are His people. Then we shall have peace, once and forever."[39]

Yet Schlatter was primarily not a political person. He despaired of political solutions. It would serve no purpose to give women the franchise;

it would do no good to vote for the Populist Party candidates. It was too late. The end of time was approaching. Schlatter predicted that in 1899 there would be a terrible war between the gold powers and the laboring classes. (He missed the McKinley-Bryan election by only three years.) After the confrontation, he said, the Lord would establish a new Jerusalem in America: it would be in Datil, New Mexico. Francis Schlatter was a product of the social unrest of the 1890s. Not without reason was he called "the democrat's Jesus."[40]

In a similar way, the 1890s also formed a great age of transition for the world of American medicine. The age of scientific medicine was dawning, but it had not yet arrived. In *Principles and Practices of Medicine* (1892), the chief textbook of the College of Physicians and Surgeons in New York, Dr. William Osler confessed that modern medicine could cure only four or five diseases.[41] Thanks to the discoveries of Louis Pasteur, Robert Koch, and Joseph Lister, medicine was able to *prevent* many infections—antiseptic measures during surgery could halt infection; clean drinking water could stop the spread of cholera and typhoid; doctors could vaccinate against smallpox; quinine could alleviate malarial fevers. But actual *cures* were limited to the fingers of one hand.[42] These were probably the "deficiency diseases," such as scurvy and beriberi, which could be corrected by proper diet.[43] The miracle drugs of sulfa, penicillin, and the like were all products of the twentieth century.[44]

The germ theory of disease had been accepted in most medical circles, but time, distance, and simple stubbornness often impeded its advance. As late as 1885, Dr. William E. Mayo of Rochester, Minnesota (father of the two famous Mayo brothers), performed his surgery without using Lister's antiseptic precautions.[45] In 1892 a famous German doctor drank a beaker full of cholera bacilli to prove that the germ theory was nonsense. He survived, presumably because he was so angry that his stomach acids killed the bacilli before they could kill him.[46] New ideas in the world of medicine spread slowly.[47]

New Mexico and Colorado in the 1890s, moreover, were hardly at the forefront of medical science. For cures, most people relied on home remedies or the numerous patent medicines that were readily available. These keynoted American medicine all through the last half of the nineteenth century. The heyday for patent medicines was from 1880 to 1900.

Every year the public spent millions of dollars on them.[48] Before federal regulation in 1906, these concoctions could, and did, promise anything. The same newspapers that scoffed at Schlatter's "cures" simultaneously ran advertisements for the cure-all Payne's Celery Compound; Hood's Sarsaparilla, a "true blood purifier"; Dr. Louden's Cholera Compound ("the only known preventative"); Dr. Miles's Heart Nervine ("permanently cures every kind of nervous disease"); and Dr. McLean's Liver and Kidney Balm (which reminded readers: "You can't live without a liver").[49]

Moreover, in the rush to establish medicine on a scientific, even mechanistic basis, late nineteenth-century physicians began to ignore the relationship between mind and body. By slighting a connection that the ancients had been well aware of, they opened a tremendous gap in the healing process.[50] Into this gap poured a whole body of ideas, which, collectively, were known as "New Thought." In the East, "New Thought" institutionalized itself as Christian Science; in the Middle West, as John A. Dowie's Zion City, Illinois; in the Far West, as Unity and the Church of Divine Science. New Thought ideas were much in evidence during the 1890s.[51]

The origins of New Thought were varied. It borrowed from Swedish mystic Emanuel Swedenborg, from Ralph Waldo Emerson and American transcendentalism, and, especially, from the Quaker idea of the "Christ consciousness" within. New Thought groups differed considerably, one from the other, but all stressed, first, that one could alter one's circumstances simply by changing one's ideas toward them and, second, the legitimacy of divine healing. They argued that God is omnipotent and perfect, that man is part of God, and, therefore, that there could be no illness if one were in the right relationship to God. As Denver Divine Science minister Nona Brooks said, "God is everywhere, therefore God is here. God is health. Health is everywhere. Therefore, health is here."[52]

Francis Schlatter drew heavily on New Thought ideas. Although his critics liked to portray him as an ignorant shoemaker, Schlatter was no fool. His spoken English may have been imperfect, but it is clear from his comments that he had read widely in the literature of his time. He left a large box of books with his landlord in Denver, but, unfortunately, these have disappeared. He confessed that he had read New Thought writings, and he was also known to have attended several gatherings of "Spiritualists" when he lived in Denver. Healer Malinda E. Cramer, one founder of the Church of Divine Science, moved to Denver in 1887, and it is likely he knew of her or the Brooks sisters.[53] Their messages were very similar.

Once a reporter asked Schlatter if he cured people by the Christian Science method, but he deflected the answer. "My mission is to cure the afflicted when The Father directs me," said Schlatter, "but unless they have faith my efforts are useless. The greater the faith the quicker they get well. Some have more disease than others. It doesn't come in a day, and it will not go in a day. When The Father doesn't want it, they cannot get it. When He sends it, they have it. It all depends upon what He sends. God is the giver of all things."[54]

Did Francis Schlatter really cure people? Definitely yes. Hundreds of claims of cures emerged, many of them signed and verified; not all of these people could have been mistaken. Modern physicians know that confidence in one's doctor forms an important part of the healing process. Few people today doubt that suggestion and autosuggestion can indeed remove certain symptoms. Several types of hysterias, neuroses, and even certain types of paralyses are directly related to mental attitude. So, yes, Francis Schlatter did cure some of those who came to see him.

Were the cures permanent? There is no way of knowing for certain, of course, for no follow-up studies were ever done. Often he assured people that if they had sufficient faith, their ailment would improve within a certain period. It seems safe to say that some were permanently helped and some were not. Since the *source* of the neurotic illness was not affected, the symptoms might, perhaps, have moved around the body. A woman cured of headaches, say, might well have developed stomach pains a few weeks later. A man who lost the pain in his arm might well have developed another in his leg, and so forth.[55] But the real miracles came from the workings of the mind and body themselves.[56] Most people feel better in the morning, the old medical adage has it, and most people get well eventually. Time heals the majority of illnesses on its own. Schlatter was well aware of this. To the many people who felt no instantaneous improvement, he said that the cures were gradual. They came "as the faith comes."

Did Francis Schlatter actually reverse such maladies as cancer, permanent blindness, deafness, or tuberculosis? Almost certainly not. Those were beyond the ken of the medicine of his time and, unfortunately, are often beyond our present-day knowledge also. But, as Walter C. Hadley of Albuquerque said of Schlatter, he was not an imposter. He was just as he represented himself—a poor shoemaker doing the bidding of The Father. Where his power came from, Hadley could not say, but: "I do know the man is honest in his intentions, consistent in all things, and that he is doing many men good and no man harm."[57] After more than a century, his story remains one of the enduring mysteries of the great Southwest.

CHAPTER NINE

The Tolar, New Mexico, Munitions Train Explosion, November 30, 1944

Since much of twentieth-century warfare hinges on the manufacture, shipping, and handling of high-level munitions, accidental home-front disasters have become an all-too-familiar part of modern conflicts. Probably the worst of these detonations occurred on December 6, 1917, when a French munitions vessel, *Mont Blanc*, loaded to the gills with a cargo of TNT, collided with the freighter *Imo* in the bustling harbor of Halifax, Nova Scotia.

The collision caused flaming fuel to seep into the ship's hold, and when the *Mont Blanc* exploded, it leveled three hundred acres of Halifax, setting off further blasts among the various caches of munitions scattered along the compact waterfront. The combined detonations killed sixteen hundred people, injured perhaps six thousand more, and left over ten thousand without housing. Although the Nova Scotia port city was eventually rebuilt, the Halifax blast is still considered the worst accidental wartime explosion in the history of the world.[1]

The even more sophisticated munitions of World War II only increased the danger. On April 9, 1945, an American Liberty ship accidentally detonated its cargo of aerial bombs in the Italian Adriatic port city of Bari, killing 360 and injuring about 1730.[2] The worst American home-front disaster, however, had occurred about fifteen months earlier. On July 17, 1944, the U.S. naval base at Port Chicago, California—northeast of San Francisco on the Sacramento River—was heavily damaged when two ships filled with bombs intended for the Pacific theater accidentally detonated in a blinding roar. This blast, later estimated as equivalent to five kilotons of TNT (about a fourth of the Hiroshima atomic bomb), injured several hundred people and took the lives of 322 navy personnel. Since the vast majority of those killed were low-ranking African American sailors assigned to load the bombs onto ships heading for the Pacific, numerous black seamen refused to return to work. For this they were charged with mutiny, and after lengthy legal proceedings, fifty black sailors were jailed at the Terminal Island Disciplinary Barracks in Southern California.[3] Thus, the Port Chicago explosion ranked not only as a tragic home-front munitions accident but also served as a symbol of the persistent racial inequalities in the armed services. Perhaps not surprisingly, the U.S. Navy razed the Port Chicago site in 1968.

■

Although far less recognized than the sagas of Halifax, Bari, or Port Chicago, the tiny hamlet of Tolar (pronounced Tol′er), New Mexico—located in the Roosevelt County panhandle about fifty miles west of the Texas line—joined those ranks on November 30, 1944. On that fateful Thursday, an Atchison, Topeka and Santa Fe train hauling a munitions car derailed in the middle of town. Within about twenty minutes, it caught fire and exploded with devastating force. Although the blast took only one life, the town never recovered from this tragedy, and today Tolar is only a wide spot on New Mexico highway 60/84 between Melrose and Fort Sumner.[4]

But the fallout from the Tolar explosion did more than simply dominate the front pages of regional newspapers during the fall of 1944. Eight months later, the Tolar blast provided the top-secret Manhattan Project with the perfect "smoke screen" to hide a far more powerful New Mexico explosion—the atomic detonation at Trinity Site on the Alamogordo Bombing Range.

The world's first atomic bomb exploded at Trinity on July 16, 1945, at 5:30 A.M., mountain war time. Thousands of people saw the blast, but the following days' papers assured citizens that the penetrating sound and strange light were caused by the accidental explosion of a nearby ammunition dump. Thus, Tolar plays a unique role in the history of the New Mexico/Texas region. Not only does it rank as the only New Mexico town to be (literally) blown off the map, it also served as a three-week camouflage for the opening of the atomic age.

The Wartime Situation in Late 1944

British politician Sir Anthony Eden once described the year 1944 as "slightly exceptional times."[5] Certainly that proved true for both the European and Pacific theaters. June 6, 1944, marked the launch of the Allied invasion of the continent, and shortly thereafter Allied B-29s inaugurated their reign of destruction over the Japanese home islands. Although the Axis military leaders found themselves much on the defensive, neither Germany nor Japan showed any signs of surrender.

By November of 1944, the U.S. military had completely rebuilt Port Chicago, and it continued to serve as a major departure point for munitions ships heading to the Pacific. Indeed, November 1944 proved particularly trying all through the Pacific theater. Using both conventional bombing and daring kamikaze attacks, the Japanese military had severely damaged the U.S. carrier *Lexington*. Shortly thereafter, the gigantic aircraft carrier *Shinano*, considered unsinkable from above because of its steel deck and concrete underpinnings, joined the Japanese fleet. [6]

That same month, the Special Balloon Regiment at Otsu began to release the first of approximately nine thousand balloon bombs, which were intended to spread both fires and panic along the American West Coast. (In five months of operation, about 285 balloon bombs reached the states—carried there by prevailing westerly winds—but because the U.S. Government kept their presence secret, there was no widespread panic.)[7] Although U.S. submarines had reduced the Japanese merchant marine to about half of its 1940 carrying capacity and Allied B-29s based in Saipan in the Mariana Islands had started to bomb Tokyo on a regular basis, few predicted an early end to the conflict. Thus, the munitions cars that rolled through Tolar on a regular basis were deemed vital to the nation's war effort.

The Story of Tolar

Prior to November 30, 1944, hardly anyone outside of the Llano Estacado had ever heard of Tolar. Begun in 1905 as a tent city on the Santa Fe Railroad line, Tolar supplied so much needed sand and gravel for construction that early settlers hoped the tiny hamlet might eventually grow into a major railroad center (which went, instead, to nearby Clovis).

Early Tolar carried a somewhat seamy reputation. The town boasted three saloons, and prostitutes filled the various tents of "Casanova Alley." "Every man was his own lawman, then," one early resident recalled.[8] But the town matured swiftly, and by 1911 it harbored about 600 people; a decade later it claimed a post office, grade school, high school, newspaper, and even a racetrack. But the rise of good roads and relatively inexpensive automobiles during the 1920s and early 1930s made it much easier to shop in nearby Fort Sumner, Melrose, Portales, or Clovis. The famed WPA *New Mexico: A Guide to the Colorful State* (originally published in 1940) failed to mention Tolar, and by 1941 the population had fallen to around 350. By 1944 it had dropped to below 300. Historian F. Stanley once described the little community as "always an orphan child of sorts."[9]

As the collected oral reminiscences of former area residents show, life on New Mexico's eastern Great Plains involved many struggles. Marvie Jeter Cline, who was born in the Tolar area in 1903, lived in a primitive half dugout while her father worked as a cowboy on neighboring ranches. Before the railroad arrived, the family journeyed by wagon to Portales for supplies—a five-day trip—only twice a year. Mary Lou Bagwell shared the same circumstances. She traveled from Texas to New Mexico by covered wagon, lived in a half dugout, raised chickens, and milked cows on the family farm. Her family hardly ever bought commercial supplies other than flour, sugar, and other staples.

The Great Depression of the 1930s hit the region especially hard. During one bleak year, Bagwell's father whittled Christmas stilts and gifts from wood for the boys while her mother sewed dolls from scrap cloth for the girls, since the family had no funds for "boughten toys." As Bagwell recollected, "It was bad times, real bad times."[10] Still, abundant artesian water lay just below the surface—many early wells could be dug by hand—and the virgin soil of Tolar produced extensive crops: potatoes, popcorn, melons, and beans, as well as orchards laden with peaches, apples, plums, and pears. Most farmers kept hogs, chickens, and milk cows, and a few ran herds of cattle as well. "I don't remember ever going hungry," Cline recalled.[11]

Out of necessity, early Tolar residents shared responsibility for the welfare of their neighbors. Church services—Southern Methodist, Southern Baptist, and those of the Latter-day Saints—played vital social roles. Neighbors always kept track of one another's health because, as Cline phrased it, "There wasn't no doctors no where!"[12]

By the early 1940s, however, most of the young men had drifted away in search of wartime work. Without radios and with only a semiweekly newspaper, the few girls would often entertain themselves by going down to the railway tracks to wave as the enlisted men on troop trains roared by. Thus, Tolar was gradually dying on the vine even as that fateful November day approached.

Around noon on November 30, 1944, an eighty-one-car train containing peanuts, cans of corned beef, cotton mattresses, airplane engines, fuel oil, and various munitions arrived in Tolar from Clovis. Right in the middle of town, the "journal" (axel) of an oil car—seventh in line—broke, and this caused thirty-six cars to jump the track. Several of these piled into the oil car and caught it on fire. The engineer pulled the few undamaged freight cars west, and the engineer from the following train hauled a number of other cars to the east. The fires burned among the derailed cars for about twenty to thirty minutes until the twenty-first car—filled with an estimated 165 unfused five-hundred-pound bombs—reached detonation temperature. It then exploded in the largest accidental blast in New Mexican history.[13]

The earth literally shook as the explosion gouged a hole five to ten feet deep and several feet across under the wreckage. Train wheels, broken axles, and other heavy metal objects were catapulted thousands of feet in the air in all directions. A complete boxcar ended up semi-intact astride

The approximate site of the 1944 Tolar explosion.
Photo by author.

the neighboring highway. Indeed, a long metal rod from the blast can still be seen sticking out of a corner of Johnny Eastwood's pasture.[14]

A gigantic shock wave roared through the flat countryside for over one hundred miles. It shook dishes off the shelves in Elida, over thirty miles to the southeast, and broke windows in Melrose, fifteen miles directly east. The force of the shock wave actually stalled a truck traveling between Taiban and Tolar, and it cracked the adobe wall of a ranch house situated about ten miles south of Taiban, scattering jugs of milk to the floor in so doing.

People in Portales—over forty miles away—initially believed that the blast had destroyed their own downtown. When Robert Eastwood, then a student at Eastern New Mexico University, discovered the truth, he raced back to his Tolar home to see if his parents had been injured. On the way he passed scores of overturned automobiles. "That was some explosion," said a man as he crawled out of his flipped vehicle.[15]

Since the munitions car derailed right in the middle of town, Tolar itself bore the brunt of the blast. The shock wave shattered the glass in all nearby ranch houses, destroyed five vehicles, and injured a woman driving on Highway 60/84, parallel to the tracks. Flying debris and/or the shock wave leveled most of the town buildings: C. A. Watkins's general store, where an errant axle slightly injured Mrs. Watkins; the Smith store; the currently unoccupied schoolhouse; the post office; the railroad depot; and the homes of six other families.

Remarkably, considering the magnitude of the blast, only one person lost his life. Jess Brown, who had been watching the fires from about one hundred yards away, was hit in the head by a flying piece of metal. He died while en route to the Melrose hospital. The death toll would have been far higher except that the Tolar children had all been attending a consolidated school in Taiban, and, because of severe gas rationing, most of the town's women had picked that Thursday to go shopping and do laundry in Melrose. The next day Mrs. J. F. Harris—whose home held the sole telephone to survive the blast—complained that she was coming down with a cold because all the windows had been blown out of her house.

Given the tense wartime situation, the government's first thought was sabotage, and it quickly dispatched FBI agent R. J. Untreiner from El Paso to investigate. After surveying the situation, however, Untreiner concluded that the blast had simply been an industrial accident. Although the story never made the national newspapers, striking photos of burning freight cars appeared in the Portales and Clovis press. Most New Mexico papers carried the Associated Press version of the incident on their front pages.[16]

Santa Fe Railroad officials immediately began rerouting all rail traffic until emergency crews could construct a "shoe-fly" line around the blast area. Within weeks, however, the track had been replaced, and other munitions trains continued to make their way through Tolar to ports on the Pacific Coast.

The Tolar explosion scattered an enormous amount of debris all through the region. Countless bits of mattress—many burned to a crisp—littered the area for miles around. Residents could walk up to their ankles in raw peanuts, still in their shells, and several families feasted on peanut brittle as long as their sugar rations held out. Hundreds of cans of corned beef hash were splattered on nearby trees and rocks, providing local dogs and cats with a banquet beyond their wildest dreams. The railroad salvaged what materials it could and then buried the rest in a large pit. Scrap metal hunters had a field day, however, and local collectors eventually sold several hundred tons to a nearby junkyard.[17]

But residents in this region were no strangers to hardship, and overall, they viewed the situation philosophically. As Edgar Sparks remarked, "All the people [in Tolar] were getting along as well as could be expected."[18]

Conclusion

Given Tolar's declining population, plus the relative proximity of much larger eastern New Mexico towns, it is probable that the November 30, 1944, accident simply hastened the inevitable. But the Tolar explosion assumed another important regional role as well. In July of 1945, Manhattan Project security officials desperately needed a red herring to divert local attention away from the nuclear experiments being conducted at the secret city of Los Alamos and at Trinity Site, east of Socorro on the Alamogordo Bombing Range. Since nothing of the Tolar accident had been hidden from the public—even before the FBI determined that no sabotage had been involved—virtually everyone in the area was well aware of what an accidental munitions explosion involved.

Thus, the Manhattan Project officials easily tapped into this frame of reference and used it to briefly conceal the true meaning of the Trinity Site atomic detonation. Immediately after the Trinity shot, virtually all regional newspapers printed an "official" statement. Allegedly sent from the commanding officer of the Alamogordo Air Base, William O. Eareckson, it read:

> Several inquiries have been received concerning a heavy
> explosion which occurred on the Alamogordo Air Base
> reservation this morning. A remotely located ammunition
> magazine containing a considerable amount of high explosives
> and pyrotechnics exploded. There was no loss of life or injury
> to anyone, and the property damage outside of the explosives

A view of Tolar today. Photo by author.

magazine itself was negligible. Weather conditions affecting
the content of gas shells exploded by the blast may make
it desirable for the Army to evacuate temporarily a few
civilians from their homes.[19]

Obviously, "another Tolar."

This charade lasted for about three weeks. Then on August 7, 1945,
President Harry S Truman announced the dropping of the atomic bomb
on Hiroshima. With that, New Mexicans instantly realized that the
Trinity Site explosion involved far more than simply a wayward ammunition dump. A new era had begun, with New Mexico strangely in the
forefront. And with this new era, the hamlet of Tolar faded slowly back
into the vast expanse of New Mexico's eastern Great Plains, from which
it had emerged only two generations before.

CHAPTER TEN

The Saga *of* Chaco Canyon's "Threatening Rock"

CA. 550 B.C.E.–22 January, 1941

*I*f New Mexico is officially known as "the Land of Enchantment," the haunting ruins of Chaco Canyon arguably rank as the most enchanted spot within its borders. Established as a national monument in 1907, the now-designated Chaco Culture National Historical Park ranks among the state's best-known tourist destinations. In spite of often-impassible dirt roads, about ninety thousand visitors a year brave the ruts to ponder its enduring mysteries.

These mysteries lie everywhere. The now-deserted ruins of Pueblo Bonito, with its seven hundred rooms, once formed the largest "apartment house" in the world; it held this record until surpassed by a New York City apartment building in the 1880s. An overhang near the Great House of Peñasco Blanco contains an image of an ancient red ocher star, a human hand, and a crescent moon—a cluster that probably depicts the historic explosion of a supernova in A.D. 1054.[1]

In 1977 archaeoastronomer Anna Sofaer discovered that the towering Fajada Butte, near the park's south entrance, contains three gigantic rock slabs that allowed a "sun dagger" of light to slice through the center of an etched spiral petroglyph on the summer solstice. Unfortunately, the eager arrival of an endless stream of visitors caused the rocks to shift, and since 1980 the ancient solar calendar no longer functions as it once did. In the words of famed anthropologist Alfonso Ortiz, this meant the loss of an "irreplaceable cultural treasure" for the people of New Mexico.[2]

Home to a thriving community of approximately five thousand people from about A.D. 800 to about A.D. 1100, the Chaco region boasts over ninety outlier sites and about 250 miles of man-made roads, as well as what appear to be several roadside "shrines." These geometric roads—some apparently going nowhere—suggest that Chaco may well have served chiefly as a major administrative/ceremonial center (the Rome of the Southwest?) rather than as a permanent residential community.

Chaco Canyon evokes almost as many questions as answers. Given the high estimated population figures, why have archaeologists found no massive human burial sites? Did the ancient ones practice a ritual form of cannibalism, as some anthropologists have alleged? And especially, since there is no obvious evidence of enemy attack, why did the ancestral Puebloans desert their beloved canyon around the year 1150?

Today Chaco has been declared a World Heritage site, which ranks it with Machu Picchu, the Egyptian pyramids, and Stonehenge. This designation is well deserved, for both first-time visitors and seasoned National Park Service rangers stand in awe of its grandeur. In the words of *New Mexico Magazine*, Chaco Canyon remains a spot of "Enduring Mystery."[3]

■

For over two thousand years, one of the persistent "enduring mysteries" of Chaco Canyon revolved around a gigantic block of sandstone that loomed directly behind Pueblo Bonito. It stood 150 feet long by 100 feet high by 20 to 30 feet wide, and its estimated weight approached thirty thousand tons. At some time during the first millennium B.C.E., this huge block began to separate from the sandstone cliff behind it. It was much in evidence when the ancient Chacoans began erecting their buildings, and they realized full well that if it fell, it would crush much of the rear

Threatening Rock, Pueblo Bonito, Chaco Canyon, New Mexico.
Photographer unknown. Courtesy of the Palace of the Governors
(MNM/DCA). Neg. no. 59377.

of Pueblo Bonito. Some anthropologists have speculated that the ancestral Puebloans left Chaco precisely because they feared that the rock
might crash at any moment.[4]

We will never know what the first Chacoans termed the rock, but
later arrivals knew it by a variety of names. At various times, Anglo-
Americans termed it "the Elephant," "Leaning Rock," "Shored-Up Cliff
Block," "Balanced Rock," or "Leaning Cliff." Local Navajos knew it as Tsé
Bíya ãAnii´áhí, or "the place where the rock is propped up from beneath."
Robert Young and William Morgan translate it as "rock under which
something extends up supporting it."[5] An unknown Park Service official
in the early 1930s coined the phrase "Threatening Rock," and this decidedly inelegant term unfortunately stuck.

*Native engineering efforts at the base of Leaning Rock,
Pueblo Bonito, Chaco Canyon (October 1921). Photographer
unknown. Courtesy of the Palace of the Governors (MNM/DCA).
Neg. no. 81152.*

Famed British medievalist J. R. R. Tolkien once observed that if a
dragon lives in your neighborhood, it is wise not to leave him out of your
calculations. Everyone who lived in Chaco Canyon had to confront the
dragon of Threatening Rock. The ancient builders were the first to
respond. Sometime around A.D. 1000, they began to erect an elaborate
timber-rock-dirt retaining wall, perhaps two hundred yards long, directly
at its base. Segments of this wall are clearly visible today.

When the National Park Service took over custodial care of Pueblo
Bonito in the early twentieth century, they confronted the same dragon.
During the 1930s, Park Service officials spent a great deal of time discussing the dilemma. They commissioned a number of surveys, installed
metal rods between rock and cliff to measure its shifting movement, and

seriously considered the possibility of permanently anchoring the rock back to the mesa wall or even removing it entirely.

Although a number of geologists and engineers dutifully filed their reports, few showed much sense of urgency. After all, the rock had stood in place for over two thousand years, they argued, and probably would remain in place for a thousand more.

But Nature seemed to have a timetable all her own. On the Wednesday afternoon of January 22, 1941, Threatening Rock began to rumble ominously. Several hours later, it crashed with a gigantic roar and, as the ancient Chacoans had long feared, tore out a sizable portion of the back side of Pueblo Bonito. Dismayed Park Service archaeologists rushed in during the next several days to assess the damage. Their sense of resignation may be seen in Superintendent Hugh M. Miller's official report: "Deeply regretted, the fall of the Rock and the damage to Pueblo Bonito represents the operation of natural forces over which, in a broad view, it may not have been the function of this Service to exercise control." Lewis T. McKinney, custodian for Chaco, reflected the same mood. Rangers raced in, hoping to set the rock back in place, but "couldn't find all the pieces," he wryly noted, and thus left when "the beans ran out."[6] Since they could do little, the Park Service decided to create the present trail that today winds between the huge fragments that once constituted Pueblo Bonito's most immediate menace.

Just why the ancestral Puebloans sited Pueblo Bonito precisely where they did can never be determined, but they probably chose their location primarily for spiritual reasons. The presence of Threatening Rock may even have played a role here, for anthropologist Niel Judd's dramatic 1958 description of it must have echoed back through time. Said Judd: the rock "was indeed a fearful awe-inspiring body. It was a living, breathing thing! As one stood to admire, it seemed actually to lean forward to engulf one."[7]

No one was more aware of the power of Threatening Rock than the ancient builders, who spent months, perhaps years, in erecting their retaining wall. A ca. 1920 postcard celebrated this effort as "our first great engineering feat—25,000 tons of sandstone supported by terraces and retaining walls—1063 A.D."[8]

During the 1930s, National Park Service engineers gave the early builders' efforts very high marks. Although their ancient masonry retaining wall could never have held back thirty thousand tons of sandstone, it did effectively halt wind erosion at the rock's base. This proved no small matter, for later studies noted that the rock rested on a six-to-eight-inch layer of low-grade coal or oil shale, which at times could prove slippery. Indeed, one of the Park Service's own proposed plans involved erecting a wall with massive grouting of horizontal cracks near the base of the rock—a scheme that followed along those exact same early engineering lines.[9]

Rumors of a hulking block of sandstone poised to crush Pueblo Bonito at any moment enticed a number of early photographers to Chaco Canyon. Unfortunately, none of William H. Jackson's 1877 images came out, so Victor Mindeleff took perhaps the first photo of the rock in 1887; numerous other photographers followed suit. Romantic author Charles F. Lummis made several photographs in 1901, and during the 1920s photographers descended on the canyon in droves. The Museum of New Mexico files contain about thirty images that clearly reveal photographers' fascination with the awesome power of Threatening Rock.

Probably the most spectacular early photo of the rock came in the summer of 1929, when archaeologist A. V. Kidder invited famed aviator Charles A. Lindbergh and his new wife, Anne Morrow Lindbergh, to take aerial photographs of key southwestern archaeological sites.

Flying in an open cockpit, two-seater Curtis Falcon biplane, the Lindberghs shot a number of aerial photos of ruins in the Pecos region, and it is highly probable that Anne should be given credit for snapping the first aerial photograph of Pueblo Bonito, one that revealed the power of Threatening Rock in all its horrific splendor.[10]

Shortly after the Lindberghs snapped their famous image, the Park Service began seriously to explore various solutions to the dilemma of Threatening Rock. In September 1933, John Y. Keur wrote a thorough report detailing the Anasazi attempts to shore it up.[11] For the next several years, the Park Service regularly debated what (if any) actions they should take. Archaeologists expressed concern over potential irreparable damage to Pueblo Bonito if it fell, but the proposed schemes that arrived from the Engineering Division all carried high price tags, and Depression-era administrators never had much money to work with.

Aerial view of Pueblo Bonito and Threatening Rock, Chaco
Canyon, 1929. Photo traditionally credited to Charles A.
Lindbergh but probably taken by Anne Morrow Lindbergh.
Courtesy of the Palace of the Governors (MNM/DCA).
Neg. no. 130232.

In spite of these restrictions, Park Service engineers proved very innovative. J. B. Hamilton and Frank Kittredge recommended coating over the extensive debris lodged between the rock and the back wall to prevent the freeze-and-thaw of winter moisture. Others suggested removing thirty feet or so from the top to lower the rock's high center of gravity. Hamilton joined with engineer T. C. Miller to suggest an even more dramatic approach. They argued that the Park Service should drill seventy-two half-inch-by-six-foot holes into both cliff face and rock and install seventy-two massive steel rods to link the two back together. Hamilton even recommended that because of the value of Pueblo Bonito, the Park Service should seriously consider removing Threatening Rock altogether.[12]

But lack of agreement, as well as lack of funds, determined that the various Chaco custodians could introduce only two small preventive measures. First, in 1935–36, they installed three movement gauges that linked rock to cliff. These consisted of calibrated steel rods set carefully within steel pipes so that the rods could slide easily within the pipes if any movement occurred.[13] Two Civilian Conservation Corps workers had the unenviable task of climbing the Anasazi stairs behind Pueblo Bonito twice a day to measure this movement. This assignment demanded that they leap the harrowing gap from cliff to rock and back again.[14] Finally, from 1937 to 1940 a CCC crew directed by landscape architect Claire J. Mueller used wheelbarrows, buckets, and eventually a donkey engine sledge to remove several tons of rock that had fallen into the back crevice. Mueller's crew found only occasional artifacts in the debris—a few pottery shards and an ancient planting stick, which ended up in the Chaco Museum. Removal of the backfill debris incidentally caused the top of the rock to tilt toward the cliff by about a quarter of an inch.

But few expressed any immediate concern. Both engineers and geologists agreed that the situation was unlikely to change in the near future. One observer, V. W. Vandiver, pointed to other "balanced rocks" in the region, such as those at Chiricahua National Monument in Arizona, which had precariously stood their ground for centuries. Geologist Charles N. Gould, who made two extensive surveys of the Chaco region, agreed. Although the rock would fall eventually, he said, the threat was not immediate: "It has stood 1,000 years since the Old People first attempted to strengthen the foundation, and bids fair to stand for another 1,000 years."[15] A general consensus prevailed that the rock was safe from all but strong earthquakes, which were relatively rare in the region.[16]

But here the ancient builders proved wiser than contemporary geologists. In 1938–39, the measuring rods showed that the rock had moved in and out about the same distance. But by late 1940, the CCC crew noted that the rock was sliding out far more than it was retreating. They also observed a black substance oozing from the layer of coal or oil shale on which the rock sat. The weather during the months of December 1940 to January 1941 proved especially challenging as well. Temperatures ranged from minus five degrees to sixty-two degrees, and the canyon received an unusually large amount of moisture—7.46 inches of rain and 5 inches of snow. No outside visitors braved the corduroy roads for the first three weeks of January. The muck proved so pervasive that none of the Navajo workmen or CCC crews could do much of anything for almost two months.

During the night of January 21, 1941, Threatening Rock started to pop and crack. An approximately fifteen-ton fragment split off from the east end and hit the ground with such force that Lewis and Carolie McKinney felt they had experienced an earthquake. The next morning McKinney discovered that several tons of sandstone had tumbled back into the gap between rock and cliff and that the rock had moved outward over ten inches during the night. The ominous rumbling continued for several more hours, during which time McKinney took a number of photographs. But then he ran out of film. Hopping into his car, he drove to the trading post in Pueblo del Arroyo to replenish his supply, but while there, at precisely 3:24 P.M., he heard the rock fall.[17] Thus, we have no photographs of the actual collapse.

The small crew of rangers, Navajo workmen, and wives raced over when they heard the crash. A huge cloud of dust covered the ruins and hung in the air for almost two minutes.[18] The sound of several thousand tons of sandstone striking the frozen earth reverberated throughout the canyon, probably the most penetrating noise New Mexicans would hear until the world's first nuclear explosion at Trinity Site (July 16, 1945) over four years later. "Boy, was it exciting," wrote Carolie McKinney.[19]

It seems clear that both Navajo and Pueblo people viewed the rock as a living object with strong spiritual power. The Navajos told the rangers that their ancestors had placed baskets of turquoise and white shell behind the rock as an offering. Many accounts dismiss this as fiction, but Claire J. Mueller later recalled that both corn pollen and turquoise dust mysteriously appeared in the new crevices on the morning of January 22. Although Neil Judd argued in 1958 that the ancient Puebloans had relied solely on engineering, not prayer, to keep the rock in place, it is now known that Pueblo prayer sticks were also found amid the rubble.[20] An unsubstantiated legend states that the rock fell after an unsympathetic governmental agent removed other Pueblo prayer sticks (lodged in a nearby kiva) that were designed to keep the rock in place.

The chief goal of Navajo life revolves around the quest for "balance," or harmony, both in the personal as well as the natural world. But a fall of rock on the reservation signifies disharmony, an unexpected disruption of nature. Thus, from the Navajo perspective, all major rockfalls were bad omens, although it was never precisely clear what form the evil would assume. In the early 1860s, for example, a large section of the rim of Black Mesa crumbled away; shortly thereafter, the U.S. Army, under Colonel Kit Carson, marched the Navajos to the Bosque Redondo in central New Mexico for their four-year captivity. The scar on the cliff face is still visible today. About the same time as the collapse of Threatening Rock, a huge boulder fell near Rough Rock, Arizona. Some Navajo leaders later interpreted this event as pointing to America's entry into World War II.

Because of its size and reputation, the fall of Threatening Rock carried even more symbolic significance. The majority of those who watched the cliff collapse were Navajo workmen, and one Navajo reportedly became hysterical as he feared that the fall signified the end of human time. Park Service architect Claire Mueller, who had directed the earlier bracing efforts, recalled that the Navajo workmen all blamed him for the "death" of the rock. For several days, every time Mueller walked near a Navajo, the man would mutter, "*Chindi*," and change his course. Once when he entered Arthur Tanner's trading post to get his mail, a large group of Navajos looked the other way, whispered, "Chindi," and immediately disappeared. This situation lasted for several weeks.[21] The contrast between the Native and Park Service views of Threatening Rock speaks volumes.

Pueblo Bonito as damaged by the fall of Threatening Rock.
Photo by author.

One Park Service engineer had earlier suggested that if the rock fell as a complete block, rather like a domino, it would miss Pueblo Bonito by about twenty feet. But that did not happen. Instead, the rock shattered into countless fragments and cascaded onto the walls of the pueblo with such force that it crushed four stories and tore about 125 feet away from the back wall. The total damage affected over eighty rooms: sixty were partially destroyed and twenty-one essentially demolished. The fall also shook the vigas at the Pueblo del Arroyo trading post and cracked the walls over the windows in the McKinney house. The inevitable had finally happened. In the words of McKinney on January 25, 1941: the danger of Threatening Rock was "none, no-threat, no-more. Thanks to all of the technicians who helped me with this minor problem."[22]

Word of the fall soon spread throughout the region. On January 26, eight visitors braved the frozen roads to assess the situation. Several

The remains of Threatening Rock today. Photo by author.

archaeologists, including veteran Charlie Steen, expressed their dismay at the damage to Pueblo Bonito. But little could be done. As the Museum of New Mexico journal *El Palacio* noted the next month, "The National Park Service, which administers the ruin, does not at the present time contemplate any repair to the damage."[23]

Four months later, McKinney observed in his official report that "the noise that Threatening Rock made when it fell must have been heard all over the U.S. because we still continue to receive inquiries concerning it."[24] In truth, however, the publicity proved relatively modest—only a few magazine and newspaper articles. When spring arrived, the visitors returned to explore the ruins, but tight budgets meant that McKinney received only modest sums to help repair the damage to Pueblo Bonito walls and begin work on a new trail amid the debris. In 1960, geologists S. A. Schumm and R. J. Chorley made an extensive survey of the scene. They concluded that the rock had first separated from the sandstone cliff around 550 B.C. Thus, Threatening Rock had remained in place for almost two and a half millennia.[25]

Contemporary National Park Service pamphlets on Pueblo Bonito give only the briefest mention of the story of Threatening Rock. But, in all fairness, it is hard to appreciate something that is no longer there. As modern visitors wend their way amid the fragments, only those with the keenest imaginations can re-create the hulking presence of a thirty-thousand-ton sandstone rock that held Chaco Canyon in general, and Pueblo Bonito in particular, in its powerful, mysterious embrace for almost twenty-five hundred years.[26]

AFTERWORD

$\mathcal{A}$s these essays have attempted to show, the story of modern New Mexico is both fascinating and complex. The vast spaces and relatively sparse population have allowed powerful personalities to leave their imprint on the region. Charles and Anne Morrow Lindbergh helped lay the grounds for the state's now-extensive airway system. Robert H. Goddard's sojourn in Roswell during the 1930s forever marked that city as the home of American rocket research. The periodic high profiles accorded to Trinity Site and Los Alamos suggest that the name of J. Robert Oppenheimer will be connected to New Mexico essentially forever. Congressman Bill Richardson first honed his famed negotiation skills in 1982 by resolving a tortuous land-use issue in the San Juan Basin. In so doing, he also set aside some of the most dramatic badlands scenery for future generations to enjoy. If—as is widely rumored—Richardson eventually plans to seek higher office, the main arena where he perfected his political skills remains the Land of Enchantment.

Even in the twenty-first century, the state harbors more than its share of mysteries. The sacred sites of Tomé Hill, Chaco Canyon, Chimayó, Taos Pueblo's Blue Lake, St. Francis Cathedral in Santa Fe, and the four sacred mountains of Dinetah all help mark the region as a land of widespread spiritual appeal. The often haunting topography and stunning clarity of light speak to this issue as well. As the twenty-first century seems to be engaged in some form of "spiritual realignment," it is likely that the reputation of the state along these lines will only continue to grow.

Finally, one comes to the elephant under the rug: the omnipresence of federal science. Late nineteenth-, early twentieth-century New Mexico had some links to the world of science and medicine. Biologists combed the Southwest to chart the native uses of various plants, and for years New Mexico was touted as the ideal location to cure tuberculosis and other health problems. Both St. Joseph's and Presbyterian Hospital in Albuquerque were founded to aid tuberculars in their recovery. The administration building at the University of New Mexico, Scholes Hall, is named for historian France V. Scholes, a World War I veteran who arrived in Albuquerque in the early 1920s on a stretcher. Doctors gave him six months, but he recovered to live into his late seventies. Scores of others, including Senator Clinton P. Anderson, were equally fortunate. Part of the high survival rate undoubtedly lay with the skills of New Mexican physicians and nurses, but part of the success must be credited to the magic of the climate as well.

Most of the links between science and New Mexico, however, have been forged since World War II. The arrival of federally funded "big science" to a poor, semi-isolated region inaugurated a wide variety of social changes. It helped "realign"—although it could never completely replace—the traditional interactions between the historic three cultures: Native American, Hispanic, and Anglo-pioneer.

When the war ended, it seemed clear to the federal government that the role of science had been paramount. The inventions of radar, sonar, the proximity fuse, the Higgins landing craft, and the atom bomb all had proved decisive in the Allied victory. It also seemed clear that the key to the success lay with the combination of U.S. Government funding, civilian scientists, and the rise of both university and national laboratories. With security issues foremost in their minds, government officials hoped to keep this alliance alive. But some of the great wartime installations, such as the Radiation Laboratory at MIT in Cambridge, Massachusetts, began to phase themselves out. There was talk that Los Alamos might follow suit. Yet General Leslie R. Groves, Commander Norris Bradbury, and others said no.

They argued that if Los Alamos National Laboratory were ever dismantled, it could never again be reassembled except in wartime. Consequently, Los Alamos became a permanent part of northern New Mexico.

While Los Alamos was never the largest of the great wartime laboratories, after 1945 it assumed the highest profile. In part that was due to the fact that the story of Los Alamos turned into high theater. Los Alamos from 1943 to 1945 proved a unique moment in the history of the human race. Never before in humankind's recorded history have so many brilliant people been gathered together in one spot for such a period of time. It was the "American Athens." It has never been duplicated before, and one doubts if it will ever be duplicated again. The story of Los Alamos and its cadre of brilliant scientists possessed a drama that the other wartime installations, such as Hanford, Washington, or Oak Ridge, Tennessee, could never approach. Moreover, Los Alamos lost only a little of that luster in the years that followed.

Consequently, Los Alamos and New Mexico became home to over fifty years of sustained federal scientific presence. True, other states may have received more federal monies for science in the postwar era. One thinks of Washington State, California, and South Carolina, all of which received greater dollar amounts. But in terms of per capita spending, New Mexico is probably number one. The presence of two powerful senators in Washington—Clinton P. Anderson and Pete V. Domenici—ensured that the federal government continued to channel large amounts of atomic-related funds to the state (about $2.7 billion in 2004).[1] The federal government emerged as absolutely essential because Los Alamos, Sandia, and other defense-related laboratories needed gigantic equipment such as cyclotrons, proton accelerators, and so on. Only the federal government had the budget to provide this equipment.

Today Los Alamos joins Santa Fe as one of the two New Mexico cities that are recognized around the world. Santa Fe has been termed "America's Salzburg," but how does one characterize Los Alamos? Is it a town to be cursed? Is it a town to be praised? It is fair to say that Los Alamos is probably one of the most controversial cities in the entire nation, ranking with Oak Ridge, Tennessee; Hanford, Washington; and Las Vegas, Nevada. There are those who curse Los Alamos. Every time international tensions rise, the curses increase. If on drives up the Hill, one may witness graffiti, "DOE Kills," on the underside of various bridges. Large billboards on heavily traveled I-25 urge lab employees to seek other work. Los Alamos's noted resident protestor, Ed Grothus, has spent decades opposing the city's nuclear assignment.

Yet this is not the whole story. Historian Chris Dietz and others who praise Los Alamos argue that the presence of the federal economy has allowed both the Indians and the Hispanos of the region the choice to maintain or change their lifestyles. The presence of the lab has also fueled such local cultural attractions as the Santa Fe Opera and the Santa Fe art world. Indeed, without the presence of Los Alamos, it is doubtful if the Santa Fe Opera would have survived. Others note that the Cold War is officially over and since 1945 atomic weapons have never again been used in anger. Surely the various weapons designs that emerged from lab scientists played a role in this situation. In the early twenty-first century there is no question that the West, if this is a proper verb, "won" the Cold War. The Bradbury Science Museum in Los Alamos, perhaps the best example of creative museology in the nation, has an antinuclear room where one can write pro or con responses to the exhibits. The comments are fascinating to read.

So, it seems safe to say that the ultimate legacy of Los Alamos to the world is "ambiguous." How then should we confront the ambiguity of the atomic world as represented by Los Alamos? Perhaps the best way to accommodate it is through what has been termed the "poetry of remembered words." Here one turns to Cherokee poet Marilou Awiakta. She writes primarily about the Oak Ridge area, as that is her home region, but her comments can be applied to any other section of atomic culture. Awiakta's "Test Cow," from her book *Abiding Appalachia*, reads:

> She'd like to be a friendly cow, I know
> But she's radioactive now and locked
> behind a fence. It makes sense to use
> her instead of us. But does she care
> she cannot share her cream with me
> to eat an apple tart? And does she know
> she's "hot" and dying? It hurts my heart
> that I can't even stroke her head

but as mother said,
radiation's just not friendly.[2]

Awiakta has also noted in another essay that the best response to the creation of the atomic world is simply to accept it. It has become, in her phrase, part of God's creation. The atomic bomb was conceived at Los Alamos in 1943–45. It was birthed at Trinity Site on July 16, 1945. It was announced to the world at Hiroshima and Nagasaki, Japan, on August 6 and 9. But it is now here, and, she argues, it should be accepted as part of creation. To accept it, however, does not necessarily mean to love it, for there are parts of nature one may or may not love. The same botanical family produces both the potato and the deadly nightshade. The vineyards of New Mexico produce both wine for table as well as for drunk drivers. But, as Awiakta has noted, the atomic age needs to be accepted.

And, of course, the story of the atomic age is forever linked with the story of New Mexico.[3]

NOTES

❖

Introduction

1. Ernie Pyle, "Why Albuquerque?" *New Mexico* 20 (January 1942): 16–17, 56.
2. W. Scott Olsen and Scott Cairns, eds., *The Sacred Place* (Salt Lake City: University of Utah Press, 1996), 346; Momaday quotation from a talk in Albuquerque, January 17, 2003.
3. This idea was first suggested to me by Dr. Mark Banker of the Webb School in Knoxville, TN.

Part One: People—Introduction

1. On Baca, see Larry D. Ball, *Elfego Baca in Life and Legend* (El Paso: Texas Western Press, 1992); Howard Bryan, *Incredible Elfego Baca: Good Man, Bad Man of the Old West* (Santa Fe: Clear Light Books, 1993); and Michael Hayes, "Socorro's Elfego Baca: Six-Guns Were His Calling Card," *New Mexico Magazine* (April 1999): 62–65.
2. WPA interview available at http://lcweb2.loc.gov/ammem/wpa/20040209.html (accessed January 2005).
3. Conversation with Larry D. Ball and Durwood Ball, summer 2005.
4. Gregory Lalire, "With One's Baca to the Wall," *Wild West* (June 2004), at http://www.thehistorynet.com/we/editorial_06_04 (accessed January 2005).
5. Robert M. Utley, *Billy the Kid: A Short and Violent Life* (Lincoln: University of Nebraska Press, 1991).
6. Kathleen P. Chamberlain, *Billy the Kid and the Lincoln County War: A Bibliography* (Albuquerque: University of New Mexico Center for the American West, 1997).

Chapter One

1. A. Scott Berg, *Lindbergh* (New York: Berkeley Books, 1999), 207–8. Berg's prizewinning account is the most complete biography, but see also Tom D. Crouch, ed., *Charles A. Lindbergh, An American Life* (Washington: National Air and Space Museum/Smithsonian Institution, 1977), and Walter Nixon, *Charles A. Lindbergh: Lone Eagle* (New York: HarperCollins College Publishers, 1996). A fine overview—loaded with photographs—can be found in Von Hardesty, *Lindbergh: Flight's Enigmatic Hero* (New York: Harcourt, 2002). A classic, early interpretation can be found in John William Ward, "The Meaning of Lindbergh's Flight," *American Quarterly* 10 (spring 1958): 3–16.

2. Perry D. Luckett, *Charles A. Lindbergh: A Bio-Bibliography* (New York: Greenwood Press, 1986), 29; Hardesty, *Lindbergh*, 160, 169.

3. Reeve Lindbergh, *Under a Wing: A Memoir* (New York: Simon and Schuster, 1998); Reeve Lindbergh, *No More Words: A Journal of My Mother* (New York: Simon and Schuster, 2001); *Guardian Weekly*, 7–13 August 2003; *Albuquerque Journal*, November 29, 2003.

4. Marion Davies, *The Times We Had: Life with William Randolph Hearst* (New York: Ballantine Books, 1925), 95–97.

5. Charles A. Lindbergh, *"We"* (New York: G. P. Putnam's Sons, 1927); see also Harry F. Guggenheim, "How Lindbergh Wrote '*We*,'" in *Santa Fe New Mexican*, September 28, 1928.

6. Actually, Albuquerque did have an airfield, but tour officials considered it unsatisfactory. See Don E. Alberts, *From Balloons to Bombers: Aviation in Albuquerque, 1882–1945* (Albuquerque: Albuquerque Museum, 1987), 26.

7. Copies available from the Lordsburg Public Library, Lordsburg, NM.

8. *Lordsburg Liberal*, September 29, 1928. See also the coverage of September 9 and September 13, 1928.

9. Donald E. Keyhoe, "Seeing America with Lindbergh," *National Geographic Magazine* 53 (January 1928): 1–46.

10. *Lordsburg Liberal*, September 29, 1928; October 13, 1928.

11. *Santa Fe New Mexican*, September 26, 1928; September 27, 1928; Charles Bennett, "Sixty-two Years Ago Charles Lindbergh Landed 'The Spirit of St. Louis' in Santa Fe," *Santa Fean Magazine* (September 1989): 30–32.

12. *Santa Fe New Mexican*, September 26, 1928.

13. Keyhoe, "Seeing American with Lindbergh," 36–37.

14. *Santa Fe New Mexican*, September 27, 1928.

15. *Albuquerque Journal*, September 22, 1928.

16. Don Alberts, *From Balloons to Bombers*, 17–22; 26; 35–37.

17. *Santa Fe New Mexican*, September 22–28, 1928; quotation from September 24, 1928.

18. Berg, *Lindbergh*, 207.

19. Keyhoe, "Seeing American with Lindbergh," 46.

20. Reeve Lindbergh, *Under a Wing: A Memoir*, 29.

21. Dan Murphy, *New Mexico: The Distant Land* (Northridge, CA: n.p., 1985), 143; Wally Begay (nephew), interview by the author, August 22, 2002.

22. "American Archaeology: Earl Morris on Early Pueblos," *El Palacio* 27 (December 7–14, 1929): 279–83.

23. *Santa Fe New Mexican*, September 13, 1932.

24. David H. Snow, "Charles A. Lindbergh's Air Photography of the Southwest," *El Palacio* 87 (fall 1981): 27–31.

25. Richard B. Woodburg, "From Chaos to Order: A. V. Kidder at Pecos," in *Pecos Ruins: Geology, Archaeology, History, and Prehistory*, ed. David Grant Noble (Santa Fe: Ancient City Press, 1993), 15–22; Alfred Vincent Kidder, *The Artifacts of Pecos* (New Haven: Yale University Press, 1932), 10.

26. *Hour of Gold, Hour of Lead: Diaries and Letters of Anne Morrow Lindbergh, 1929–1932* (New York: Harcourt Brace Jovanovich, 1973), 64–65.

27. The originals can be found in the School of American Research Collection in the Museum of New Mexico, Santa Fe, NM. Copies at Pecos National Monument, Pecos, NM.

28. Snow, "Charles A. Lindbergh's Air Photographs of the Southwest," 29.

29. Morris, as cited in Snow, "Charles A. Lindbergh's Air Photographs of the Southwest," 31.

30. Edward M. Weyer, Jr., "Exploring Cliff Dwellings with the Lindberghs," *World's Work* (December 1929): 52–57, quoted on p. 53; a slightly different wording can be found in Florence C. Lister and Robert H. Lister, *Earl Morris and Southwestern Archaeology* (Albuquerque: University of New Mexico Press, 1960), 137.

31. Weyer, "Exploring Cliff Dwellings," 54.

32. Florence C. Lister and Robert H. Lister, *Earl Morris*, 136.

33. "American Archaeology: Lindbergh's Aerial Survey of Maya World," *El Palacio* 27 (November 2, 1929): 174–79.

34. Cited in Charles A. Lindbergh, *Autobiography of Values* (New York: Harcourt Brace Jovanovich, 1977), 204n. (probably included by William Jovanovich).

35. Douglas R. Givens, *Alfred Vincent Kidder and the Development of American Archaeology* (Albuquerque: University of New Mexico Press, 1992), 100–102, 119, 146; see also Berg, *Lindbergh*, 209–10.

36. Dorothea Magdalene Fox, "Dr. Goddard," *New Mexico Magazine* 28 (September 1960): 1–8.

37. Milton Lenman, *This High Man: The Life of Robert H. Goddard*, with a preface by Charles A. Lindbergh (New York: Farrar, Straus and Co., 1963), remained the only biography for four decades until replaced by the far more analytical David A. Clary, *Rocket Man: Robert H. Goddard and the Birth of the Space Age* (New York: Theia, 2003). I would especially like to thank David Clary for allowing me to read his manuscript before publication. See also Goddard's brief "Autobiography," as reprinted in *Astronautics* (April 1959): 1–5. Richard Rhodes has written a brief overview in "'God Pity a One-Dream Man,'" *American Heritage* 31 (1986): 24–33.

38. Esther C. Goddard, ed., *The Papers of Robert H. Goddard*, 3 vols. (New York: McGraw-Hill Book Co., 1970), 2:727; *Early Years: Goddard Space Flight Center: Historical Origins and Activities Through December 1962* (Washington, DC: NASA, 1997), 3. Richard P. Hallion, *Legacy of Flight: The Guggenheim Contribution to American Aviation* (Seattle and London: University of Washington Press, 1977), details the crucial role the Guggenheims played in the Goddard story.

39. R. H. Goddard to John C. Merriam, July 14, 1930; RHG to Wallace W. Atwood, July 14, 1930, in *The Papers of Robert H. Goddard*, 2:756–57; diary entry May 15, 1934, *The Papers of Robert H. Goddard*, 2:871; Esther Goddard as quoted in the *Albuquerque Tribune*, July 4, 1958.

40. Cited in *Albuquerque Journal*, September 19, 1982.

41. His work received only minor publicity in the 1930s. Virtually the only articles were G. Edward Pendray, "Number One Rocket Man," *Scientific American* 58 (May 1938): 270–72, and "Rocketry's Number One Man," *Astronautics* 37 (July 1937): 3–9.

42. Tom D. Crouch, "Robert H. Goddard," *Dictionary of American Biography*, 140–42; *Albuquerque Journal*, September 19, 1982; *Albuquerque Journal*, October 13, 1957.

43. R. H. Goddard to John C. Merriam, March 29, 1930; RHG to Charles A. Lindbergh, June 12, 1932, in *The Papers of Robert H. Goddard*, 2:732–33, 830.

44. RHG to CAL, July 23, 1938, in *The Papers of Robert H. Goddard*, 3:1177–79.

45. *The Papers of Robert H. Goddard*, 3:1064.

46. RHG to CAL, May 1, 1937, in *The Papers of Robert H. Goddard*, 3:1059.

47. Cited by Geoffrey C. Ward in his review of the books by A. Scott Berg and Reeve Lindbergh, *New York Times Book Review*, September 27, 1998.

48. Lindbergh, "Preface," *This High Man*, xiii. See also F. C. Durant III, *Robert H. Goddard: The Roswell Years* (Roswell: Roswell Rotary Club, ca. 1973), and *Congressional Recognition of Goddard Rocket and Space Museum, Roswell, New Mexico, with Tributes to Robert H. Goddard* (Washington, DC: GPO, 1970).

CHAPTER TWO

1. With the end of the Cold War, the range of speakers at the lecture series now includes eminent Russian scientists such as the former director of Arzamas-16. See the pamphlet "Academician Yuli Borišovich Kharíton" (Los Alamos, July 1995). Copy generously sent by Roger Meade, archivist of the Los Alamos National Laboratory; *Los Alamos Monitor*, April 17, 1983, as found in Fern Lyon and Jacob Evans, *Los Alamos: The First Forty Years* (Los Alamos: Los Alamos Historical Society, 1984), 171.

2. Pavel Sudoplatov, *Special Tasks: The Memoirs of an Unwanted Witness— A Soviet Spymaster* (Boston: Little, Brown and Co., 1994); *Time*, April 25, 1994, 65–72; *New York Times*, April 19, 1944; *Albuquerque Tribune*, April 18, 1974.

3. There has been a sudden upsurge of interest in Oppenheimer. See Peter Goodchild, *J. Robert Oppenheimer: Shatterer of Worlds* (Boston: Houghton Mifflin, 1981); James W. Kunetka, *Oppenheimer: The Years of Risk* (Englewood Cliffs, NJ: Prentice Hall, 1982); Jack Rummel, *Robert Oppenheimer: Dark Prince* (New York: Facts on File, 1992); and Jeremy Bernstein, *Oppenheimer: Portrait of an Enigma* (Chicago: Ivan R. Dee, 2004). The latest studies are Kai Bird and Martin Sherwin's long-awaited *American Prometheus: The Triumph and Tragedy of J. Robert Oppenheimer* (New York: Alfred A. Knopf, 2005) and Jennet Conant, *109 East Palace: Robert Oppenheimer and the Secret City of Los Alamos* (New York: Simon and Schuster, 2005). Robert F. Bacher's brief pamphlet *Robert Oppenheimer, 1904–1967* (Los Alamos: Los Alamos Historical Society, 1972, 1999), is still valuable. The lengthy AEC hearings are available in *In the Matter of J. Robert Oppenheimer: Transcript of the Hearing Before Personnel Security Board and Texts of Principal Documents and Letters* (Cambridge: MIT Press, 1971). Oppenheimer appears as a central figure in Herbert York, *The Advisors: Oppenheimer, Teller, and the Superbomb* (San Francisco: W. H. Freeman and Co., 1976); Gregg Herken, *Brotherhood of the Bomb: The Tangled Lives and Loyalties of Robert Oppenheimer, Ernest Lawrence, and Edward Teller* (New York: Henry Holt and Co., 2002); and S. S. Schweber, *In the Shadow of the Bomb: Oppenheimer,*

Bethe, and the Moral Responsibility of the Scientist (Princeton: Princeton University Press, 2000). The Preliminary Proceedings of the Atomic Heritage Foundation's symposium, "Oppenheimer and the Manhattan Project" (June 25–26, 2004), are available in typescript form from the Los Alamos Historical Society.

4. Alice Kimball Smith and Charles Weiner, eds., *Robert Oppenheimer: Letters and Recollections* (Cambridge, MA: Harvard University Press, 1980), 7–10; Charles Weiner, interview by Herbert W. Smith, August 1, 1974, copy deposited at the American Institute of Physics, College Park, MD.

5. "Erna Fergusson," *Albuquerque Review*, February 8, 1962; *Albuquerque Journal*, February 12, 1962; March 5, 1954; March 7, 1965.

6. C. H. Gellenthien, MD, with Anna Nolan Clark, "Climate for Health," *New Mexico* 15 (September 1937): 12. See also Gellenthien with Clark, "Climate: The Magic Difference," *New Mexico* 15 (November 1937): 14–15, 41.

7. Goodchild, *J. Robert Oppenheimer*, 14–15.

8. Quoted in Smith and Weiner, *Letters and Recollections*, 10.

9. For descriptions of the region see Roy Allen Stamm, "Jaunt in July," *New Mexico Magazine* (March 1937): 16–17, 34–35; "Trail Riders Plan Trek," *New Mexico Magazine* 27 (March 1949): 26; and Stamm, "The Peaks of the Pecos," *New Mexico Magazine* 5 (September 1937): 22–23ff.

10. Lou Hernandez, "High Country Waterfalls," *New Mexico Magazine* 45 (August 1967): 3.

11. For a vigorous defense of his scientific accomplishments, see John S. Rigden, "J. Robert Oppenheimer: Before the War," *Scientific American* 273 (July 1995): 76–82. Historians Gregg Herken and Barton Bernstein argue that he was a Communist; Martin Sherwin and Kai Bird do not agree. See Charles Burress, "Expert: Oppenheimer Was Communist," AP article in the *Albuquerque Tribune*, April 24, 2004. Herken makes his case in *Brotherhood of the Bomb: The Tangled Lives and Loyalties of Robert Oppenheimer, Ernest Lawrence, and Edward Teller* (New York: Henry Holt and Co., 2002), esp. 43–62.

12. Smith and Weiner, *Oppenheimer*, 8. Paul Horgan, interview by Alice Kimball Smith, March 3, 1976, Institute Archives and Special Collections, MIT Libraries, Cambridge, MA; Francis Fergusson, interview by Alice Kimball Smith, April 21, 1976, ibid.

13. Bernice Brode, *Tales of Los Alamos: Life on the Mesa, 1943–1945* (Los Alamos: Los Alamos Historical Society, 1997), 120–28.

14. Alice Kimball Smith, interview by Helen Homans Gilbert, at Radcliffe College, 1987, copy supplied by the Radcliffe Institute for Advanced Study, Schlesinger Library, Cambridge, MA, 63; 1945 Christmas Letter, Edith Warner Manuscripts, Angelico Chavez Historical Library, Santa Fe, NM.

15. Patrick Burns, ed., *In the Shadow of Los Alamos: Selected Writings of Edith Warner* (Albuquerque: University of New Mexico Press, 2001), 31.

16. Frank Waters, *The Woman at Otowi Crossing* (Chicago: Swallow Press, 1966).

17. Peggy Pond Church, *The House at Otowi Bridge: The Story of Edith Warner and Los Alamos* (Albuquerque: University of New Mexico Press, 1959, 1960).

18. Alice Kimball Smith, interview.

19. Robert S. Norris, *Racing for the Bomb: General Leslie R. Groves, the Manhattan Project's Indispensable Man* (South Royalton, VT: Steerforth Press, 2002), is a first-rate biography.

20. *LASL News* (January 1, 1963): 13.

21. Norris, *Racing for the Bomb*, 242.

22. For a superb memoir of life at the school, see John D. Wirth and Linda Harvey Aldrich, *Los Alamos: The Ranch School Years, 1917–1943* (Albuquerque: University of New Mexico Press, 2003). See also Roland A. Pettitt, *Los Alamos Before the Dawn* (Los Alamos: Pajarito Publications, 1972), 42–43.

23. Alice and Cyril Smith, telephone interview by the author, copy of transcript in Los Alamos National Laboratory Archives.

24. *Los Alamos Monitor 50th Anniversary Guide*, Sunday, March 28, 1999, 6. The majority of the text for this special edition came from Marjorie Bell Chambers, "Technically Sweet Los Alamos: The Development of a Federally Sponsored Scientific Community" (PhD diss., University of New Mexico, 1974).

25. John Marble, "First Medical Staff Couldn't Keep Up . . . ," *Los Alamos Monitor 50th Anniversary Guide*, Sunday, March 28, 1999, 22.

26. Charles L. Crutchfield, "The Robert Oppenheimer I Knew," in *Behind Tall Fences: Stories and Experiences about Los Alamos at Its Beginning* (Los Alamos: Los Alamos Historical Society, 1996), 173. The best book on the Manhattan Project remains Richard Rhodes, *The Making of the Atomic Bomb* (New York: Simon and Schuster, 1986). See also the official AEC history, Richard G. Hewlett and Oscar E. Anderson, Jr., *The New World, 1939/1946* (University Park, PA: Pennsylvania State University Press, 1962).

27. Gilbert, interview.

28. *Albuquerque Journal*, April 3, 1965.

29. See Lillian Hoddeson, Paul W. Henriksen, Roger A. Meade, and Catherine Westfall, *Critical Assembly: A Technical History of Los Alamos during the Oppenheimer Years, 1943–1945* (Cambridge, MA: Cambridge University Press, 1993).

30. Terry L. Rosen, *The Atomic City: A Firsthand Account by a Son of Los Alamos* (Austin: Sunbelt Eakin, 2002), quoted on p. 8; on Teller, see Edward Teller with Judith Shoolery, *Memoirs: A Twentieth-Century Journey in Science and Politics* (Cambridge, MA: Perseus, 2001), and Peter Goodchild, *Edward Teller: The Real Dr. Strangelove* (London: Weidenfeld and Nicolson, 2004).

31. Cited in Ellen D. McGehee, "The Women of Project Y: Working at the Birthplace of the Bomb, Los Alamos, New Mexico, 1942–1946" (master's thesis in history, University of New Mexico, 2004), 106, and "J. Robert Oppenheimer: As Los Alamos Knew Him," *The Atom* (March 1967): 2.

32. Glenn T. Seaborg, "Los Alamos: 25 Years in the Service of Science and the Nation," *The Atom* 5 (March 1965): 5.

33. Tuck is quoted in Noel Pharr Davis, *Lawrence and Oppenheimer* (New York: Simon and Schuster, 1968), 187; unnamed scientist quoted in Lincoln Barnett, "J. Robert Oppenheimer," *Life* 27 (October 10, 1949): 133.

34. Marjorie Bell Chambers, "Technically Sweet Los Alamos."

35. General T. E. Farrell's account in *The Atomic Age Opens*, ed. Donald Porter Geddes (New York: Pocket Books, 1945), 32.

36. For the saga of this event, see Ferenc Morton Szasz, *The Day the Sun Rose Twice: The Story of the Trinity Site Nuclear Explosion, July 16, 1945* (Albuquerque: University of New Mexico Press, 1984, 1995).

37. Smith and Weiner, *Letters and Recollections*, 310–11.

38. Ibid., 315–25.

39. Crutchfield, "Oppenheimer," 172–76.

40. Rosen, *The Atomic City*, 45.

41. FDR Memorial Address, Box 262, J. Robert Oppenheimer Papers, Manuscript Division, Library of Congress, Washington, DC.

42. Quoted in Robert V. Pound's obituary of Kenneth Thompkins Bainbridge, *Physics Today* (January 1997): 81.

43. *Santa Fe New Mexican*, August 17, 1945, as found in War Records Library Collection, Scrapbook 71, New Mexico State Records Center and Archive, Santa Fe, NM.

44. Truman statement, misquoted in Goodchild, *J. Robert Oppenheimer*, 174; *Santa Fe New Mexican*, March 27, 1946, Scrapbook 71, New Mexico State Records and Archive Center, Santa Fe, NM.

45. J. Robert Oppenheimer, untitled tape recording, ca. 1947, Audio Division, Library of Congress, Washington, DC.

46. J. K. McCaffery video interview with J. Robert Oppenheimer, Audio Division, Library of Congress, Washington, DC. Many Oppenheimer quotations can be found at http://www.quotations.com and in *The Little, Brown Book of Anecdotes*, ed. Clifton Fadiman (Boston: Little, Brown and Co., 1985), 435. Most compilations of twentieth-century quotations include one or more of his observations, and, incidentally, they rarely cite the same ones.

47. Eric Sevareid interview with J. Robert Oppenheimer, December 2, 1963, Oppenheimer Papers, Manuscript Division, Library of Congress, Washington, DC. See also "The Oppenheimer Years, 1943–1945, *Los Alamos Science* 4 (winter/spring 1983): 6–25.

48. Norris, *Racing for the Bomb*, 446.

49. *Albuquerque Journal*, June 8, 1947.

50. Charmain Schaller, "General Groves Demanded a Miracle—And Got It," *Los Alamos Monitor 50th Anniversary Guide*, Sunday, March 28, 1999, 7.

51. J. P. Wernette to J. Robert Oppenheimer, June 11, 1947, Box 227, Oppenheimer Papers, Manuscript Collection, Library of Congress, Washington, DC; JRO to Wernette, ibid.

52. *Albuquerque Journal*, June 8, 1947.

53. Jane A. Sanders, "The University of Washington and the Controversy over J. Robert Oppenheimer," *Pacific Northwest Quarterly* 70 (January 1979): 8–19; "Oppenheimer to Speak Here," *The Atom* (April 1964): 1.

54. "Los Alamos Revisited," *The Atom* (June 1964): 11–13; quotation on p. 12.

55. *Albuquerque Journal*, May 19, 1964. A version of the speech appeared in the *New York Review of Books*, December 17, 1964, 6–8.

56. "J. Robert Oppenheimer," *The Atom* (March 1967): 4.

57. Robert R. Lansford, et al., *The Economic Impact of Los Alamos National Laboratory on North-Central New Mexico and the State of New Mexico, Fiscal Year 1996* (Albuquerque: Office of Technology and Site Programs, 1997), 13.

58. Stephen I. Schwartz, ed., *Atomic Audit: The Costs and Consequences of U.S. Nuclear Weapons Since 1940* (Washington, DC: Brookings Institution Press, 1998), 356.

59. Laura Paskos, "New Mexico Goes Head to Head with Nuclear Juggernaut," *High Country News*, November 24, 2003, 7–12.

60. *Albuquerque Journal*, August 20, 1975; August 23, 1975.

61. See the concise summary "The Legacy of Los Alamos" in Hoddeson et al., *Critical Assembly*, 402–17.

CHAPTER THREE

1. Clinton, as quoted on http://www.emailyourgovernor.com /nm-governor.html.

2. Laura Blumenfeld, "A Little Diplomacy Goes a Long Way," *Washington Post*, December 13, 1996, C1.

3. The best overview of the region can be found in *Bisti*, photographs by David Scheinbaum with essays by Spencer G. Lucas, Garrick Bailey, and Andrew David, foreword by Beaumont Newhall (Albuquerque: University of New Mexico Press, 1987).

4. Bob Miles, "The Bisti," *Denver Post Empire Magazine*, October 12, 1969; "Battle for the Badlands," *Santa Fe Reporter*, September 26, 1982.

5. Mark Clayton, "Hot Coal," *Albuquerque Tribune*, February 28, 2004.

6. "History of Natural Gas Seeps in the Northern San Juan Basin," as found at http: //oil-gas.state.co.us/Library/sanjuanbasin/blm /Background/hngseeps.htm.

7. Jess Price, "Where Giants Walked," *New Mexico Magazine* 57 (September 1979): 47.

8. Meade F. Kemrer, ed., *Archaeological Variability Within the Bisti-Star Lake Region, Northwestern New Mexico* (Albuquerque: U.S. Department of Interior, Bureau of Land Management, 1982), 5.

9. Frederick F. York, "An Ethnohistory of Human Occupation and Land Area Use Activities on the PNM Project Area of the Bisti," appendix D of Margaret Powers, *An Inventory and Analysis of Archaeological Resources on 3.8 Sections of Land Near the Bisti Badlands, Northwestern New Mexico for Public Service Company of New Mexico*, submitted by Meade F. Kemrer, PhD, principal investigator (Farmington: Division of Conservation Archaeology, 1980), 2–3.

10. See Powers and also *Final Environmental Impact Statement on Public Service Company of New Mexico's Proposed New Mexico Generating Station and Other Possible End Uses of the Ute Mountain Land Exchange* (Santa Fe: Bureau of Land Management, November 1983).

11. Peter John Hutchison, "Stratigraphy and Paleontology of the Bisti Badlands Area, San Juan County, New Mexico" (master's thesis, University of New Mexico, 1981).

12. A summary can be found in *Final San Juan Basin Cumulative Overview and Comment Letters* (Santa Fe: Bureau of Land Management, 1983).

13. Hannah Huse, Bradley A. Noiszt, and Judith A. Halasi, *The Bisti–Star Lake Project—A Sample Survey of Cultural Resources in Northwestern New Mexico* (Albuquerque: Bureau of Land Management, 1978), 70.

14. *Oversight Hearings before the Subcommittee on Mining, Forest Management, and Bonneville Power Administration and the Subcommittee on Interior and Insular Affairs, House of Representatives, Ninety-eighth Congress, First Session on Federal Coal Leasing Policies and to Designate the Bisti Badlands Wilderness in the State of New Mexico* (Washington, DC: GPO, 1984), 3.

15. Ibid., 45–59, 94–100.

16. Ibid., 68.

17. Ibid., 5, 13.

18. Ibid., 21.

19. Ibid., 88–89.

20. Ibid., 512.

21. Ibid., 114; 118–19; 123–25.

22. Ibid., 72–74.

23. Governor Bill Richardson, interview by the author, March 22, 2004, Albuquerque, NM.

24. *The San Juan Wilderness Protection Act of 1983*, HR 3766, 98th Cong., 1st sess.

25. *U.S. Statutes at Large*, 98th Cong., 2d sess., 98, pt. 3 (1984).

26. *Congressional Record—House*, 98th Cong., 2d sess. (June 12, 1984–June 19, 1984): vol. 130, pt. 12, 16836–16841.

27. *Congressional Record—Senate*, 98th Congress, 2d sess. (October 5, 1984): 29498.

28. Richardson quoted in Judith Gaines, "BLM Wilderness Designations End 15 Years of Debate," *Denver Post*, May 6, 1985, 4A.

29. *Congressional Record—House* (October 5, 1984): 30337; *Congressional Record—Senate*, 98th Cong., 2d sess. (October 5, 1984): 30469–30471.

30. David Liss, "Bill Richardson: 'Find the Common Thread,'" *BusinessWeek* online, November 13, 2003, at http://www.businessweek.com/bwdaily /dnflash/nov2003/nf 20031113_7589_db074.htm. See also *Farmington Daily Times*, October 31, 1984.

31. *Farmington Daily Times*, May 5, 1985.

32. Deborah Sease (Washington, DC–based national legislative director of the Sierra Club), telephone interview by the author, March 25, 2004; Judith Gaines, "BLM Wilderness Designations and 15 Years of Debate," *Denver Post*, May 6, 1985, 4A.

33. *Bisti and De-Na-Zin Wilderness Areas* (Farmington: Bureau of Land Management, November 1984).

34. Robert Moore (Farmington Office of the Bureau of Land Management), telephone interview by the author, February 26, 2004.

35. John Fleck, "Dinosaur Species was a Real Bonehead," *Albuquerque Journal*, January 14, 2003; John Fleck, "Eve of Destruction," *Albuquerque Journal Venue*, January 17, 2003.

36. *Santa Fe New Mexican*, June 27, 1991; Taffeta Elliot, "Between an Oil Lease and a Hard Place," *High Country News*, September 14, 1998.

37. Bob Moore (BLM Farmington office), telephone interview by the author, February 26, 2004.

38. "Beauty and the Bisti," *New Mexico Magazine* 63 (February 1965): 61–68; H. L. James, "Sculptured Badlands," *New Mexico Magazine* 45 (October 1967): 6–9.

39. *Bisti and De-Na-Zin Wilderness Areas.*

40. Eduardo Fuss, *Wonderland: A Photographer's Journey into the Bisti* (Santa Fe: New Mexico Magazine Photo Series, 2003).

41. Michael Reichmann, "The Bisti Badlands," on the "Luminous Landscape" Web site, http://www.luminous-landscape.com. Several photographers offer Bisti Badlands images for sale as well.

42. Jay W. Sharp, "New Mexico's Bisti Badlands: Nature's Sculpture Garden," http://www.desertusa.com/mag00/may/stories/bisti.html. See also "Bisti Wilderness Area," http://www.hanksville.org/voyage/misc/bisti.html.

43. "The Bisti Badlands," http://www.americansouthwest.net/new_mexico /bisti_badlands/.

44. Reichmann, "The Bisti Badlands," on the "Luminous Landscape" Web site.

45. *Bisti*, vii; Fuss, *Wonderland*, 9–10, 13, 87; Noll, "Beauty and the Bisti," *New Mexico Magazine*, 60.

46. Sease, interview.

47. Liss, "Bill Richardson: Find the Common Thread," 1–7.

PART THREE: CULTURES—CHAPTER FOUR

For Further Reading on "Cultures"

The original form of this bibliography—compiled to accompany the publication of an earlier version of "The Cultures of Modern New Mexico"—was largely the work of my former colleague and premier western bibliographer, Richard W. Etulain. In this revised version, I have kept much of Etulain's work but have added a number of publications that have appeared since 1990. Indeed, the literature has mushroomed so rapidly during recent years that one can only hint at the variety of works now available.

All studies of New Mexico and western history should begin with Etulain's numerous bibliographies, especially his *The American West in the Twentieth Century: A Bibliography* (with Pat Devejian, Jon Hunner, and Jacqueline Etulain Partch) (Norman: University of Oklahoma Press, 1994), which contains over eight thousand entries. One should also consult his more recent "The American West: A Bibliographical Essay," in *Western Lives: A Biographical History of the American West*, ed. Etulain (Albuquerque: University of New Mexico Press, 2004), as well as the numerous, more specific bibliographies published under his direction at UNM's Center for the American West, such as Maria Szasz, *Theatre in the American West* (Albuquerque: Center for the American West, 1998).

Cultures

Most state histories, such as Calvin and Susan Roberts, *New Mexico* (Albuquerque: University of New Mexico Press, 1988), and Frank D. Reeve and Alice Ann Cleaveland, *New Mexico: Land of Many Cultures* (Boulder, CO: Pruett Publishing Co., 1969), have appropriate if brief sections on cultural issues. The broad concept is explored in more depth in *The Lore of New Mexico*, ed. Marta Weigle and Peter White (Albuquerque: University of New Mexico Press, 1988), and, in abbreviated form, in *New Mexico: A New Guide to the Colorful State* (Albuquerque: University of New Mexico Press, 1989). See also Hal Rothman, ed., *The Culture of Tourism, the Tourism of Culture: Selling the Past to the Present in the American Southwest* (Albuquerque: University of New Mexico Press, 2003), and Rothman's *Devil's Bargains: Tourism in the Twentieth-Century American West* (Lawrence: University Press of Kansas, 1998). A fine collection of pictorial images can be found in Thomas E. Chávez, *An Illustrated History of New Mexico* (Albuquerque: University of New Mexico Press, 1992). Richard W. Etulain covers a good deal of ground in his edited work *New Mexican Lives: Profiles and Historical Stories* (Albuquerque: University of New Mexico Press, 2002). William deBuys and Alex Harris, *River of Traps* (Albuquerque: University of New Mexico Press, 1990), has achieved the status of classic for its descriptions of life in the northern part of the state. The Pueblo perspective can be found in Joe S. Sando, *Pueblo Profiles: Cultural Identity Through the Centuries of Change* (Santa Fe, NM: Clear Light, 1988).

The Arts

Ever since the early twentieth century, New Mexico has boasted a close connection with the art world. A. M. Gibson, *The Santa Fe and Taos Colonies: Age of the Muses, 1900–1942* (Norman: University of Oklahoma Press, 1983), details the origins of this movement, but there is no comparable survey for the post–World War II era. Consequently, one must go largely to biographies of individual artists. Roswell native Paul Horgan discusses San Patricio's Peter Hurd in *Peter Hurd: A Portrait from Life* (Austin: University of Texas Press, 1965), while the artist's early work can be seen in Peter Hurd, *Portfolio of Landscapes and Portraits* (Albuquerque: University of New Mexico Press, 1950). The Roswell Museum and Art Center contains the best collection of Hurd's paintings, as well as those of his talented wife, Henriette Wyeth.

The most famous contemporary Indian woman artists are treated in Sally Hyer's essay "Pablita Velarde," in *The Cultural Broker: Link Between Indian and White Worlds*, ed. Margaret Connell Szasz (Norman: University of Oklahoma Press, 1994; 2001), and in Alice Lee Marriott, *María: The Potter of San Ildefonso* (Norman: University of Oklahoma Press, 1968).

The state's most celebrated woman painter, Georgia O'Keeffe, has been the subject of three biographies: Laurie Lisle, *Portrait of an Artist: A Biography of Georgia O'Keeffe* (Albuquerque: University of New Mexico Press, 1986); Roxana Robinson, *Georgia O'Keeffe: A Life* (New York: Harper and Row, 1989); and Benita Eisler, *O'Keeffe and Stieglitz: An American Romance* (New York: Doubleday, 1991). The story of New Mexico's Tamarind Institute and its role in the revival of lithography can be found in Garo Antreasian and Clinton Adams, *The Tamarind Book of Lithography: Art and Techniques* (New York: Harry N. Abrams, 1971).

Architecture

Four UNM Press books detail the story of contemporary state architecture. Bainbridge Bunting, *Of Earth and Timbers Made: New Mexico Architecture* (1974), provides a good introduction to the subject. Carl D. Sheppard has penned *Creator of the Santa Fe Style: Isaac Hamilton Rapp, Architect* (Albuquerque: University of New Mexico Press, 1988). The most controversial state architect is the subject of a study by Christopher

Mead, *Houses by Bart Prince: An American Architecture for the Continuous Present* (Albuquerque: University of New Mexico Press, 1991). Noted critic Chris Wilson explores the impact of perhaps the most influential architect in *Facing Southwest: The Life and Houses of John Gaw Meem* (New York: W. W. Norton and Co., 2001). Wilson also analyzes the mix of art, architecture, and culture in his best-selling *The Myth of Santa Fe: Creating a Modern Regional Tradition* (Albuquerque: University of New Mexico Press, 1996). See also Henry Tobias and Charles Woodhouse, *Santa Fe: A Modern History, 1880–1990* (Albuquerque: University of New Mexico Press, 2001).

Photography

The world of photography has been intimately linked with New Mexico. One should begin with Van Deren Coke's *Photography in New Mexico: From the Daguerreotype to the Present* (Albuquerque: University of New Mexico Press, 1979). For images by the most famed New Mexico photographers, see Laura Gilpin, *The Pueblos: A Camera Chronicle* (New York: Hastings House, 1941); Gilpin, *The Enduring Navajo* (Austin: University of Texas Press, 1965); and Ernest Knee, *Santa Fe, New Mexico* (New York: Hastings House, 1942).

The two foremost nature photographers of the twentieth century, Eliot Porter and Ansel Adams, both have strong New Mexico links. For Porter, see *Eliot Porter's Southwest* (New York: Holt, Rinehart and Winston, 1985), and for Adams, *Ansel Adams: Images, 1923–1974*, foreword by Wallace Stegner (Boston: New York Graphic Society, 1974), and James Alinder, *Ansel Adams: Classic Images* (Boston: Little, Brown and Co., 1986).

The University of New Mexico Press has achieved an international reputation in the field of photography books. The versatility of the photographic wing of the UNM Fine Arts Department can be seen in two recent studies: *Silver Lining: Photographs by Anne Noggle* (Albuquerque: University of New Mexico Press, 1983), and Patrick Nagatani's *Nuclear Enchantment* (Albuquerque: University of New Mexico Press, 1991). Newcomers Debra Bloomfield, *Four Corners* (Albuquerque: University of New Mexico Press, 2004), and Lucian Niemeyer, *New Mexico: Images of a Land and Its People*, with an essay by Art Gómez (Albuquerque: University of New Mexico Press, 2004), have continued this tradition. Laguna Pueblo photographer Lee Marmon provides a Native perspective in *The Pueblo Imagination: Landscape and Memory in the Photography of Lee Marmon* (Boston: Beacon Press, 2003), while Miguel Gandert has photographed the Hispanic community of the Rio Grande in *Tesoros del Espíritu: A Portrait in Sound of Hispanic New Mexico* (Albuquerque:

El Norte/Academic Publications, 1994) and *Nuevo Mexico Profundo: Rituals of an Indo-Hispano Homeland* (Santa Fe: Museum of New Mexico Press, 2000). As a contemporary eastern photographer once observed, New Mexico has become "almost synonymous with photography."

Science

Although there have been relatively few studies of the theme, big science has shaped modern New Mexico in a myriad of ways. One should begin with David M. Hsi et al., eds., *From Sundaggers to Space Exploration—Significant Contributions to Science and Technology in New Mexico*, special issue of the *New Mexico Journal of Science* 26 (February 1986). Ever since 1942, the state has been synonymous with the early atomic age, a theme discussed in James W. Kunetka, *City of Fire: Los Alamos and the Atomic Age* (Albuquerque: University of New Mexico Press, 1979); Ferenc Morton Szasz, *The Day the Sun Rose Twice: The Story of the Trinity Site Nuclear Explosion, July 16, 1945* (Albuquerque: University of New Mexico Press, 1984; 1995); and Szasz, *British Scientists and the Manhattan Project* (New York and London: St. Martin's Press/Macmillan, 1992). David A. Clary has written the first analytical biography of Robert Goddard in *Rocket Man: Robert H. Goddard and the Birth of the Space Age* (New York: Theia, 2003). A fascinating memoir of growing up in Los Alamos when it was a boys' school can be found in John D. Wirth and Linda Harvey Aldrich, *Los Alamos: The Ranch School Years, 1917–1943* (Albuquerque: University of New Mexico Press, 2003). An equally intriguing account of growing up in the atomic city of the 1950s is Terry L. Rosen, *The Atomic City: A Firsthand Account by a Son of Los Alamos* (Austin: Sunbelt Eakin, 2002). For the story of uranium, see Raye C. Ringholz, *Uranium Frenzy: Boom and Bust on the Colorado Plateau* (New York: W. W. Norton and Co., 1989); Peter H. Eichstaedt, *If You Poison Us: Uranium and Native Americans* (Santa Fe: Red Crane Books, 1994); Eric W. Mogren, *Warm Sands: Uranium Mill Tailings Policy in the Atomic West* (Albuquerque: University of New Mexico Press, 2002); and Michael A. Admundson, *Yellowcake Towns: Uranium Mining Communities in the American West* (Boulder: University Press of Colorado, 2002); for Sandia, see Necah Stewart Furman, *Sandia National Laboratories: The Post War Decade* (Albuquerque: University of New Mexico Press, 1990), and Leland Johnson, with Carl Mora, John Taylor, and Rebecca Ullrich, *Sandia National Laboratories: A History of Exceptional Service in the National Interest* (Albuquerque: Sandia National Laboratories, 1997).

Religion and Music

In the field of modern religious history, see Richard W. Etulain, ed., *Religion in the Twentieth-Century American West: A Bibliography* (Albuquerque: University of New Mexico, Center for the American West, 1991). We still need a full history of the Roman Catholic Church for the modern era, but the various works by Thomas J. Steele, SJ, provide a good start. See his *Santos and Saints: The Religious Folk Art of Hispanic New Mexico* (Santa Fe: Ancient City Press, 1994) and (with several other editors) *Seeds of Struggle/Harvest of Faith: The Papers of the Archdiocese of Santa Fe Catholic Church Cuarto Centennial* (Albuquerque: CPD Press, 1998). Carol Lovato has detailed the life of New Mexico's most prominent post–World War II religious figure in *Brother Mathias: Founder of the Little Brothers of the Good Shepherd* (Huntington, MD: Our Sunday Visitor, 1987). Henry Tobias, *A History of Jews in New Mexico* (Albuquerque: University of New Mexico Press, 1990), carries the story up to the present day. See also *Jewish Pioneers of New Mexico*, ed. Tomas Jaehn and Thomas E. Chavez, introduction by Henry J. Tobias (Santa Fe: Museum of New Mexico Press, 2003). Although there is no modern account of the impact of the Methodists, Presbyterians, or Pentecostals on the state, Daniel Richard Carnett has provided a fine overview of the Baptists in *Contending for the Faith: Southern Baptists in New Mexico, 1938–1995* (Albuquerque: University of New Mexico Press, 2002).

The musical heritage of the state has deep roots. In 1946, Arthur Campa collected *Spanish Folk Poetry in New Mexico* (Albuquerque: University of New Mexico Press), and John Donald Robb followed him with *Hispanic Folk Songs of New Mexico* (1954), better known in the expanded version, *Hispanic Folk Music of New Mexico and the Southwest: A Self-Portrait of a People* (Norman: University of Oklahoma Press, 1980). Producer Jack Loeffler and historian Enrique Lamadrid have combined to create *Tesoros del Espiritu: A Portrait in Sound of Hispanic New Mexico*, with three CDs (Albuquerque: El Norte Publications, 1996). Loeffler, Katherine Loeffler, and Lamadrid have also written *La Música de Los Viejitos: Hispano Folk Music of the Rio Grande del Norte* (Albuquerque: University of New Mexico Press, 1999). See also Ned Sublette, compiler, *A Discography of Hispanic Music in the Fine Arts Library of the University of New Mexico* (Westport, CT: Greenwood Press, 1973).

The story of Native American music remains less well documented. The U.S. Bureau of Ethnology created a bulletin in 1957 that served as the basis for Francis Densmore, *Music of Acoma, Isleta, Cochiti, and Zuni Pueblos* (New York: Da Capo Press, 1972). Aided by Antonio Garcia,

Gertrude Prokosch Kurzth wrote *Music and Dance of the Tewa Peoples* (Santa Fe: Museum of New Mexico Press, 1970), and Jill D. Sweet compiled *Dances of the Tewa Pueblo Indians: Expressions of New Life* (Santa Fe: School of American Research Press, 1985).

Ever since the 1950s, the Santa Fe Opera has achieved worldwide fame. On this, see Ronald L. Davis, *A History of Opera in the American West* (Englewood Cliffs, NJ: Prentice Hall, 1965), and, especially, Eleanor Scott, *The First Twenty Years of the Santa Fe Opera* (Santa Fe: Sunstone Press, 1976). Scott Meredith has written an essay on New Mexico's foremost composer in "Many-Sided Man: John Donald Robb and Music in New Mexico, 1892–1989," found in *La Crónica de Nuevo México* 60 (October 2003). The story of Roswell-based western singer/composer Louise Massey and Her Westerners remains locked in the archives of the Historical Center for Southeast New Mexico in Roswell.

Literature

Historian Erna Fergusson helped introduce New Mexico to the nation with her *New Mexico: A Pageant of Three Peoples* (New York: Alfred A. Knopf, 1951), a theme picked up by Paul Horgan in *The Heroic Triad: Essays in the Social Energies of Three Southwestern Cultures* (New York: Holt, Rinehart and Winston, 1970). Prolific southwestern author Marc Simmons has also penned a brief survey in *New Mexico* (New York: W. W. Norton and Co., 1977).

The contemporary Native American voice can be found in Simon Ortiz, *From Sand Creek* (New York: Thunder Mouth Press, 1981); N. Scott Momaday, *House Made of Dawn* (New York: Harper and Row, 1968); and Leslie Marmon Silko, *Ceremony* (New York: Viking, 1977).

Other writers who have captured the spirit of the region include Angélico Chavez, *My Penitente Land: Reflections on Spanish New Mexico* (Albuquerque: University of New Mexico Press, 1974), and UNM graduate Edward Abbey, whose chronicle of his two years as a ranger at Arches National Park in Utah, *Desert Solitaire: A Season in the Wilderness* (New York: McGraw-Hill Co., 1968), has probably reached the widest audience. Rudolfo Anaya's *Bless Me, Ultima* (Berkeley: Tonatiuh International, 1972), of course, is acknowledged as a New Mexico classic.

Local mystery writing has also flourished during the past decades. Rudolfo Anaya has penned four Sonny Baca thrillers, while the mysteries by Judith Van Giesen (*The Stolen Blue*, 2000), Michael McGarrity (*Under the Color of Law*, 2002), and Virginia Swift (*Bye, Bye, Love*, 2004) continue to reach wide audiences. Of course, popular mystery writer Tony Hillerman stands in a class by himself. Through his works, millions of readers have become acquainted with the various cultural traditions of the American Southwest. In 2001 he penned his autobiography, *Seldom Disappointed: A Memoir* (New York: HarperCollins Publishers).

Popular Culture

"Popular culture" is, perhaps, the most elusive aspect of any discussion of contemporary cultural traditions. Melinda M. Snodgrass has edited *A Very Large Array: New Mexico Science Fiction and Fantasy* (Albuquerque: University of New Mexico Press, 1987), and Richard C. Sandoval has compiled a delightful collection of outsider misunderstandings of the state in *One of Our Fifty Is Missing* (Santa Fe: New Mexico Magazine, 1986). Popular western novelist Max Evans has written of the state's most famous madame in *Madame Millie: Bordellos from Silver City to Ketchikan* (Albuquerque: University of New Mexico Press, 2002).

The counterculture of the post-1960s generation receives analysis in Iris Keltz, *Scrapbook of a Taos Hippie* (El Paso: Cinco Puntos Press, 2000), and Arthur Kopecky, *New Buffalo: Journals from a Taos Commune* (Albuquerque: University of New Mexico Press, 2004). Former *Albuquerque Journal* reporter Toby Smith has penned *Little Gray Men: Roswell and the Rise of a Popular Culture* (Albuquerque: University of New Mexico Press, 2000), while Jack Kutz has compiled *Mysteries and Miracles of New Mexico: Guide Book to the Genuinely Bizarre in the Land of Enchantment* (Corrales, NM: Rhombus Pub. Co., 1988), as well as *More Mysteries and Miracles* a decade later. We still need a book—presumably filled with photographs—on the numerous sacred places of New Mexico.

PART THREE:
ATOMIC NEW MEXICO—INTRODUCTION

1. A number of recent books have much enriched our understanding of this era. See especially Jon Hunner, *Inventing Los Alamos: The Growth of an Atomic Community* (Norman: University of Oklahoma Press, 2004), and the memoirs of McAllister Hull, *Rider of the Pale Horse* (Albuquerque: University of New Mexico Press, 2005).

CHAPTER FIVE

1. *LASL News*, January 1, 1963, quoted on p. 20.
2. See the fine account by Dorothy Cave, *Beyond Courage: One Regiment Against Japan, 1941–1945* (Las Cruces: Yucca Tree Press, 1992).

3. For Pyle's regional impact, see Richard Melzer, *Ernie Pyle in the American Southwest* (Santa Fe: Sunstone, 1996). The older account by Lee G. Miller, *The Story of Ernie Pyle* (New York: Viking Press, 1950), is still worth reading.

4. Bill Mauldin, *Up Front* (New York: Henry Holt and Co., 1945).

5. See Evan Haywood Antone, *Tom Lea: His Life and Work* (El Paso: Texas Western Press, 1987).

6. See Ferenc Morton Szasz, *The Day the Sun Rose Twice: The Story of the Trinity Site Nuclear Explosion, July 16, 1945* (Albuquerque: University of New Mexico Press, 1984; 1995).

7. Al Christman, *Target Hiroshima: Deke Parsons and the Creation of the Atomic Bomb* (Annapolis: Naval Institute Press, 1998).

8. Will Lane, "New Mexico's Atom Site: National Monument Planned for Crater of First Atomic Bomb," *Holiday* (November 1946): 52–55.

9. Colonel William J. Penly, typescript of diary, July 31, 1946, Los Alamos National Archives, Los Alamos, New Mexico (hereafter LANL).

10. U.S. Congress, Senate, *Committee Hearings*, 79th Cong., Senate Library, vol. 809, 1946 (Special), 206, 275.

11. Spaatz to Baker, August 8, 1945, LANL.

12. T. F. Ferrell to Groves, August 24, 1945, LANL. The best biography of Groves is Robert S. Norris, *Racing for the Bomb: General Leslie R. Groves, the Manhattan Project's Indispensable Man* (South Royalton, VT: Steerforth Press, 2002).

13. Lenore Fine and Jesse A. Remington, *The Corps of Engineers: Construction in the United States* (Washington, DC: Office of the Chief of Military History, 1972), quoted on p. 695.

14. *Santa Fe New Mexican*, October 17, 1945, Scrapbook 71, State Records Center and Archives, Santa Fe, NM (hereafter SRCA).

15. "Years of Decision...," *LASL News*, January 1, 1963, 31.

16. Kathleen Mark, "A Roof Over Our Heads," in "The Atom and Eve," unpublished manuscript, LANL.

17. *Santa Fe New Mexican*, July 10, 1947, Scrapbook 71, SRCA.

18. Marjorie Bell Chambers considers it a fait accompli, but I believe it needs the adjective. See Marjorie Bell Chambers, "Technically Sweet Los Alamos: The Development of a Federally Sponsored Community" (PhD diss., University of New Mexico, 1974), 159–63.

19. J. Robert Oppenheimer to All Division Leaders, August 9, 1945, LANL.

20. Baldwin in the *New York Times*, August 7, 1945, 10.

21. Donald Porter Geddes, ed., *The Atomic Age Opens* (New York: Pocket Books, 1945), 164, 206.

22. Paul Boyer, *By the Bomb's Early Light: American Thought and Culture at the Dawn of the Atomic Age* (New York: Pantheon Books, 1985). See also Allan M. Winkler, *Life Under a Cloud: American Anxiety About the Atom* (New York: Oxford University Press, 1993), and Spencer R. Weart, *Nuclear Fear: A History of Images* (Cambridge, MA: Harvard University Press, 1988).

23. Bernice Brode, *Tales of Los Alamos: Life on the Mesa, 1943–1945* (Los Alamos: Los Alamos Historical Society, 1997), 129–36.

24. Wendell L. Willkie, *One World* (New York: Pocket Books, 1943), 2. In the first year of publication alone, the book sold 1,224,000 copies.

25. J. Robert Oppenheimer to All Division and Group Leaders, August 20, 1945, LANL.

26. Richard G. Hewlett and Oscar E. Anderson, Jr., *The New World, 1939/1946* (University Park: Pennsylvania State University, 1962), 435–36. See also Alice Kimball Smith, *A Peril and a Hope: The Scientists' Movement in America: 1945–1947* (Chicago: University of Chicago Press, 1965).

27. Hewlett and Anderson, *The New World*, quoted on pp. 445, 508, 499.

28. W. S. Parsons to A. A. Burke, October 15, 1945, LANL.

29. Stephen I. Schwartz, ed., *The Costs and Consequences of U.S. Nuclear Weapons Since 1940* (Washington, DC: Brookings Institution Press, 1998), 60–61n.

30. Leslie R. Groves, *Now It Can Be Told: The Story of the Manhattan Project* (New York: Da Capo Press, 1962), 378–79.

31. Groves to Bradbury, January 4, 1946, LANL.

32. *Santa Fe New Mexican*, January 5, 1946, Scrapbook 71, RCA.

33. Groves to the Chief of Ordinance, May 31, 1946, LANL.

34. Typed excerpts from the diary of Colonel L. E. Seeman, April 22, 1946, LANL; Manley to Groves, September 24, 1946, LANL.

35. Groves, *Now It Can Be Told*, 377–78.

36. Terry L. Rosen, *The Atomic City: A Firsthand Account by a Son of Los Alamos* (Austin, TX: Sunbelt Eakin, 2002), quoted on p. 38.

37. "Norris Bradbury, 1909–1997," LANL *Daily News Bulletin*, August 21, 1997 (accessed at http://nuclearweaponarchive.org/News/Bradburyobit.html).

38. Bradbury's relatives allegedly told a PBS reporter that he advised them to stay upwind during testing; see also Vera Norwood, "Disturbed Landscape/Disturbing Processes: Environmental History for the Twenty-First Century," *Pacific Historical Review* 70 (February 2001): 77–89.

39. Stewart L. Udall, *The Myths of August: A Personal Exploration of Our Tragic Cold War Affair with the Atom* (New York: Pantheon Books, 1994); LANL *Daily News Bulletin*, August 21, 1997.

40. Notes on talk given by Commander N. E. Bradbury at Coordinating Council, October 1, 1945, LANL.

41. Bradbury to Groves, September 17, 1946, LANL.

42. L. E. Seeman to Division and Group Leaders, November 23, 1945, LANL.

43. Edith C. Truslow and Ralph Carlisle Smith, *Beyond Trinity*, pt. 2 of *Project Y: The Los Alamos Story* (Los Alamos: Tomash Publishers [1946, repr., 1983], 265, 419; Norris Bradbury, "Los Alamos—The First 25 Years," in *Reminiscences of Los Alamos, 1943–1945*, ed. Lawrence Badash, Joseph O. Hirschfelder, and Herbert P. Broida (Dordrecht: D. Reidel, 1980), 154.

44. Hawkins to Bradbury, August 7, 1946, LANL.

45. Richard G. Hewlett and Francis Duncan, *Atomic Shield, 1947/1952*, vol. 2 of *A History of the United States Atomic Energy Commission* (University Park: Pennsylvania State University Press, 1969), 133.

46. G. B. Kistiakowsky to Group and Section Leaders of X Division, "What to Do Now," August 13, 1945, LANL.

47. *Project Y: The Los Alamos Story*, 370–79.

48. Bradbury to Groves, May 18, 1946, LANL.

49. *Project Y: The Los Alamos Story*, 380–429.

50. Ibid., 273–77; Richard G. Hewlett and Oscar E. Anderson, Jr., *The New World, 1937/1946*, vol. 1 of *A History of the United States Atomic Energy Commission* (University Park: Pennsylvania State University Press, 1962), 580–82.

51. J. Carson Mark, "A Maverick View," in *Behind Tall Fences: Stories and Experiences About Los Alamos at Its Beginning* (Los Alamos: Los Alamos Historical Society, 1996), 155–67. See Jonathan Weisgall, *Operations Crossroads: The Atomic Tests at Bikini Atoll* (Annapolis: Naval Institute Press, 1994), and Necah Stewart Furman, *Sandia National Laboratories: The Postwar Decade*, chap. 6, "Crossroads: Impact and Legacy" (Albuquerque: University of New Mexico Press, 1990), 181–206.

52. *Santa Fe New Mexican*, August 2, 1946.

53. A. W. Betts, Memorandum for the Diary, October 30, 1946, LANL.

54. Colonel A. W. Betts to All Division Leaders, January 10 1946, LANL.

55. Rosen, *The Atomic City*, quoted on p. 15.

56. Colonel A. W. Betts to All Division Leaders, January 15, 1946; Betts to All Division Leaders, January 22, 1946; Betts to All Division Leaders, February 23, 1946, LANL.

57. Brode, *Tales of Los Alamos*, 149.

58. "Los Alamos: Past and Present," *LASL News*, November 1947, 7.

59. Alice Kimball Smith, interview by Helen Homans Gilbert, typescript, Radcliffe College, 1987, copy in author's possession.

60. *LASL News*, January 1, 1963, 20–21.

61. Smith, interview.

62. Craig Martin, *Quads, Shoeboxes, and Sunken Living Rooms: A History of Los Alamos Housing* (Los Alamos: Los Alamos Historical Society, 2000), 3. See also Peter Bacon Hales, *Atomic Spaces: Living on the Manhattan Project* (Urbana: University of Illinois Press, 1997).

63. Additional Comments by the Director, January 18, 1946, LANL.

64. E. J. Denson to Group and Division Leaders, May 14, 1946; to [Group Leaders] from Colonel L. E. Seeman, November 6, 1946, LANL.

65. A. W. Betts, diary, December 9, 1946, LANL.

66. Colonel L. E. Seeman, diary, April 17, 1946; April 16, 1946, LANL.

67. To: Colonel A. W. Betts. From: Tech Maintenance Group [George L. Williams], April 16, 1946, LANL.

68. Henry R. Hoyt, diary, November 11, 12, 1946, LANL.

69. Six-part summary of discussion of Interim Council, August 9, 1946, LANL.

70. Chambers, "Technically Sweet Los Alamos," 173–74.

71. For the history of Sandia, see Furman, *Sandia National Laboratories: The Postwar Decade*, and Leland Johnson, *Sandia National Laboratories: A History of Exceptional Service in the National Interest*, ed. Carl Morz, John Taylor, and Rebecca Ullrich (Albuquerque: Sandia National Laboratories, 1997).

72. United States Atomic Energy Commission response to query: "Will Los Alamos Be Permanent?" March 8, 1951, copy Reynolds Electrical and Engineering Co., Las Vegas, Nevada (hereafter REECO).

73. AEC Resume of Laboratory Planning, November 2, 1948, REECO.

74. Glenn T. Seaborg, "Los Alamos: 25 Years in the Service of Science and the Nation," manuscript, February 15, 1968, REECO.

75. Roland Sawyer, "Los Alamos: The Town Few Can See—but the Whole World Watches," *Christian Science Monitor*, November 18, 1949.

76. *Albuquerque Tribune*, July 31, 1950, quoting H. F. Brown of Zia Company. See also "The Bradbury Years, 1945–1970," *Los Alamos Science* 4 (winter/spring 1983): 27–53.

CHAPTER SIX

1. On Trinity, see Lansing Lamont, *Day of Trinity* (New York: Atheneum, 1965), and Ferenc Morton Szasz, *The Day the Sun Rose Twice: The Story of the Trinity Site Nuclear Explosion, July 16, 1945* (Albuquerque: University of New Mexico Press, 1984; 1995).

2. Stafford Warren, "Reminiscences of Stafford Warren," typescript, UCLA Oral History Project, UCLA, 811.

3. Mary Ellen Glass, *Nevada's Turbulent '50s: Decade of Political and Economic Change* (Reno: University of Nevada Press, 1981), 43–47.

4. On the Alaska tests, see Melvin L. Merritt and R. Glen Fuller, eds., *The Environment of Amchitka Island, Alaska* (Springfield, VA: National Technical Information Service, 1977), and Frank Kreith and Catherine B. Wrenn, *The Nuclear Impact: A Case Study of the Plowshare Program to Provide Gas by Underground Nuclear Stimulation in the Rocky Mountains* (Boulder, CO: Westview Press, 1976). Colorado witnessed four detonations but at only two locations—Rulison and Rio Blanco.

5. Major General Niles J. Fulwyler, "Early History of White Sands Missile Range," in *Victory in World War II: The New Mexico Story*, ed. Gerald W. Thomas, et al. (Las Cruces: New Mexico State University Press, 1994), 36–41.

6. *Albuquerque Journal*, September 18, 1945.

7. Office of Environmental Management, *Closing the Circle on the Splitting of the Atom: The Environmental Legacy of Nuclear Weapons Production in the United States and What the Department of Energy Is Doing About It* (Washington, DC: U.S. Department of Energy, 1996), 74. The photographs by Robert Del Tredici in this volume are stunning.

8. Carl R. Gerber, Richard Hamburger, and E. W. Seabrook Hull, *Plowshare* (Oak Ridge, TN: United States Atomic Energy Commission [USAEC] Division of Technical Information Extension, 1966), 23.

9. Richard G. Hewlett and Jack M. Holl, *Atoms for Peace and War, 1953–1961: Eisenhower and the Atomic Energy Commission* (Berkeley: University of California Press, 1989), 528–30.

10. *Engineering with Nuclear Explosives: Proceedings of the Third Plowshare Symposium* (Washington, DC: USAEC), 1964.

11. Lawrence Badash, *Scientists and the Development of Nuclear Weapons: From Fission to the Limited Test Ban Treaty, 1939–1963* (Atlantic Highlands, NJ: Humanities Press International, 1995), 176.

12. Copies of the statue were placed in several cities, and the figure was prominently featured in the AEC film on Plowshare, *Gnome*. The statue is also on the cover of Carl R. Gerber, et al., *Plowshare* (Washington, DC: USAEC Division of Technical Information, 1966).

13. *Projects Gnome and Sedan: The Plowshare Program* (Washington, DC: Defense Nuclear Agency, 1973), 24.

14. Gerald W. Johnson and Harold Brown, "Non-military Uses of Nuclear Explosives," *Scientific American* 199 (December 1956): 29.

15. David B. Lambert, "Plowshare," *Physics Today* (October 1961): 27–28.

16. Quoted in ibid., 28.

17. Spencer R. Weart, *Nuclear Fear: A History of Images* (Cambridge, MA: Harvard University Press, 1988), quoted on p. 211.

18. Dan O'Neill, *The Firecracker Boys* (New York: St. Martin's Press, 1994), 19–50.

19. Alice Kimball Smith, *A Peril and a Hope: The Scientists' Movement in America, 1945–1947* (Chicago: University of Chicago Press, 1965).

20. Ferenc Morton Szasz, *British Scientists and the Manhattan Project: The Los Alamos Years* (New York: St. Martin's Press, 1992), 69, 80, 99.

21. O'Neill, *The Firecracker Boys*; Paul Brooks and Joseph Foote, "The Disturbing Story of Project Chariot," *Harper's* 222 (April 1962): 60–67.

22. Clinton Anderson (with Milton Viorst), *Outsider in the Senate: Senator Clinton Anderson's Memoirs* (New York and Cleveland: World Publishing Co., 1970), 1. See also Anthony Mora, "Senator Clinton P. Anderson's Service on the Joint Committee on Atomic Energy" (senior thesis, University of New Mexico, 1996).

23. *Current-Argus*, October 8, 1961, Carlsbad Public Library, Carlsbad, NM.

24. *Capitan Reef* 4 (spring 1996): 12.

25. *Current-Argus*, January 25, 1959.

26. Ibid., February 2, 1959.

27. Ibid., February 16, 1959.

28. Undated clipping, "Businessmen Give Solid Support to Next Year's Project Gnome," *Current-Argus*, Carlsbad Public Library, Carlsbad, NM.

29. *Current-Argus*, February 17, 1959.

30. *Projects Gnome and Sedan*, 2.

31. *The Stars and Stripes* (European ed.), December 11, 1961, Carlsbad Public Library.

32. *Current-Argus*, October 23, 1961.

33. Ibid., December 10, 1961.

34. Ibid.

35. Ibid.

36. *Information for Project Gnome Visitors*, December 9, 1961, pamphlet copy, Carlsbad Public Library.

37. *Current-Argus*, December 23, 1961.

38. AEC press release, March 16, 1960, San No. 159.

39. David B. Lambert, "Plowshare," *Physics Today* 14 (October 1961): 27–29.

40. *Current-Argus*, January 25, 1959.

41. *Albuquerque Journal*, July 7, 1991; Melvin L. Merritt, interview by the author, June 1996.

42. Lawrence Livermore Laboratory in Livermore, California, has the best collection of photographs.

43. AEC press release, August 6, 1959.

44. *Current-Argus*, December 10, 1961.

45. *Time* (December 22, 1961): 29; *Current-Argus*, December 11, 1961.

46. Wendell Weart, interview with the author, May 13, 1996.

47. *Current-Argus*, December 11, 1961; *Projects Gnome and Sedan*, 2.

48. Weart, interview.

49. Anecdote heard from several sources in Carlsbad, May 13–14, 1996.

50. *Current-Argus*, December 11, 1961.

51. Anecdote told by Craig Newbill, June 25, 1996.

52. *Time* (December 22, 1961): 29.

53. Donald E. Rawson, "Review and Summary of Some Project Gnome Results," *Transactions* (*American Geophysical Union*) 214 (March 1963): 129–35.

54. *Current-Argus*, December 20, 1961.

55. AEC press release (D-340), December 14, 1961.

56. *Current-Argus*, December 11, 1961.

57. "Power Gathering Phase of Gnome May Be Washout," *Current-Argus*, December 22, 1961.

58. D. Rawson, C. Boardman, and N. Jaffe Chazam, *Project Gnome Final Report* (Livermore, CA: Lawrence Radiation Laboratory, April 20, 1965).

59. *Current-Argus*, March 6, 1962; *Current-Argus*, September 9, 1962.

60. Jim W. Kenney, et al., *Radionuclide Baseline in Soil Near Project Gnome and the Waste Isolation Pilot Plant* (Carlsbad, NM: Environmental Evaluation Group, July 1995), 6.

61. Chuck McCutcheon, "New Mexico Blast from the Past," *Albuquerque Journal*, July 7, 1991.

62. Kenney, *Radionuclide Baseline*, 6.

63. Ibid., 23, 111.

64. *Albuquerque Tribune*, April 22, 1996, 1, 2.

65. USAEC, January 1968 press release (NV 68–5); Frank Kreith and Catherine B. Wrenn, *The Nuclear Impact: A Case Study of the Plowshare Program to Produce Gas by Underground Nuclear Stimulation in the Rocky Mountains* (Boulder, CO: Westview, 1976). See also Arthur R. Gomez, *Quest for the Golden Circle: The Four Corners and the Metropolitan West, 1945–1970* (Albuquerque: University of New Mexico Press, 1994), 87–88, 158, 163.

66. AEC, *Project Gasbuggy*, September 15, 1967, 2–3 (NUP-1).

67. *Project Gasbuggy: Preshot Symposium on the Gasbuggy Experiment,* Elks Club, Farmington, NM, September 19–20, 1967 (abstracts), 7, 8. Data provided by San Juan College Library.

68. Gomez, *Quest for the Golden Circle*, 64–65.

69. *Project Gasbuggy*, 16.

70. In addition to the over two hundred tests at the NTS, by this time Mississippi (2), central Nevada near Fallon (1), and Amchitka, Alaska (1), had all experienced underground blasts. None quite fulfilled expectations.

71. Kreith and Warren, *The Nuclear Impact*, 49–69; *Albuquerque Journal*, December 3, 1967.

72. Fred Holzer, *Gasbuggy Preliminary Postshot Summary Report*, NE-1003 (January 1966), 1–16.

73. *Farmington Daily Times*, April 30, 1995.

74. Holzer, *Gasbuggy Preliminary Postshot Summary Report*, 13.

75. AEC, release of January 25, 1968, JO1–21.

76. R. F. Lemon and H. J. Patel, "The Effect of Nuclear Stimulation on Formation Permeability and Gas Recovery at Project Gasbuggy," *Journal of Petroleum Technology* (October 1972): 1199–1206.

77. Holzer, *Preliminary Postshot Summary Report*, 12–13.

78. See Weart, *Nuclear Fear*, and Allan M. Winkler, *Life Under a Cloud: American Anxiety About the Atom* (New York: Oxford University Press, 1993).

79. *Farmington Times*, April 30, 1995.

80. Fred Holzer, *Gasbuggy Preliminary Postshot Summary Report*, 12.

81. Project Gasbuggy Site Restoration Final Report, July 1983, 8, copy in author's possession.

82. *Long-Term Hydrologic Monitoring Program: Project Gasbuggy, Rio Arriba County, New Mexico* (October 1966), N110-277, 2; S. H. Faller, "Surface Radioactivity at the Plowshare Gas-Stimulation Test Sites: Gasbuggy, Rulison, Rio Blanco, Co.," U.S. Environmental Protection Agency, Las Vegas, NV, 600/R-95/002 (January 1995), 1.

83. For the poles of the argument, see Robert P. Newman, *Truman and the Hiroshima Cult* (East Lansing: Michigan State University Press, 1995), and Robert Jay Lifton and Greg Mitchell, *Hiroshima in America: Fifty Years of Denial* (New York: G. P. Putnam's Sons, 1995).

84. Kreith and Wrenn, *The Nuclear Impact*, 1.

85. On Trinity, see Richard L. Douglas, *Levels and Distribution of Environmental Plutonium Around the Trinity Site* (Las Vegas: U.S. Environmental Protection Agency, 1976).

86. *Current-Argus*, April 6, 1979.

CHAPTER SEVEN

1. Julian Ellis Mack and Berlyn Brixner, "Photographing the Atomic Bomb," copy, A-84-019-Box 43, Folder 10, Los Alamos; David Hawkins, pt. 1, *Toward Trinity*, Edith Truslow and Ralph Carlisle Smith, *Beyond Trinity*, pt. 2 of *Project Y: The Los Alamos Story* (Los Angeles/San Francisco: Tomash Publishers), 1983, 206.

2. Rachael Fermi and Esther Samra, *Picturing the Bomb: Photographs from the Secret World of the Manhattan Project* (New York: Harry N. Abrams, 1995), 148.

3. Berlyn Brixner, "A Scientific Photographer at Project Y," in *Behind Tall Fences: Stories and Experiences About Los Alamos at Its Beginning* (Los Alamos: Los Alamos Historical Society, 1996), 90–100; quotation on p. 97.

4. Fermi and Samra, *Picturing the Bomb*, 123–64. Aeby image on p. 158.

5. Ibid., 182, and George R. Caron and Charlotte Meares, *Fire of a Thousand Suns* (Westminster, CO: Web Publishing Co., 1995), 29.

6. Robert Del Tredici, "Only Five Photographs: An Interview with Yoshito Matsushige," *Photo Communiqué* 7 (summer 1985): 9–14.

7. Ferenc Morton Szasz, *The Day the Sun Rose Twice: The Story of the Trinity Site Nuclear Explosion, July 16, 1945* (Albuquerque: University of New Mexico Press, 1984; 1995), 161–62, and Joe O'Donnell, *Japan 1945: A U.S. Marine's Photographs from Ground Zero* (Nashville: Vanderbilt University Press, 2005).

8. On Bikini, see especially David Bradley, *No Place to Hide* (Boston: Little, Brown and Co., 1948).

9. Peter B. Hales, "The Atomic Sublime," *American Studies* (spring 1991), 5–31; quotation on p. 5. See also Vincent Leo, "The Mushroom Cloud Photo: From Fact to Symbol," *Afterimage* (summer 1965), 6–12, and Michael J. Strada, "Kaleidoscopic Nuclear Images of the Fifties," *Journal of Popular Culture* 22 (winter 1986): 179–97.

10. Jon Hunner, interview by the author, spring 2002.

11. *The Atomic Photographers Guild* (pamphlet); *De Facto: Atomic Photographers Guild Newsletter #2*, copies in the author's possession.

12. *Bombensicher* (1991), copy in author's possession.

13. Blake Fitzpatrick and Robert Del Tredici, eds., *Visibility and Invisibility in the Nuclear Era* (Toronto: Gallery TPW/Toronto Photographers Workshop, 2001).

14. *De Facto: Atomic Photographers Guild Newsletter #2*; Doug Brugge, *Memories Come to Us in the Rain and the Wind: Oral Histories and Photographs of Navajo Uranium Miners and Their Families* (Jamaica Plain, MA: Red Sun Press, 1997).

15. *The People of Three Mile Island: Interviews and Photographs by Robert Del Tredici* (San Francisco: Sierra Club Books, 1980).

16. Robert Del Tredici, *At Work in the Fields of the Bomb* (New York: Harper and Row, 1982). Also simultaneously published by Harrap of London and Douglas & McIntyre of Vancouver; translated into German and published in 2001 as *Unsere Bomb*.

17. *Closing the Circle on the Splitting of the Atom: An Environmental Legacy of Nuclear Weapons Production in the United States and What the Department of Energy Is Doing About It* (Washington, DC: U.S. Department of Energy, Office of Environmental Management, 1996), ix.

18. *Visibility and Invisibility in the Nuclear Era*, quoted on p. 3.

19. *Canada's Atomic Atlas: A Publication of the Radioactive Inventory Project* (pamphlet, September 1996) and *The Nuclear Map of Canada Project: An Exhibition of Photographs by Robert Del Tredici* (museum catalog, 1998), courtesy of Robert Del Tredici.

20. Peter Goin, *Nuclear Landscapes* (Baltimore: Johns Hopkins University Press, 1991). Goin also has an interesting essay, "The Nuclear Past in the Landscape Present," in *Atomic Culture: How We Learned to Stop Worrying and Love the Bomb*, ed. Scott C. Zeman and Michael A. Amundson (Boulder: University of Colorado Press, 2004), 81–100.

21. Patrick Nagatani, *Nuclear Enchantment* (Albuquerque: University of New Mexico Press, 1991).

22. Carole Gallagher, *American Ground Zero: The Secret Nuclear War* (Cambridge, MA: MIT Press, 1993).

23. Terry Tempest Williams, *Refuge: An Unnatural History of Family and Place* (New York: Vintage Books, 1991; 2001), 287.

24. Ibid., "The Clan of the One-Breasted Women," epilogue of *Refuge*, 281–90.

25. Gallagher, *American Ground Zero*, 137, 151, 179, 191, 277.

26. "Science Gone Bad," *Seattle Post-Intelligencer*, June 29, 1993.

27. Fermi and Samra, *Picturing the Bomb*, passim.

28. Michael Light, *100 Suns* (New York: Alfred A. Knopf, 2003).

29. Stephen I. Schwartz, ed., *Atomic Audit: The Costs and Consequences of U.S. Nuclear Weapons Since 1940* (Washington, DC: Brookings Institution Press, 1998), 3.

30. Just six examples from this extensive literature: Richard Rhodes, *The Making of the Atomic Bomb* (New York: Simon and Schuster, 1986); Peter Bacon Hales, *Atomic Spaces: Living on the Manhattan Project* (Urbana and Chicago: University of Illinois Press, 1997); Allan M. Winkler, *Life Under a Cloud: American Anxiety About the Atom* (New York: Oxford University Press, 1993); Phillip Fradkin, *Fallout: An American Nuclear Tragedy* (Tucson: University of Arizona Press, 1989); Lillian Hoddeson, Paul W. Henriksen, Roger A. Meade, and Catherine Westfall, *Critical Assembly: A Technical History of Los Alamos During the Oppenheimer Years, 1943–1945* (Cambridge: Cambridge University Press, 1993); and Stephane Groueff, *Manhattan Project: The Untold Story of the Making of the Atomic Bomb* (Boston: Little, Brown and Co., 1967). See also Ferenc M. Szasz, "Downwind from the Bomb: A Review Essay," *Nevada Historical Society Quarterly* XXX (fall 1987): 183–87.

PART FOUR: MYSTERIES—INTRODUCTION

1. On regional treasure tales, see J. Frank Dobie, *Coronado's Children: Tales of Lost Mines and Buried Treasures of the Southwest* (New York: Grosset and Dunlap, 1930); John D. Mitchell, *Lost Mines of the Great Southwest* (Glorieta, NM: Rio Grande Press, 193, 1970); Thomas Penfield, *Dig Here!* (Tucson: Treasure Chest Publications, 1962; 1968); W. C. Jameson, *New Mexico Treasure Tales* (Caldwell, ID: Caxton Press, 2003); and Peter White and Mary Ann White, eds., *"Along the Rio Grande": Cowboy Jack Thorp's New Mexico* (Santa Fe, NM: Ancient City Press, 1988), especially chap. 3.

2. Michael Welsh, "Lost Mines and the Myth of the American West," in *Great Mysteries of the West*, ed. Ferenc Morton Szasz (Golden, CO: Fulcrum Publishing, 1993), 233–43.

3. Martin Gray, "Sacred Sites of the United States," http://www.sacredsites.com (accessed January 2005).

4. John L. Kessell, "Miracles or Mystery: María de Agreda's Ministry to the Jumano Indians of the Southwest in the 1620s," in *Great Mysteries of the West*, 121–44.

5. On La Llorona, see http://legendsofamerica.com/HC-weepingwoman1.html (accessed January 2005).

6. "The Mysterious Staircase, Santa Fe: Miracle or Legend?" http://www.funtripslive.com/santa_fe/miracle_staircase/staircase.htm.

7. Brendan Smith, "DA Investigating Mysterious Cow Deaths in New Mexico," *Albuquerque Journal*, June 9, 1999; *Las Vegas Sun*, March 21, 1998. See also Jack Kutz, *Mysteries and Miracles of New Mexico: Guide Book to the Genuinely Bizarre in the Land of Enchantment* (Corrales, NM: Rhombus Publishing Co., 1988), 201–15.

8. "The Zamora Case, Socorro, New Mexico, 1964," http://ufologie.net/htm/zamora.htm; "Socorro/Zamora UFO Incident—1964," http://www.cufon.org/contributors/chrisl/socorro.htm.

9. The literature on the Roswell incident is enormous. See Kevin D. Randle and Donald R. Schmitt, *UFO Crash at Roswell* (New York: Avon Books, 1991); David M. Jacobs, *The UFO Controversy* (Bloomington: Indiana University Press, 1975); and William E. Gibbs, "The Roswell Incident," in *Great Mysteries of the West*, 145–60.

CHAPTER EIGHT

1. *Albuquerque Morning Democrat*, July 22, 1895; Harry Byron Magill, *Biography of Francis Schlatter, The Healer, with His Life, Works, and Wanderings* (Denver: Schlatter Publishing Company, 1896), 8; and Francis Schlatter, *The Life of the Harp in the Hand of the Harper* (Denver, 1897), 86. Alice Bullock, "Francis Schlatter: A Fool for God," *El Palacio* 81(1975): 38–43, offers a good short synopsis of his career. I would like to thank the staff of the Western History Department, Denver Public Library, Charles A. Truxillo, and Margaret Connell Szasz for their assistance in the preparation of this chapter.

2. Fitz Mac, "The 'Christ Man' of Denver," *The Great Divide* 12 (November 1895): 253–54. See also Richard Melzer, "The Healer," *Valencia County (NM) News-Bulletin*, December 25–26, 1999.

3. Anon., *The Divine Healer* (Denver, 1895), 21–30, and Schlatter, *The Life of the Harp*, 17–38. The *Denver Times* twice printed a map showing his various travels (October 7, November 14, 1895), and reporter Harry B. Magill described his journey in some detail in Magill, *Biography of Francis Schlatter*.

4. *Albuquerque Morning Democrat*, July 17, 1895. Some people felt he was the "wandering Jew" of legend. Charles Truxillo, interview by the author,

March 1978, Albuquerque. Florence Ellis, "Tomé and Father J. B. R.,"
New Mexico Historical Review 30 (1955): 215. As a Mr. Chaves said later,
Schlatter "clearly possessed a mysterious, unexplainable power over men."
Santa Fe Daily New Mexican, August 22, 1895.

5. *Albuquerque Morning Democrat*, July 17, 1895.

6. Ibid. A woman said, "O! It's wonderful, wonderful, wonderful. Christ on earth in our day." *Albuquerque Weekly Citizen*, December 21, 1895.

7. *Albuquerque Morning Democrat*, July 21, 1895. Only much later, when the excitement over Schlatter had begun to fade, did the Catholic priests speak out against him. *Santa Fe Daily New Mexican*, December 28, 1895.

8. *Albuquerque Morning Democrat*, July 23, 1895.

9. Ibid., August 13, 1895.

10. Ibid., July 24, 1895; July 25, 1895; July 27, 1895.

11. William A. Keleher took his crippled younger brother, Lawrence, to see Schlatter, but with no effect. Keleher, *Memoirs: 1892–1969* (Santa Fe: Rydall Press, 1969), 34–36. "Old timer once held hands with Francis Schlatter, but got no wallop," *Santa Fe New Mexican*, October 20, 1922. William Jones Wallrich, "'Christ Man' Schlatter," *New Mexico Folklore Record* 4 (1949–1950): 28–30, is a very critical modern account.

12. *Albuquerque Weekly Citizen*, July 27, 1895.

13. *Albuquerque Morning Democrat*, July 25, 1895.

14. Ibid., August 13, 1895; August 16, 1895.

15. Ibid., August 10, 1895.

16. *Santa Fe Daily New Mexican*, August 12, 1895; *Albuquerque Morning Democrat*, August 11, 1895.

17. *Albuquerque Morning Democrat*, August 12, 1895; August 23, 1895; *Santa Fe Daily New Mexican*, August 24, 1895.

18. *Albuquerque Morning Democrat*, August 22, 1895.

19. *Denver Times*, September 17, 1895.

20. Ibid., October 12, 1895.

21. Ibid., September 17, 1895.

22. Ibid., September 19, 1895, October 26, 1895.

23. *Catholic Register*, August 7, 1941; *Denver Post*, November 9, 1895.

24. *Santa Fe Daily New Mexican*, September 21, 1895.

25. *Denver Times*, October 22, 1895.

26. Ibid., November 28, 1895; September 24, 1895; September 21, 1895.

27. Millard T. Everett, "Strange Cures Verified by Skeptical Newsmen," *Catholic Register*, August 21, 1941, 1–2; August 28, 1941; *Denver Republican*, October 26, 1895; Wesley B. French, "Denver's Mystery Messiah," *Empire Magazine* (September 30, 1951); M. Rayon, *Fads or Facts?* (Chicago: M. S. Publishing Company, 1905), 67–73; *Colorado Sun*, October 29, 1895.

28. *Denver Post*, November 4, 1895.

29. Gene Fowler, *Timberline: A Story of Bonfils and Tammen* (New York: Covici, Friede, 1933), 220. Thomas F. Dawson, "Francis Schlatter— Denver Healer of the '90's," *The Trail* 11 (October 1918): 11–14.

30. *Santa Fe Daily New Mexican*, December 20, 1895; December 18, 1895; December 19, 1895; "The constant inquiry of all persons yesterday was 'Where is Schlatter?'" said the *Albuquerque Morning Democrat*, December 19, 20, and 21, 1895.

31. Schlatter is quoted in Agnes Morley Cleaveland, *No Life for a Lady* (Boston: Houghton Mifflin, 1941), 223. Copies of Schlatter, *The Life of the Harp*, are in the New York Public Library, the Denver Public Library, and a private residence in Santa Fe.

32. *Silver City Enterprise*, April 10, 1896.

33. *Denver Catholic Register*, June 7, 1945; *Denver Republican*, October 27, 1909, October 22, 1909; Frank McClelland, "Denver's Famous Healer Francis Schlatter and His Many Imitators," *Rocky Mountain News*, March 18, 1928; *Denver Times*, December 6, 1900, July 8, 1901, September 5, 1901, September 20, 1901, January 28, 1903; *Denver Post*, May 9, 1909, August 1, 1904, October 22, 1909, April 4, 1916. The police mug shot in Tom Sharpe's article is clearly of another person. Tom Sharpe, "Mystery Still Surrounds Eccentric Faith Healer," *New Mexico Magazine* 71 (March 1993): 70–74.

34. *Denver Times*, July 17, 1901. Edgar L. Hewett, *Campfire and Trail* (Albuquerque: University of New Mexico Press, 1943), 69–75.

35. Harry B. Magill, *Biography of Francis Schlatter, "The Healer"* (Denver: Schlatter Publishing Co., 1896; repr., Pomeroy, WA: Health Research, 1968); and Norman Cleaveland, ed., *The Healer: The Story of Francis Schlatter* (Santa Fe, NM: Sunstone Press, 1989).

36. As found at http://www.voverlee.com/healing.html.

37. Charles Hoffman, "The Depression of the Nineties," *Journal of Economic History* 16 (1956): 137–64.

38. Adelia Haberski French, ed., *The Social Reform Papers of John James McCook* (Hartford: Antiquarian and Landmarks Society of Connecticut, 1977), 8.

39. Schlatter, *The Life of the Harp*, 134, 142, 153–54; quotation on p. 149.

40. Ibid., 117–22, 167, 168, 174–76.

41. Simon Flexner and James Thomas Flexner, *William Henry Welch and the Heroic Age of American Medicine* (New York: Dover Publications, 1941), 269–70.

42. Paul De Kruif, *Microbe Hunters* (New York: Harcourt Brace and Co., 1926), 57–184; Kenneth Walker, *The Story of Medicine* (New York: Oxford University Press, 1955), 182–88; Aristedes A. Moll, *Half a Century of Medical and Public Health Progress, 1890–1940* (Washington, DC: Pan American Union, 1940), 1–5; C. D. Haagensen and Wyndham E. B. Lloyd, *A Hundred Years of Medicine* (New York: Sheridan House, 1943), 17.

43. Walker, *The Story of Medicine*, 282–86.

44. John C. Burnham, "Will Medical History Join the American Mainstream?" *Reviews in American History* 6 (1978): 43–49. See also Erwin H. Ackerknecht, MD, *A Short History of Medicine* (New York: Ronald Press Co., 1908), 228–39.

45. Helen Clapesattle, *The Doctors Mayo* (New York: Minneapolis: University of Minnesota Press, 1943), 234.

46. William H. McNeill, *Plagues and Peoples* (New York: Anchor Books, 1976), 236.

47. Phyllis Allen Richmond, "American Attitudes Toward the Germ Theory of Disease (1860–1880)," *Journal of the History of Medicine* 9 (1954): 428–54. In the late 1880s, a distinguished doctor, Alfred Loomis, stood on a New York University Medical College lecture platform and said, "People say there are bacteria in the air, but *I* cannot see them." For this, he was greeted with applause! Flexner and Flexner, *William Henry Welch and the Heroic Age of Medicine*, 119.

48. Guenter B. Risse, Ronald L. Numbers, and Judith Walker Leavitt, *Medicine Without Doctors: Home Health Care in American History* (New York: Science History Publications, 1977), offers the best study of this subject; Clapesattle, *The Doctors Mayo*, 28–29. Adelaide Hechtlinger, *The Great Patent Medicine Era* (New York, Grosset and Dunlap, 1970), offers a colorful panorama. James Harvey Young, *The Toadstool Millionaires: A Social History of Patent Medicines in America Before Federal Regulation* (Princeton: Princeton University Press, 1961), is the best scholarly account; see 191–208. See also James Harvey Young, "Patent Medicines and the Self-Help Syndrome," in Risse et al., ed., *Medicine Without Doctors*, 95–115; also William G. Rothstein, *American Physicians in the Nineteenth Century: From Sects to Science* (Baltimore: Johns Hopkins University Press, 1972), 187.

49. *Albuquerque Weekly Citizen*, July 20, 1895; November 2, 1895; *The [Socorro] Citizen*, August 10, 1894; *Albuquerque Morning Democrat*, July 17, 1895.

50. Henry E. Sigerist, *Civilization and Disease* (Ithaca, NY: Cornell University Press, 1943), 144–45.

51. Ferenc M. Szasz, "'New Thought' and the American West," *Journal of the West* 23 (January 1984): 83–90; Lloyd C. Taylor, Jr., *The Medical Profession and Social Reform* (New York: St. Martin's Press, 1974), 19; Brian Inglis, *A History of Medicine* (Cleveland, 1965), 133–40, 179.

52. Virginia Culver, "Divine Science Origins Traced," *Denver Post*, August 19, 1972. Historian David Edwin Harrell, Jr., *All Things Are Possible: The Healing and Charismatic Revivals of Modern America* (Bloomington: Indiana University Press, 1975), presents a rather sympathetic account of such healings, while William A. Nolen, MD, *Healing: A Doctor in Search of a Miracle* (New York: Random House, 1974), looks at healers from a medical point of view and is quite critical.

53. *Denver Post*, August 19, 1972; Schlatter, *The Life of the Harp*, 157, 174.

54. *Albuquerque Morning Democrat*, July 17, 1895; *Colorado Sun*, October 4, 1895; *Albuquerque Morning Democrat*, July 22, 1895.

55. Sigerist, *Civilization and Disease*, 136–37; Nolen, *Healing*, 235–44, 270–73.

56. An excellent restatement of this thesis is Ronald J. Glasser, MD, *The Body Is a Hero* (New York: Random House, 1976).

57. *Albuquerque Morning Democrat*, July 27, 1895.

CHAPTER NINE

1. James Cornell, *The Great International Disaster Book* (New York: Pocket Books, 1974), 255–57. I would like to thank Chris G. Bradley for her assistance in the preparation of this chapter.

2. Robert Goralski, *World War II Almanac, 1931–1945: A Political and Military Record* (New York: G. P. Putnam's Sons, 1981), 394; Peter Young, *The World Almanac of World War II* (New York: Pharos, 1981), 306–10.

3. Robert L. Allen, *The Port Chicago Mutiny: The Story of the Largest Mass Mutiny Trial in U.S. Naval History* (New York: Amistad, 1973).

4. Don McAlavy and Harold Kilmer, *High Plains History of East-Central New Mexico* (n.p.: High Plains Historical Press, 1980), 82.

5. Sir Anthony Eden in the *Observer*, as cited in *The Penguin Dictionary of Modern Quotations*, ed. J. M. and M. J. Cohen (New York: Penguin Books, 1980: rev. ed.), 106.

6. The *Shinano* was sunk by a torpedo before it could do any real damage.

7. See Robert C. Mikesh, *Japan's World War II Balloon Bomb Attacks on North America* (Washington, DC: Smithsonian Institution Press, 1973).

8. F. Stanley, *The Tolar New Mexico Story* (Pep, TX: n.p., 1967), 8–9. For a history of the entire region, see Henry E. Morgan, *A Brief History of Roosevelt County, New Mexico* (master's thesis, University of New Mexico, 1938), and Jean M. Burroughs, ed., *Roosevelt County History and Heritage* (Portales: Bishop Printing Co., 1975). See also Wendel Sloan, "Tolar before the Explosion," *New Mexico Magazine* 65 (October 1987): 73.

9. F. Stanley, *The Tolar New Mexico Story*, 1, 16.

10. Mary Lou Bagwell, interview by Craig Newbill, June 6, 1992, Caprock Oral History Project, Center for Southwest Research, Zimmerman Library, University of New Mexico.

11. Marvie Jeter Cline (Mrs. Hardy Houstin), oral history interview by Mary Jo Walker, June 18, 1986, Special Collections, Golden Library, Eastern New Mexico University, Portales, NM (copy sent by Gene Bundy, archivist at Eastern New Mexico University).

12. Cline, interview.

13. *Albuquerque Journal*, December 1, 1944, and December 5, 1993.

14. Don McAlavy, "Nature, Military Aggression Tests Curry County Residents," *Clovis News Journal* (July 18, 2005).

15. *Portales Daily News*, December 1, 1944.

16. *Hobbs Daily News*, December 1, 1944; *Clovis News Journal*, December 1, 1944; *Roswell Daily Current-Argus*, December 1, 1944; *Albuquerque Tribune*, November 30, 1944, December 1, 1944; *Gallup Independent*, December 1, 1944; *Portales Daily News*, November 30, 1944.

17. Robert Parsons (local historian), interview by the author, Fort Sumner, NM, December 20, 2002.

18. *Portales Daily News*, December 1, 1944.

19. For examples, see *Silver City Daily Press*, July 16, 1945, and *Las Cruces Sun News*, July 16, 1945. For a fuller account, see also Ferenc Morton Szasz, *The Day the Sun Rose Twice: The Story of the Trinity Site Nuclear Explosion, July 16, 1945* (Albuquerque: University of New Mexico Press, 1984; 1995).

CHAPTER TEN

1. Steve Larese, "Chaco's Supernova Pictograph," *New Mexico Magazine* 77 (October 1999): 24. See also the superb account in Kendrick Frasier, *People of Chaco: A Canyon and Its Culture* (New York: W. W. Norton and Co., 1986). Thanks to Joyce M. Raab, Charlie R. Steen, Dave Brugge, and Nathan Wilson for their assistance in the preparation of this chapter.

2. Ortiz quoted in Byron Spice, "Chaco Canyon Treasure Lost," *Albuquerque Journal*, June 26, 1980.

3. Ann Moore, "Pueblo Pintado Holds Secrets of Chaco's Past," *New Mexico Magazine* 77 (September 1999): 32–37; the quotation is from the front cover.

4. The best account of Threatening Rock is Neil M. Judd, "The Braced-Up Cliff at Pueblo Bonito," *Annual Report of the Board of Regents of the Smithsonian Institution (1958)* (Washington, DC: GPO, 1959), 501–11. An unidentified clipping, January 24, 1941, suggests the rock caused the move (copy, Chaco Culture NHP Chaco Archive, Zimmerman Library, University of New Mexico).

5. Judd, "The Braced-Up Cliff at Pueblo Bonito," 501–2; Robert W. Young and William Morgan, Sr., *The Navajo Language: A Grammar and Colloquial Dictionary* (Albuquerque: University of New Mexico Press, rev. ed., 1987), 729, 973.

6. Hugh M. Miller, "Opening," *Southwest National Monuments Monthly Report for January 1941* (Washington, DC: U.S. Department of the Interior, 1941), 1; L. T. McKinney, Custodian, to Hugh M. Miller, Superintendent, Southwest National Monuments, Coolidge, Arizona, February 26, 1941. *Superintendent's Monthly Narrative Reports*, copy at visitors' center, Chaco Culture National Historic Park, Chaco Canyon, NM.

7. Judd, "The Braced-Up Cliff," 501.

8. Postcard photo, G. Frasher's, Inc., Pomona, CA, Palace of the Governors, Museum of New Mexico Photo Archives, folder "Monuments and Parks."

9. J. B. Hamilton and Frank A. Kittredge, "Cliff Dwellers of 1000 A.D. as Underpinning Experts," *Engineering News-Record* 110 (June 15, 1933): 774–75.

10. See A. Scott Berg, *Lindbergh* (New York: Basic Books, 1998), 207–11.

11. John Y. Keur, "Primitive Indian Engineering Methods at Threatening Rock," in *Supplement to Southwestern Monuments Monthly Reports* (1938), 352–66, copy, Center for Southwest Research, Zimmerman Library, University of New Mexico.

12. T. C. Miller, "Proposed Stabilization of Threatening Rock" (January 27, 1937), *Supplement to Southwest Monuments*, 361–62.

13. Charles E. Andrews, "Threatening Rock," *Supplement to Southwest Monuments Monthly Reports* (September 1936), 209.

14. "A synopsis of the activities of the CCCers of Camp NP-2-N, 14. Chaco Canyon, NM, as recalled by Claire J. Mueller, Senior Foreman, Landscape Architect," copy Chaco Archive, Zimmerman Library; Robert H. Lister

and Florence C. Lister, *Chaco Canyon: Archaeology and Archaeologists* (Albuquerque: University of New Mexico Press, 1981), 120–28.

15. V. W. Vandiver, "A Letter," April 7, 1937, *Supplement to Southwest Monuments Monthly Reports* (1938): 365.

16. Ibid., 376; J. B. Hamilton and Frank Kittredge, "Cliff Dwellers."

17. Robert H. Lister and Florence C. Lister, *Chaco Canyon*, 124.

18. National Park Service ranger G. B. Cornucopia, interview by the author, summer 2001.

19. Carolie McKinney to Friends, January 23, 1941, copy, Chaco Archive; *New York Times*, January 29, 1967.

20. Mueller Reminiscences; *Pueblo Bonito* (Chaco Culture National Historic Park visitor pamphlet), 3.

21. Mueller Reminiscences; *Albuquerque Journal*, December 25, 1979. The information on the cosmic significance of rockfalls comes from an interview by the author of Dave Brugge, February 7, 2003.

22. McKinney to Miller, January 25, 1941, *Superintendent's Reports*, Chaco Archive, Albuquerque, NM.

23. "Chaco Threatening Rock Falls," *El Palacio* 48 (February, 1941): 25–26.

24. McKinney to Hugh M. Miller, May 21, 1941, *Superintendent's Reports*; see also McKinney to Miller, February 26, 1941, and McKinney to Miller, March 23, 1941, ibid., Chaco Archive, Albuquerque, NM.

25. S. A. Schumm and R. J. Charley, "The Fall of Threatening Rock," *American Journal of Science* 262 (November 1964): 1041–54.

26. See also David Grant Noble, ed., *New Light on Chaco Canyon*, an issue of *Exploration, the Annual Bulletin of the School of American Research* (Santa Fe, NM: School of American Research Press, 1968), 34, and Daniel P. Douglas, "The Fall of Threatening Rock: A Geomorphology Exercise Adaptation," *Journal of Geography* 101 (May/June 2002): 117–20.

Afterword

1. A strong supporter of nuclear power, Domenici recently authored *A Brighter Tomorrow: Fulfilling the Promise of Nuclear Energy* (New York: Roman and Littlefield, 2004).

2. Marilou Bonham Awiakta, *Abiding Appalachia: Where Mountain and Atom Meet* (Memphis, TN: St. Luke's Press, 1978).

3. This section borrows in part from my essay "Los Alamos in the Context of State and Nation," *New Mexico Historical Review* 72 (January 1997): 23–30.

INDEX

Page numbers in *italics* indicate illustrations.